Laura Baine
(914) 417-5751

COMP 360A
Special Topics:
. . .
Intro
to Automated
Reasoning

Uwe Schöning • Jacobo Torán

The Satisfiability Problem

Algorithms and Analyses

Mathematics for Applications
edited by Uwe Schöning, University of Ulm

This series of textbooks is designed to demonstrate how mathematics is more than just a collection of theorems and definitions – it is a powerful means to solve real-world problems! Intended for use in lecture courses and seminars in any field of engineering or computer science, each volume aims for a compact and didactically sound presentation of its subject matter, balancing the demands of formal correctness with the need for general accessibility. Not only students, but also those working in technical professions, teachers of high school mathematics and even their students should find these books valuable.

© Lehmanns Media • Berlin 2013 • corrected reprint 2020 • All rights reserved
Helmholtzstraße 2-9
10587 Berlin • Germany

Cover and Interior Design: Uwe Schöning / Bernhard J. Bönisch
Printed in Poland by Totem • Inowrocław

ISBN 978-3-86541-527-1   www.lehmanns.de

Preface

The satisfiability problem of propositional logic, *SAT* for short, represents a cornerstone among the NP-complete problems. The *SAT* problem (as well as its restricted, but still NP-complete version 3-*SAT*) is the starting point of most NP-completeness proofs (Garey, Johnson, 1979). The satisfiability problem, and research about *SAT*, has been compared with the leading role of drosophila in genetics (Stamatiou, 2003).

In recent years, very powerful algorithms, able to solve very large *SAT* problems containing thousands of variables, have been developed. It is often the case that instances of another difficult problem, for example the graph coloring problem, can be transformed efficiently to instances of *SAT* and solved using a *SAT* algorithm.

In this book we treat the satisfiability problem *SAT*, its structure, its elementary properties, its NP-completeness, as well as respective algorithms and calculi for its solution, and, whenever possible, their mathematical analysis. We try to keep to the thread in the main part of the book and concentrate on the design and analysis of algorithms for the *SAT* problem. Therefore, themes that would lead us too far away from this thread are placed in appendices.

It is intended that this book be a useful source for seminars and lectures about *SAT* and *SAT* solving, or just for self-study a new exciting research theme.

Several colleagues gave us useful hints and suggestions for corrections. We are very thankful to Adrian Balint, Martin Bossert, Uwe Bubeck, John Franco, Oliver Gableske, William Gasarch, Frederic Green, Walter Guttmann, Alexander Hartmann, Hans Kestler, Hans Kleine Büning, Don Knuth, Oliver Kullmann, Dominik Scheder, Thomas Thierauf, and Heribert Vollmer. Also, many thanks to Bernhard Thieme for his professional proof reading, as a lector at Lehmann's.

November 2011 (original German version)
June&Oct. 2013 (English translation of a slightly extended version)   U.S. & J.T.

Contents

Introduction

Imagine you want to organize a party. The question is whom to invite and whom not to invite. You are facing the problem that there are some quite tricky conditions regarding your circle of friends that should be considered.

- Hans and Iris are a couple. One can invite either both of them or none of them.

- Based on some incident in the past it is not advisable to invite Mary if Iris is also invited.

- Paul, Edgar and Conny should be invited in any case.

- and so on, and so on...

The underlying problem is a satisfiability problem, or can be formulated as such. Each person of your circle of friends can be understood as a variable with the two possible values **true** (to be invited) or **false** (not to be invited). Assignments of values to these variables are searched for one which satisfies all conditions.

A task which is a little more complicated, but not impossible, is to include conditions with numerical quantities, like: the party should have at least 10 guests, or there should be 50 percent female and 50 percent male invitees.

We want to indicate with this example that such a configuration (or invitation) problem can become rather complex. If your circle of friends encompasses 100 persons then there are 2^{100} potential party configurations. This is a number with 30 decimal digits. Not even a computer can check all these configurations in a brute force manner.

This book will offer several clever algorithmic possibilities to avoid such a big number of trials and still come to a solution.

Another related question concerns the number of conditions that need to be present in order for the number of admissible solutions to become so small that the search for a solution resembles the problem of searching for a needle in a haystack. Possibly, there is not a single solution left. Hence, should you not invite anyone to a party at all?

But before this happens you should keep on reading...

1   First Definitions and Results

In this chapter the necessary definitions about Boolean formulas, which are the starting point for the satisfiability problem, are given, together with the fundamental concepts like assignments, satisfiability, equivalence etc. Some first results that follow directly from the definitions will be presented.

Our interest is focused on the design and analysis of the most efficient algorithms for the *SAT* problem. Therefore, only the necessary definitions and concepts are discussed here.

1.1   Boolean Formulas and Assignments

In this section Boolean formulas and theirs uses are introduced. Simple propositions that can take the value true or false are combined by using logical connectives like "and" (∧), "or" (∨) and "not" (¬), as well as some others, into more complex propositions. The complex propositions constructed in this manner can be assigned the truth values (true or false) in a systematic way. Boolean formulas and their corresponding transformation rules can be understood as simple models for expressing deductions of logical statements.

A different mathematical perspective is to consider Boolean formulas as a certain representation for the Boolean functions $f : \{0,1\}^n \to \{0,1\}$, in the same manner as circuits or decision diagrams are also different ways to represent these functions (see the appendix for precise definitions).

Definition

A *Boolean formula* (or, formula in propositional logic) is defined inductively. The constants 0 and 1 are formulas; in addition every variable (from an unbounded pool of variables) is also a formula. If F is a formula, then $\neg F$ is also a formula (sometimes also written as $\overline{F}$). If F and G are formulas, then $(F \vee G)$ and $(F \wedge G)$ are also formulas.

Example: A formula according to this definition is

$$F = ((0 \vee (x \wedge \neg(y \vee \neg x))) \wedge 1)$$

When necessary we augment the set of formulas with $(F \to G)$, $(F \oplus G)$, $(F \leftrightarrow G)$.

We denote the set of variables that appear in a formula F as $Var(F)$. One can also define $Var(F)$ inductively by using the above inductive definition of formulas: $Var(0) = Var(1) = \emptyset$, $Var(x) = \{x\}$, $Var(\neg F) = Var(F)$, $Var((F \circ G)) = Var(F) \cup Var(G)$, for each of the given connectives $\circ$.

One can also assign a *length* to a formula F, which we denote by $|F|$. This measure is especially interesting for the complexity statements in the algorithms that receive formulas as inputs. For the definition of $|F|$ we again use the inductive formula definition: $|0| = |1| = |x| = 1$; $|\neg F| = |F| + 1$; $|(F \circ G)| = |F| + |G| + 1$.

We define for each logical symbol $\neg, \vee, \wedge$ as well as $\rightarrow$ (for "implies"), $\oplus$ (for exclusive or, xor for short), $\leftrightarrow$ (for equivalence, or "if and only if") a semantic meaning, given by the following tables. The only values that the variables, and formulas, can take are 0 and 1 which can be interpreted as the logical values "false" and "true," respectively.

$\neg$	0	1
	1	0

$\vee$	0	1
0	0	1
1	1	1

$\wedge$	0	1
0	0	0
1	0	1

$\rightarrow$	0	1
0	1	1
1	0	1

$\oplus$	0	1
0	0	1
1	1	0

$\leftrightarrow$	0	1
0	1	0
1	0	1

In writing and evaluating Boolean formulas we make use of the associativity rule, and also apply the usual priority rules for saving parenthesis ($\neg$ binds stronger than $\wedge$, and $\wedge$ binds stronger than $\vee$). In some situations the *and*-connectives ($\wedge$) are not written and the *or*-connectives ($\vee$) are denoted by $+$.

Definition

An *assignment* α is a mapping from (some of) the variables to the values 0 or 1. This is denoted as

$$\alpha = \{ x_1 = a_1,\ x_2 = a_2,\ \ldots,\ x_k = a_k \}$$

where $a_1, a_2, \ldots, a_k \in \{0, 1\}$. Let α be a given assignment. One can then *apply* α to a formula F. We denote the result of this operation by $F\alpha$.

We assume here that after the pure symbolic substitution of the corresponding variables in the formula by the constants 0 and 1, some trivial simplifications take place:

$(G \vee 0)$ (resp. $(0 \vee G)$) is simplified to G,

$(G \vee 1)$ (resp. $(1 \vee G)$) is simplified to 1,

$(G \wedge 0)$ (resp. $(0 \wedge G)$) is simplified to 0,

$(G \wedge 1)$ (resp. $(1 \wedge G)$) is simplified to G,

$\neg\neg G$ is simplified to G,

$\neg 0$ is simplified to 1,

$\neg 1$ is simplified to 0.

For example, after the application of the assignment $\{y = 0\}$, the formula $F = x \vee (y \wedge z)$ is transformed step by step to $x \vee (0 \wedge z)$, then to $x \vee 0$, and then to x. In this case $F\{y = 0\} = x$ holds. A different assignment would be $\{x = 1\}$. This produces $F\{x = 1\} = 1$.

In principle, such simplification rules also could be introduced in connection with the operators $\rightarrow, \oplus, \leftrightarrow$, but, for simplicity, we will refrain from doing so.

We say that an assignment α with $F\alpha = 1$ *satisfies* the formula F; and in case $F\alpha = 0$, we say that α *falsifies* F.

We denote by $Var(\alpha)$ the set of those variables that receive a value from α.

In the following the concept of assignment is extended. To this end, let a *literal* denote either a variable, for example x, or a negated variable, for example $\overline{x}$. Accordingly, call a variable x a *positive literal*, and an negated variable $\overline{x}$ a *negative literal*.

Let u be any literal. The notation $\{u = 1\}$ then means that the literal u is assigned value 1, which in case of a negated variable (like $u = \overline{x}$) means that the underlying variable is assigned value 0 (thus $\{x = 0\}$).

Finally, $F[u = \overline{u}]$ means, that the literal u should change its sign everywhere in F, thus u will replace $\overline{u}$, and $\overline{u}$ will replace u.

A further refinement of notation is needed to cover changes to assignments that might be caused by backtracking or local search algorithms. In the simplest case a single assignment $\{x = 0\}$ is modified from 0 to 1, resulting in $\{x = 1\}$, or the other way around. This process of changing a single bit within a given assignment is called "flip."

Let β be another assignment (for one or more variables). We denote by $\alpha[\beta]$, the assignment resulting from overwriting in α the values from β (for those variables for which β is defined):

$$\alpha[\beta](x) = \begin{cases} \beta(x), & \text{if } x \in Var(\beta) \\ \alpha(x), & \text{otherwise} \end{cases}$$

For example, let $G = F\beta$. Then, $G\alpha = F\alpha[\beta]$ holds. This is so since the formula G does no longer contain the variables in $Var(\beta)$. Applying α to G cannot have an effect on $Var(\beta) \setminus Var(\alpha)$. The same result occurs by applying the assignment $\alpha[\beta]$ to F.

As a rule, the use of the square brackets means that an already existing assignment is modified in one or more positions. Thus $\alpha[x]$ denotes the assignment that differs from α exactly in the value of variable x; the value of x is "flipped." Here it is assumed that $x \in Var(\alpha)$.

Definition

A formula F is called *satisfiable* if there exists an assignment α such that $F\alpha = 1$. Otherwise, F is called *unsatisfiable* (sometimes it is also called *contradictory*). The set of all satisfiable formulas is denoted by *SAT*. A satisfying assignment α for a formula F is often also called a *model* for F, in which case we write: $\alpha \models F$.

A formula F is called *valid* (or also a *tautology*) if, for all assignments α with $Var(\alpha) = Var(F)$, it holds that $F\alpha = 1$. The set of tautologies is denoted by *TAUT*. The notation $\models F$ expresses that F is a tautology.

A formula G *follows from* F (or, G is a *consequence* from F, or also: F *implies* G, notation: $F \models G$), if $F \rightarrow G$ (or equivalently: $\neg F \vee G$) is a tautology.

The following equivalence statements follow directly from the definitions:

$$F \text{ is a tautology if and only if } \neg F \text{ is unsatisfiable.}$$

$$G \text{ follows from } F \text{ if and only if } F \wedge \neg G \text{ is unsatisfiable.}$$

Moreover, the following is also true. If F is a formula and $x \in Var(F)$. Then, F is satisfiable if and only if either $F\{x = 1\}$ is satisfiable or $F\{x = 0\}$ is satisfiable. Analogously, F is unsatisfiable if and only if $F\{x = 1\}$ and $F\{x = 0\}$ are both unsatisfiable.

Definition

Two formulas F and G are called (semantically) *equivalent* if, for all assignments α with $Var(\alpha) = Var(F) \cup Var(G)$, it holds that $F\alpha = G\alpha$.

Two formulas F and G are called *sat-equivalent* if it holds that F is satisfiable if and only if G is satisfiable.

The last definition appears a little strange. It will make sense when we describe algorithmic methods that transform a given formula F (for which it is unknown whether it is satisfiable or not) to another formula G in such a way that the satisfiability or unsatisfiability is preserved.

There are many rules for the equivalence-preserving transformation of Boolean formulas (associativity, distributivity, etc.) Probably the most important rules of this kind are the DeMorgan rules, which are

$$\neg(F \vee G) = (\neg F \wedge \neg G) \quad \text{and} \quad \neg(F \wedge G) = (\neg F \vee \neg G).$$

We have used the equality symbol, in order to denote semantic equivalence between formulas. This means, that in the following we do not to want to differentiate strictly between syntactic identity and semantic equivalence.

A formula can be transformed using the DeMorgan rules to an equivalent one in such a way that the negation symbols are pushed "inwards", until they are directly in front of the variables.

Finally, double negations are removed according to the expression $\neg\neg F = F$. This means that one can find for every formula F an equivalent one in which the negation symbols are placed only in front of variables. A formula which is in this form is called a *negation normal form* of F (for short: *NNF*).

The set of satisfiable formulas *SAT* is often referred to as an algorithmic decision problem. This means, given an arbitrary Boolean formula F, decide whether F is satisfiable (i.e. $F \in SAT$) or not. This problem is NP-complete (see appendix). This implies, under the hypothesis $P \neq NP$, that there is no algorithm which, given a formula F with n variables, can decide satisfiability in running time $p(n)$, where $p(n)$ is an arbitrary polynomial, i.e. $p(n) = O(n^k)$ for some constant k.

This is the bad news. On the other hand, without trying to question that $P \neq NP$, one can try to find algorithms for *SAT* with a tolerable running time, at least for *many* input formulas. Furthermore, an algorithm that has exponential complexity is not necessarily impractical. An exponential algorithm with running time 1.3^n is much better than one with running time 2^n. When the 2^n algorithm can solve problems with an input size of n_0 in a given time, an algorithm with running time 1.3^n can solve problems with input size $2.64 \cdot n_0$ in the same time. The search for such more efficient algorithms is a central topic in this book.

Let us start with some easy observations: in order to decide on the satisfiability or tautological properties of a formula F with $\text{Var}(F) = \{x_1, x_2, \ldots, x_n\}$, one can generate systematically a list of all possible assignments α_i for these n variables, and apply each of these 2^n assignments to F and obtain $F\alpha_i$.

$$F\{x_1 = 0, x_2 = 0, \ldots, x_n = 0\} = a_1$$
$$F\{x_1 = 1, x_2 = 0, \ldots, x_n = 0\} = a_2$$
$$F\{x_1 = 0, x_2 = 1, \ldots, x_n = 0\} = a_3$$
$$F\{x_1 = 1, x_2 = 1, \ldots, x_n = 0\} = a_4$$
$$\vdots$$
$$F\{x_1 = 1, x_2 = 1, \ldots, x_n = 1\} = a_{2^n}$$

This is called a *truth table* of F. F is now satisfiable if and only if there exists at least one i with $a_i = 1$. Furthermore, F is a tautology if and only if, for all $i \leq 2^n$, $a_i = 1$ holds.

Consider for example the formula $F = (\overline{x} \vee y) \wedge z$. It is reasonable to construct a column in the truth-table for every subformula in F.

x	y	z	$\overline{x}$	$\overline{x} \vee y$	F
0	0	0	1	1	0
0	0	1	1	1	1
0	1	0	1	1	0
0	1	1	1	1	1
1	0	0	0	0	0
1	0	1	0	0	0
1	1	0	0	1	0
1	1	1	0	1	1

Inspecting the rightmost column it is clear that this formula is satisfiable, but is not a tautology.

The computational cost for this way of testing satisfiability is $O^*(2^n)$ (for the different asymptotic notations used in this book, see the appendix). The same asymptotic computational cost results, when in a recursive manner the variables are assigned successively with the values 0 and 1, as is the case in the following program:

> **proc** test (F : formula) : **bool**
> // outputs 1 if and only if F is satisfiable
> **if** $F = 1$ **then return** 1
> **if** $F = 0$ **then return** 0
> // Let $x \in \text{Var}(F)$
> **if** test($F\{x = 0\}$) **then return** 1
> **else return** test($F\{x = 1\}$)

In the worst case two recursive calls occur in every procedure execution. This results in the recursion equality $T(n) = 2 \cdot T(n-1)$ with the solution $T(n) = O(2^n)$. For more on recursion relations see the appendix.

This algorithm is in fact the basis for much better algorithms called DPLL algorithms, after the initials of the authors from (Davis, Putnam, 1960) and (Davis, Logemann, Loveland, 1962) that will be treated in a later chapter.

1.2   Conjunctive Normal Form and CSP

In the following we will assume, almost without exception, that the Boolean formulas to analyze are given in conjunctive normal form.

Definition

A Boolean formula F is in *conjunctive normal form* (abbreviated: $F \in CNF$), when it is written as:
$$F = C_1 \wedge C_2 \wedge \cdots \wedge C_m$$
The subformulas C_i are called *clauses* and must have the following form
$$C_i = (u_{i,1} \vee u_{i,2} \vee \cdots \vee u_{i,k_i})$$
where the $u_{i,j}$ are *literals*, that is, variables or negated variables:
$$u_{i,j} \in \{x_1, x_2, \ldots, x_n\} \cup \{\overline{x_1}, \overline{x_2}, \ldots, \overline{x_n}\}$$
The *size* (or width) of a clause is the number of literals it contains, which we denote by $|C|$. If $|C_i| \leq k$ for some constant k and all i, then formula F is said to be in *k-conjunctive normal form* (abbreviated: $F \in k\text{-}CNF$).

A formula in *CNF* is therefore a *conjunction* (and-connection) of *clauses*, while the clauses are *disjunctions* (or-connections) of *literals*.

Alternatively, the following set theoretic notation is used. A formula F in *CNF* is considered as a *set* of clauses, and is written as
$$F = \{C_1, C_2, \ldots, C_m\}.$$

This notation has the advantage that some algorithmic actions like the addition or deletion of clauses to a formula can be simply expressed in set notation. Analogously, also clauses can be considered as *sets* of literals and in this way easily expressed as the addition or deletion of literals in clauses, as well as the merging of several clauses into a single one.

Definition

Let us consider the problem of deciding whether a given input formula in *CNF* is satisfiable. We call this restricted version of the *SAT* problem *CNF-SAT*. Expressed as a formula this is: $CNF\text{-}SAT = CNF \cap SAT$.
We define accordingly: $k\text{-}CNF\text{-}SAT = k\text{-}CNF \cap SAT$, and we abbreviate this by $k\text{-}SAT$.

Similar to *SAT*, the problems *CNF-SAT* and k-*SAT* (for $k \geq 3$) are NP-complete. The above observation, stating that under the hypothesis $P \neq NP$ there cannot be polynomial time algorithms for these problems, also holds here (see also the appendix on NP-completeness). On the other hand, the k-*SAT* problem for $k \leq 2$ is solvable in polynomial time. This will be shown in a later chapter.

Clauses with only one literal, $C = \{u\}$ will play a special role in the following. Because of this they receive their own name: they are called *unit clauses*.

Many times we will come across the following simplification rule, called *unit propagation*. Suppose that the set of clauses F includes a unit-clause $\{u\}$, and we are interested in deciding the satisfiability or unsatisfiability of F. If F were satisfiable, then u must necessarily be assigned the value 1. Because of this we can analyze the formula $F\{u = 1\}$ instead of F. In other words, the formulas F and $F\{u = 1\}$ are sat-equivalent.

By using this and other transformations (done by calculi or by algorithms) it can happen that the empty formula $\emptyset$ appears – or possibly, an empty clause, a clause without any literal, that we represent by $\square$. While the empty formula is equivalent to 1 (and therefore is a tautology), the empty clause $\square$ (or a formula that includes the empty clause) is equivalent to 0 and therefore is unsatisfiable.

The abbreviation *CNF* includes the expression "normal form." The following theorem shows that this term is justified.

> **Theorem**
>
> For every formula F there is an equivalent formula G in *CNF*. The transformation from F to G generally requires exponential computation time.

Proof: We show more generally, that for every Boolean function $f : \{0, 1\}^n \to \{0, 1\}$ there is a formula G in *CNF* with $Var(G) = \{x_1, \ldots, x_n\}$, so that for each assignment α with $Var(\alpha) = \{x_1, \ldots, x_n\}$ we have $f(\alpha) = G\alpha$.

For this we consider the truth-table for f. We must express G as an *and*-connection of several conditions (formulated as clauses). Every line of the truth-table corresponding to an assignment α_i with value $f(\alpha_i) = 0$, produces such a condition (clause). This clause expresses that a possible satisfying assignment α for the formula being constructed cannot coincide with α_i. Let $\alpha_i = \{x_1 = a_1, \ldots, x_n = a_n\}$. This produces the clause $(z_1 \vee \cdots \vee z_n)$ with $z_j = x_j$ if $a_j = 0$ and $z_j = \overline{x_j}$ in case $a_j = 1$. $\square$

Example: The truth-table from page 16 contains 5 lines with value 0. According to the described method, this leads to the following formula in *CNF*:

$$F = (x \vee y \vee z) \wedge (x \vee \overline{y} \vee z) \wedge (\overline{x} \vee y \vee z) \wedge (\overline{x} \vee y \vee \overline{z}) \wedge (\overline{x} \vee \overline{y} \vee z)$$

Using the usual simplification rules for Boolean formulas, the first two clauses can be transformed to $(x \vee z)$. This is nothing else than the use of resolution and subsumption, explained later. In a similar way several other clauses can be simplified to obtain

$$F = (x \vee z) \wedge (y \vee z) \wedge (\overline{x} \vee y) \wedge (\overline{y} \vee z) \wedge (\overline{x} \vee z) = (\overline{x} \vee y) \wedge z.$$

A satisfying assignment for a formula in *CNF* must satisfy all clauses *simultaneously*. Because a single clause C is a disjunction of literals, it will not be satisfied by exactly one of the possible $2^{|C|}$ assignments of the $|C|$ variables. A clause C expresses, so to speak, a "forbidden assignment", while all the other assignments are – from the point of view of the clause – allowed.

The *CNF-SAT* problem is a special case of a *constraint satisfaction problem* (abbreviated: *CSP*). Such a problem is specified by the following information:

- What are the variables $x_1, \ldots, x_n$ occurring in the problem?

- What is the domain of values D that the variables can take? Occasionally every variable x_i can have its individual domain D_i.

- What are the constraints $C_1, \ldots, C_m$? A constraint can be written as an inequality, referring to a (usually small) subset of the variables: $(x_{i_1}, x_{i_2}, \ldots, x_{i_k}) \neq (d_1, d_2, \ldots, d_k)$, with $d_i \in D$. This means, a constraint forbids exactly one concrete variable assignment. A constraint can be written as a disjunction, like a clause:

$$(x_{i_1} \neq d_1) \vee (x_{i_2} \neq d_2) \vee \cdots \vee (x_{i_k} \neq d_k)$$

The algorithmic goal of a given *CSP* is to find an assignment $(d_1, d_2, \ldots, d_n) \in D^n$ satisfying all the constraints.

In the case of $|D| = d$ we call this as a d-*CSP*, and a (d, k)-*CSP* means that, in addition, there is a constant k, so that every constraint contains at most k variables. According to this, *CNF-SAT* is a 2-*CSP*, and k-*SAT* is a $(2, k)$-*CSP*.

A further problem for which the character of a *CSP* becomes obvious is the graph colorability problem (see the appendix on graphs). The k-colorability problem (given a graph G, is there an admissible coloring of G with k colors?) is a special case of $(k, 2)$-*CSP*, in which the variables are the graph vertices, the value domain $D = \{1, 2, \ldots, k\}$ is the set of colors, and each edge $\{x, y\}$ of the graph generates the k constraints $(x, y) \neq (1, 1)$, $(x, y) \neq (2, 2), \ldots$, $(x, y) \neq (k, k)$.

In order to solve a (d, k)-*CSP* with n variables, one can randomly choose for each variable (independently from each other) a selection of 2 of the possible d values in D. By interpreting the selected values for each variable as 0, respectively 1, one can transform this restricted *CSP* to a k-*SAT*-problem. A possible satisfying assignment for the original problem "survives" this value restriction with probability $\left(\frac{2}{d}\right)^n$ (see the appendix on probabilistic algorithms for an explanation of the connection between the success probability and the running time of a probabilistic algorithm). For example, let $D = \{a, b, c, d\}$ and $n = 3$. Let $(x_1, x_2, x_3) = (a, c, d)$ be a solution for the underlying *CSP*. Let us suppose that the randomly selected restrictions to 2 values produce the following: $\{a, b\}$ for x_1, $\{b, d\}$ for x_2, and $\{a, d\}$ for x_3. In this case the solution (a, c, d) does not fulfill the selected restrictions, since for x_2 the value c is not allowed. However, with probability $\left(\frac{2}{4}\right)^3 = \frac{1}{8}$ a value restriction can be chosen for which the solution (a, c, d) is possible.

We explain with the help of the following example how a *SAT* problem is defined from the given 4-*CSP*, after the value restrictions. The intended values a, b for x_1 are now identified with 0 and 1 (and analogously for x_2 and x_3). From an initial constraint like $(x_1, x_2, x_3) \neq (b, b, b)$ respectively $(x_1 \neq b) \vee (x_2 \neq b) \vee (x_3 \neq b)$ for example, the clause $(x_1 \neq 1) \vee (x_2 \neq 0) \vee (1)$ is generated, which means: $(\overline{x_1} \vee x_2)$.

With these ideas we obtain:

Theorem

If the best (deterministic or probabilistic) k-*SAT* algorithm has running time $O^*(t_k(n))$, then, by the method described above, a probabilistic algorithm for (d, k)-*CSP* with running time $O^*((\frac{d}{2})^n \cdot t_k(n))$ can be constructed.

For example, the graph 3-colorability problem, a special case of $(3, 2)$-*CSP*, can be solved in time $O^*((\frac{3}{2})^n)$ since 2-*SAT* $\in$ P (see Beigel, Eppstein, 2005).

1.3 Tseitin Encoding and Series-Parallel Graphs

While the transformation of a formula to an equivalent one in *CNF* can produce an exponential blow-up, one can transform a formula within polynomial time to a *sat-equivalent* formula in *CNF* (even to a 3-*CNF* formula) of linear size with respect to the original formula. Notice that we have not mentioned at all *DNF-SAT* which is dual to *CNF-SAT*, i.e. it is an *or* of *and*, instead of an *and* of *or*. This is so since *DNF-SAT* is trivially in P, but transformation of *CNF* to *DNF* may yield an exponential blow-up. More details on this topic can be found in (Kleine Büning, Lettmann, 1999).

Theorem (Tseitin)

For every formula F there is a sat-equivalent formula G in 3-*CNF*. The transformation from F to G can be done efficiently (in polynomial time).

Proof: We show more generally that for every circuit S with n inputs and m gates (see the appendix on circuits) there is a formula G in 3-*CNF* that can be constructed efficiently (in polynomial time in n and m). The formula G contains the variables $x_1, \ldots, x_n$ and $y_1, \ldots, y_m$, and for all $a_1, \ldots, a_n \in \{0, 1\}$ the following holds:

$$S(a_1, \ldots, a_n) = 1 \quad \text{if and only if} \quad G\{x_1 = a_1, \ldots, x_n = a_n\} \text{ is satisfiable}.$$

We associate one of the y-variables with the output of each gate and suppose that y_1 is associated with the output of the last gate, the one defining the circuit output.

When the output of a gate (associated with variable y_i) is connected to one of the inputs of another gate, we understand this input to be also associated with variable y_i.

We consider that the input gates of the circuit S are associated with the corresponding variables x_j.

The formula G then has the following form:

$$G = (y_1) \wedge \bigwedge_{i=1}^{m} (z_{i,3} \leftrightarrow f_i(z_{i,1}, z_{i,2})).$$

Here, f_i represents the Boolean function with two inputs being computed by the i-th gate. The variables $z_{i,1}$ and $z_{i,2}$ are those x- or y-variables associated with the inputs of the i-th gate. The variable $z_{i,3}$ is the y-variable associated with the output of the i-th gate.

The formula G expresses that the truth values of the different gates in circuit S are correctly given to the corresponding variables, and that this assignment gives value 1 to the output gate.

Example: Consider the following circuit:

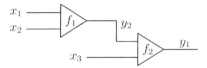

The Boolean function corresponding to this circuit is

$$G = (y_1) \wedge (y_2 \leftrightarrow f_1(x_1, x_2)) \wedge (y_1 \leftrightarrow f_2(y_2, x_3)) \, .$$

This formula is not yet in *CNF*. The subformula $(z_{i,3} \leftrightarrow f_i(z_{i,1}, z_{i,2}))$ has exactly 3 variables and can be transformed to an equivalent *CNF* that has also only 3 variables (and is therefore in 3-*CNF*).

For example let f_i be an *and*-connective. Then the subformula $(z \leftrightarrow (x \wedge y))$ is equivalent to $(x \vee \bar{z}) \wedge (y \vee \bar{z}) \wedge (\bar{x} \vee \bar{y} \vee z)$.

One obtains in this way a 3-*CNF* and the transformation can be done within polynomial time.   □

The presented transformation is also called a *Tseitin transformation* or *Tseitin encoding*, see also (Bauer, Brand, Fischer, Meyer, Paterson, 1973), (Tseitin, 1983). One can understand this as a polynomial transformation or reduction from circuit satisfiability (*CIRCUIT-SAT*) to 3-*SAT*, in symbols *CIRCUIT-SAT* $\preceq$ 3-*SAT*, see also the appendix about the NP-completeness of *SAT*. This is in fact one of the most used methods to transform hard combinatorial problems to (3-)*SAT* problems.

In doing so, it is, of course, important to introduce as few new variables (and clauses) as possible so that one can profit from the (relatively) efficient modern *SAT* solvers. Naturally, their complexity increases with the number of variables. Since the formula G always includes the unit-clause $\{y_1\}$, it is possible to obtain immediately a simplification by means of unit propagation (see page 18) to $G\{y_1 = 1\}$, from which it might be possible to apply further unit propagation simplification steps.

Let us suppose that the initial formula F is given in negation normal form (see page 15). This means that all the negations are directly in front of some variable. In other words, the circuit contains only *and* and *or* gates and the circuit inputs are literals (negated or non-negated variables). One can see that in this situation it suffices to use subformulas of the type $(z_{i,3} \rightarrow f_i(z_{i,1}, z_{i,2}))$, since the f_i are now monotone Boolean functions. This means, concretely, that for an *and*-connective, one can substitute the subformula $(z \rightarrow (x \wedge y))$ by the equivalent one $(\overline{z} \vee x) \wedge (\overline{z} \vee y)$. For an *or*-connective, from $(z \rightarrow (x \vee y))$ one obtains the equivalent one $(\overline{z} \vee x \vee y)$.

Example: Let us consider the formula in negation normal form

$$F = (x_1 \vee (\overline{x_2} \wedge \underbrace{(x_3 \vee \overline{x_1})})) .$$

where the braces mark y_3, y_2, y_1.

As explained, the corresponding subformulas are associated with 3 additional variables y_1, y_2, y_3. This generates the sat-equivalent formula G:

$$
\begin{aligned}
G \;=\; &(y_1) \;\wedge\; (y_1 \rightarrow (x_1 \vee y_2)) \\
&\wedge\; (y_2 \rightarrow (\overline{x_2} \wedge y_3)) \\
&\wedge\; (y_3 \rightarrow (x_3 \vee \overline{x_1})) \\
\;=\; &(y_1) \;\wedge\; (\overline{y_1} \vee x_1 \vee y_2) \\
&\wedge\; (\overline{y_2} \vee \overline{x_2}) \;\wedge\; (\overline{y_2} \vee y_3) \\
&\wedge\; (\overline{y_3} \vee x_3 \vee \overline{x_1})
\end{aligned}
$$

By using unit propagation we now build

$$G\{y_1 = 1\} = (x_1 \vee y_2) \wedge (\overline{y_2} \vee \overline{x_2}) \wedge (\overline{y_2} \vee y_3) \wedge (\overline{y_3} \vee x_3 \vee \overline{x_1}) .$$

In this way a formula in 3-*CNF* arises, which is sat-equivalent to F and has 4 clauses and 2 additional variables.

We include here also another construction that needs fewer clauses and fewer variables. This method was proposed in (Bubeck, Kleine Büning, 2009). Let us suppose that the initial formula F is given in negation normal form. From this formula first a series-parallel graph (see the appendix on graphs), is generated whose size is proportional to the length of the formula. On the one hand, from this graph it is possible to obtain a *CNF* equivalent to F (which generally can be exponential in $|F|$). This provides an alternative method to that of the truth table given previously.

On the other hand, it is possible to obtain from the graph a sat-equivalent formula G in 3-*CNF*. The number of clauses in G corresponds to the number of edges in the graph, which in turn corresponds to the number of literal occurrences in F.

The construction of the series-parallel graph from the formula F starts by defining a start-vertex y_1, an end-vertex y_2 and an edge labeled F between y_1 and y_2. Depending on whether F is a conjunction $F = G \wedge H$ or a disjunction $F = G \vee H$, edges running in parallel or in serial between the vertices (in this latter case including an additional vertex in between) are included.

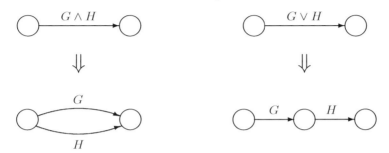

Example: Let us consider the formula $F = ((x_1 \wedge x_3) \vee \overline{x_2}) \wedge \overline{x_4}$. The following diagrams show how the desired series-parallel graph G_F, in which the edges are only labeled by literals, is generated

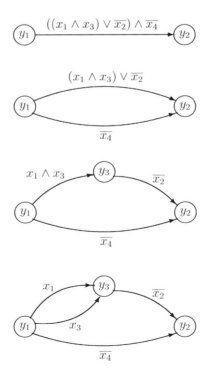

One can verify that in the transformation steps the following invariant holds: If α is an assignment satisfying the formula F, then in each path from the start-vertex y_1 to the end-vertex y_2 there is at least an edge labeled by a formula satisfied by α.

From this the following *CNF* representation equivalent to F is obtained:

$$F = \bigwedge_{\substack{p \\ \text{a path in } G_F, \\ \text{from } y_1 \text{ to } y_2}} \left(\bigvee_{\substack{u \\ \text{a literal, labeling} \\ \text{an edge on } p}} u \right)$$

For the previous example, there are 3 paths from y_1 to y_2. We obtain:

$$F = (x_1 \vee \overline{x_2}) \wedge (x_3 \vee \overline{x_2}) \wedge (\overline{x_4})$$

The *CNF* in this example is very short, but one should observe that in general there can be exponentially many different paths in the graph G_F. This is a transformation to *CNF* based on syntactic manipulations from formula F, while the original construction (given in the previous chapter) uses semantic considerations over the truth table.

Furthermore, also a sat-equivalent formula G in *CNF*, with length proportional to that of F can be constructed. This is an alternative to the Tseitin encoding. Additional Boolean variables are needed, namely the y_i, to denote the vertices in the graph G_F.

$$G = (y_1) \wedge (\overline{y_2}) \wedge \bigwedge_{\substack{(z, z') \\ \text{an edge in } G_F, \\ \text{labeled by } u}} (\overline{z} \vee u \vee z')$$

For the previous example formula we obtain:

$$G = (y_1) \wedge (\overline{y_2}) \wedge (\overline{y_1} \vee x_1 \vee y_3) \wedge (\overline{y_1} \vee x_3 \vee y_3) \wedge (\overline{y_3} \vee \overline{x_2} \vee y_2) \wedge (\overline{y_1} \vee \overline{x_4} \vee y_2)$$

By using unit propagation one can further eliminate the variables y_1 and y_2:

$$(x_1 \vee y_3) \wedge (x_3 \vee y_3) \wedge (\overline{y_3} \vee \overline{x_2}) \wedge (\overline{x_4})$$

Justification for the given formula is as follows. Due to the first two clauses, a satisfying assignment for G must set the variables y_1 to 1 and y_2 to 0. The rest of the conjunctive terms of G, each one associated to an edge (z, z'), can be written equivalently as $(z \rightarrow (u \vee z'))$. Since the first variable in such an implication chain is y_1 (with the assignment 1), and the last one is y_2 (with the assignment 0), there must be in each path from y_1 to y_2 an edge in which the corresponding literal u is set to 1 (and z' can then be set to 0). This then corresponds to a scheme as in the *CNF* representation given before.

Altogether this form of the sat-equivalent transformation to 3-*CNF* uses fewer clauses and fewer additional variables than the Tseitin encoding. The initial situation was however a formula in negation normal form, while in the case of Tseitin one can start from a circuit. In fact, the last described method of Bubeck and Kleine Büning can also be used when the Boolean function is given as a branching program (see the respective appendix). Analogously, as in the series-parallel graphs, the following holds: if α is an assignment giving value 1 to the Boolean function represented by the branching program, then in each path from the start-vertex to the 0-vertex of the branching program there is at least an edge labeled by a variable assignment $\{x_i = a\}$, contradicting the assignment α. Because of this, one can define, as in the previous construction an equivalent *CNF* in the following way:

$$F = \bigwedge_{\substack{p \\ \text{path in the branching program,} \\ \text{from start- to 0-vertex}}} \left(\bigvee_{\substack{u \\ u = 0 \text{ is the labeling} \\ \text{of an edge on } p}} u \right)$$

Corresponding to this we obtain the following sat-equivalent version of F by assigning to every edge in the branching program a new Boolean variable y_i. The edge labelings correspond to the variable queries (in accordance to the original variables of the branching program):

$$G = (y_1) \wedge (\overline{y_2}) \wedge \bigwedge_{\substack{(z, z') \\ \text{edge in the branching} \\ \text{program, labeled by } u = 0}} (\overline{z} \vee u \vee z')$$

Here y_1 is the variable assigned to the start-vertex in the branching program, and y_2 is the variable assigned to the 0-vertex.

1.4 Examples for Encoding into a *SAT* Problem

We show with some examples how algorithmic problems from various applications can be reduced to a *SAT* problem. Formally, this is nothing else than a polynomial reduction $A \preceq SAT$ where A is the problem in question (cf. the appendix about NP-completeness of *SAT*).

In the field of hardware verification, given a newly developed Boolean circuit S (see appendix about Boolean circuits), the task is to prove that the circuit complies with the requirements. Here we suppose that reference circuit S_{ref} is available whose correctness is already established. What needs to be done is to establish the equivalence between S and S_{ref}. Suppose both circuits have the input variables $x_1, \ldots, x_n$ and a single output bit. In case of more than one output bit one can handle each bit separately. The circuits S and S_{ref} are *not* equivalent if and only if there is an assignment to the input variables such that the following circuit outputs 1 (as an *XOR* of S and S_{ref}).

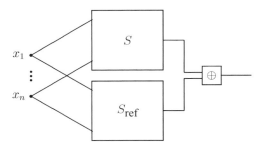

Therefore, it is possible to translate this non-equivalence problem into a 3-*SAT* problem, of size $O(|S| + |S_{ref}|)$ using the Tseitin method described in the last chapter. The solution can then be found by a 3-*SAT* solver.

Other difficult problems can be translated into a *SAT* problem as well. On the one hand, one is interested in algorithms that are as efficient as possible for as many problems as possible. On the other hand, secure cryptography relies on the "hope" that it will not be possible to find an efficient algorithm for the factorization problem. This is defined as follows. Given a composite number (in binary, can be several hundred bits long), find a non-trivial factorization, i.e., $n = p \cdot q$ where $1 < p, q < n$.

Let us consider the (tiny) number $n = 21$. We are searching for the factors 3 and 7. In binary notation we have $21 = (10101)_2$. We set up a multiplication scheme, as in school. The number 21 in binary is placed at the position where the multiplication result occurs. All other digit positions are filled with variables.

x_6	x_5	x_4	$*$	x_3	x_2	x_1
		x_9	x_8	x_7		
			x_{12}	x_{11}	x_{10}	
$+$				x_{15}	x_{14}	x_{13}
		1	0	1	0	1

We are looking for an assignment to the variables such that all elementary operations are fulfilled according to the rules of doing a school multiplication. For example, x_7 is the *AND* of x_3, x_4. Furthermore, x_{13} should be 1, and the *XOR* of x_{10} and x_{14} should result in 0, and so on (possibly one needs to introduce additional Boolean variables to take care of the carry bits). A *SAT* solver being fed with a formula representing the above multiplication table will deliver one of two (or both) of the results, $21 = 7 \cdot 3$, or $21 = 3 \cdot 7$:

```
1  1  1  *  0  1  1              0  1  1  *  1  1  1
─────────────────               ─────────────────
         0  0  0                          0  1  1
         1  1  1                          0  1  1
   +        1  1  1              +         0  1  1
─────────────────               ─────────────────
   1  0  1  0  1                    1  0  1  0  1
```

This method of multiplying two binary numbers with m bits each takes $O(m^2)$ many bit operations. There exist more efficient methods for doing the multiplication, requiring fewer circuitry, and therefore fewer Boolean variables. Such methods are described in (Wegener, 1987, chapter 3).

A large software system, like an operating system, typically includes several components: that is, packages with various functionalities. Some of these packages are not only needed in one such large program but are needed as a necessary component in several of them. If a large software system needs to be installed or deinstalled, or updated, it is a non-trivial problem to figure out which packages are still present and are needed elsewhere, and which packages are no longer needed. There is a complex structure of dependencies. Furthermore, packages exist in several versions. Not every version of one package is compatible with another version of another package.

These complex dependencies can be expressed by Boolean formulas. For example,

$$A \to (B_1 \lor B_2 \lor B_3) \quad \text{or equivalently,} \quad (\overline{A} \lor B_1 \lor B_2 \lor B_3)$$

This formula could have the interpretation that in order to install package A it is necessary to install B_1 or B_2 or B_3 first.

As another example, the formula

$$(\overline{A} \lor \overline{C_1}) \land (\overline{A} \lor \overline{C_2}) \land (\overline{A} \lor \overline{C_3})$$

could mean that the presence of package A on the system is not compliant with version $1, 2, 3$ of package C.

A unit clause such as (A) could mean that for the functionality of the whole system it is necessary to have A installed.

In the event that new packages need to be installed, or existing packages be uninstalled, a *SAT* solver can figure out whether the intended new system contains incompatibilities or not. Additionally, it would be desirable for the solver to give advice or suggest alternatives about how the functionality of the whole system can be guaranteed.

Formal software and hardware verification uses the technique of *bounded model checking* (BMC, for short). The program (or the designed piece of hardware) will be "unreeled" for a certain constant number k of times. That means, it will be transformed into a straight-line program without loops. Additionally, the property that needs to be verified must be formulated with respect to the configuration being reached after exactly k loops. Everything needs to be expressed bitwise, i.e. using Boolean variables. For the resulting formula the desired properties need to be formulated in negated form (as in a proof by contradiction). The logical consequence is that if the formula turns out (by a *SAT* solver) to be unsatisfiable, the program is correct (at least regarding the first k loops), and incorrect if the formula is satisfiable. The satisfying assignment, in this case, gives a hint about the position of the mistake in the program.

More about this theme can be found in chapter 14 of the handbook (cf. Biere et al., 2009).

1.5 Autark Assignments

In this chapter we give the definition and some first analysis of a concept that is useful when looking for sat-equivalent transformations. The concept of autark (partial) assignments allows a formula to be significantly simplified, whenever such an assignment shows up.

Definition

An assignment α is called *autark* for a given formula F in clause form (*CNF*) if, for all clauses $C \in F$, $Var(\alpha) \cap Var(C) \neq \emptyset$ implies $C\alpha = 1$.

In words: whenever the assignment α "touches" a clause C, then it should satisfy this clause.

There are some trivial autark assignments, like the empty assignment on the one hand, and an assignment that satisfies all clauses of F (provided F is satisfiable).

A simple (non trivial) case of an autark assignment occurs if there exists a *pure* literal, that is a literal u occurring in F such that $\overline{u}$ does not occur anywhere in F. In this case it is clear that $\alpha = \{u = 1\}$ is an autark assignment. All clauses containing u are set to 1 by α.

Example: The assignment $\alpha = \{x_1 = 1, x_2 = 0\}$ is autark for the following formula:

$$F = (x_1 \vee x_2 \vee x_3) \wedge (\overline{x_2} \vee \overline{x_3}) \wedge (x_3 \vee x_4)$$

The assignment α "touches" the first two clauses, and those two are satisfied by α.

Regarding the satisfiability problem, instead of F, one can continue with $F\alpha = (x_3 \vee x_4)$. This is formulated in the following theorem more generally.

Theorem

Let F be a clause set, and let α be an autark assignment for F. Then F and $F\alpha$ are sat-equivalent.

Proof: If β is a satisfying assignment for $F\alpha$ (where $Var(\alpha) \cap Var(\beta) = \emptyset$), then $\alpha \cup \beta$ satisfies the formula F too.

Conversely, suppose F is satisfiable with the assignment β. Let β' be the assignment β restricted to the set of variables $Var(F) \setminus Var(\alpha)$. Then β' satisfies all clauses in F which do not contain variables from $Var(\alpha)$. This means that $F\alpha$ is satisfied by β'. □

The typical setting in which autark assignments occur (for example, in the algorithm by Monien-Speckenmeyer, see section 4.2) is the following. Assume we have a backtracking procedure, and one of the recursive calls is intended to be applied to $F\alpha$, for some assignment α, but also other recursive calls like $F\beta$ should follow. It is easy to see that the test whether α is autark for F can be done efficiently. If this test turns out to be affirmative, then it suffices to perform the sole recursive call with $F\alpha$, while the others, like $F\beta$ are no longer necessary. This is so since F and $F\alpha$ are sat-equivalent.

But still, even if α is not an autark assignment (which is probably rather the rule) then this information brings a small advantage. Suppose all clauses in F have size k. If α is not autark for F, then there is at least one clause C in F such that $C\alpha$ has at most $k-1$ literals. At least one literal in C is set to 0. It might be an advantage if the next recursive call, applied to $F\alpha$, selects such a shortened clause C as starting point (ideally, C is even a unit clause).

Meanwhile the theory of autark assignments has been further developed, cf. chapter 11 in the handbook (Biere et al, 2009) or (Marek, 2009).

1.6 Craig Interpolants

The propositional version of Craig's interpolation theorem asserts that for every tautology of the form $F \to G$ there is a formula I whose variables are those which occur in F *and* in G, such that I is, logically, in the middle between F and G as the following theorem specifies.

Craig's Interpolation Theorem
Let $F \to G$ be a tautology. Then there is a formula I such that $Var(I) = Var(F) \cap Var(G)$ and both $F \to I$ and $I \to G$ are tautologies. The formula I is called an *interpolant* of F and G.
In general, the construction of formula I requires exponential time (at least, no better algorithms are known).

Proof: Let $Var(F) \cap Var(G) = \{x_1, \ldots, x_k\}$. We show how a truth table for the desired formula I can be defined. To this end, we cycle through all 2^k potential assignments

α of the variables $x_1, \ldots, x_k$ and we define the respective function value of I as follows.

$$I\alpha = \begin{cases} 1 & \text{if } \alpha \text{ can be extended to a satisfying assignment of } F, \\ 0 & \text{if } \alpha \text{ can be extended to an assignment which falsifies } G, \\ * & \text{otherwise} \end{cases}$$

In this case the meaning of the star $*$ is that $I\alpha$ can have any of the values 0 or 1.

This definition of I is indeed valid since by assumption $F \rightarrow G$ is a tautology. An assignment α to a set of variables $Var(I)$ can be extended to a satisfying assignment of F if and only of all extensions of α to $Var(G)$ will satisfy the formula G.

For any assignment β of $Var(F) \cup Var(G)$ we have $F\beta = 1$ implies $I\beta = 1$, and therefore, that $F \rightarrow I$ is a tautology. Similarly, if $G\beta = 0$, it follows that $I\beta = 0$, which shows that $I \rightarrow G$ is a tautology, too. Given the truth-table of I, by the standard method, it is possible to construct a (*CNF-*) formula.   □

Craig also showed that, given a proof of the formula $F \rightarrow G$ (as being a tautology) an interpolant I can be constructed (cf. the chapter on proof systems). The question then arises how large I must be, compared to the size of F and of G. Of course this depends on the kind of representation of I, either as a formula, a circuit, or a binary decision diagram. We want to consider the case of a circuit representation for I.

In a later chapter we will see that it is possible to construct interpolation circuits which have about the size of a resolution refutation of $\neg(F \rightarrow G)$, which is the same as $F \wedge \overline{G}$.

On the other hand, it is not likely that interpolants can always be polynomial in the size of F and G since this implies that all problems located in NP as well as in co-NP would have polynomial-size circuits.

Theorem

If for every tautology of the form $F \rightarrow G$ it is possible to construct an interpolant I which, when represented as a circuit, has size at most $p(|F|+|G|)$, for some polynomial p, then it follows that all sets in NP $\cap$ co-NP have polynomial-size circuits.

Furthermore, if this construction of I can be done efficiently (by a polynomial-time algorithm), it follows that NP $\cap$ co-NP $=$ P.

Proof: Let A be a decision problem (represented as a set) in NP $\cap$ co-NP. Then there is a nondeterministic polynomial-time Turing machine M_1 which accepts A, and there is another such machine M_2 which accepts the complement $\overline{A}$ (cf. (Wegener, 2005)). As in the proof of the Cook-Levin Theorem about the NP-completeness of *SAT* (see appendix), for each input length n Boolean formulas F (based on M_1) and G (based on M_2) can be constructed. The variables of formula F consist of $x_1, \ldots, x_n$ and $y_1, \ldots y_{p(n)}$, such that for all $a_1 a_2 \ldots a_n \in \{0, 1\}^n$ the following is true:

$$a_1 a_2 \ldots a_n \in A \text{ if and only if } F\{x_1 = a_1, \ldots, x_n = a_n\} \text{ is satisfiable.}$$

Analogously, G has the variables $x_1, \ldots, x_n$ and $z_1, \ldots, z_{q(n)}$ such that

$$a_1 a_2 \ldots a_n \in \overline{A} \text{ if and only if } G\{x_1 = a_1, \ldots, x_n = a_n\} \text{ is satisfiable.}$$

The existence of a polynomial-size interpolant circuit I means that I has the input variables $Var(F) \cap Var(G) = \{x_1, \ldots, x_n\}$. From the interpolation property we get: $a_1 a_2 \ldots a_n \in A$ if and only if $I\{x_1 = a_1, \ldots, x_n = a_n\} = 1$. Hence, A has polynomial-size circuits (or is even polynomial-time computable, under the stronger assumption). □

This chapter uses results from (Craig, 1957), (Mundici, 1984), (Schöning, Torán, 2006).

1.7 Satisfiability by Combinatorics

In some cases it is possible, just by counting clauses, variables, their occurrences in the clauses, by considering the size of clauses, etc. to figure out that a formula must be satisfiable. We start with some very easy observations of this kind.

Proposition

If a clause set F does not contain any clause with solely positive literals (or with solely negative literals) then F is satisfiable.

Proof: In the first case, F can be satisfied by setting all variables to 0; in the second case by setting all variables to 1. □

Proposition

Given a clause set F whose clauses all have *exactly* k literals, if F has strictly less than 2^k clauses, then F is satisfiable.

Proof: Let $n = |Var(F)|$, where $n \geq k$. For every clause $C \in F$, $|C| = k$, there are exactly 2^{n-k} assignments α with $Var(\alpha) = Var(F)$ which falsify C. Hence, altogether there are strictly less than $2^k \cdot 2^{n-k} = 2^n$ assignments which falsify F. Therefore, F must be satisfiable. □

In other words, each clause C determines a portion of $2^{-k} = 2^{-|C|}$ of all potential assignments that do not satisfy F. Altogether these portions do not add up to 1 so that there are satisfying assignments remaining. Therefore, the previous proposition can be generalized as follows.

Theorem

Let $F = \{C_1, C_2, \ldots, C_m\}$ be a clause set. If $\displaystyle\sum_{j=1}^{m} 2^{-|C_j|} < 1$, then F is satisfiable.

This theorem states the satisfiability of F in a non-constructive way, by a counting argument. The question remains how such a satisfying assignment can be found (efficiently). Let x be a variable occurring in F. Under the given assumption, the formula F is satisfiable. Therefore, either $F\{x = 0\}$ or $F\{x = 1\}$ is satisfiable (or both). The problem is for which one we should decide. The sum $\sum_{C \in F} 2^{-|C|}$ can be divided in 3 terms: one sum which deals with those clauses in F which contain x, another sum which deals with those clauses in F which contain $\overline{x}$, and finally, another sum which contains the clauses without x or $\overline{x}$. Let us write this a follows.

$$\sum_{C \in F} 2^{-|C|} \;=\; S_x + S_{\overline{x}} + S \;<\; 1$$

Plugging in $x = 0$ and $x = 1$ yields the following.

$$\sum_{C \in F\{x=0\}} 2^{-|C|} = 2S_x + S \qquad \sum_{C \in F\{x=1\}} 2^{-|C|} = 2S_{\overline{x}} + S$$

It is not possible that both sums are ≥ 1 (otherwise we could add both inequalities and obtain a contradiction to the assumption). Therefore, at least one of the sums is strictly less than 1. By the theorem, the corresponding formula $F\{x = 0\}$ or $F\{x = 1\}$ is then satisfiable. The value of x can be set accordingly and one can continue with this method to obtain a satisfying assignment of F at the end.

This was an application of the self-reducibility property of *SAT* (see the appendix about P and NP).

Next we look at another class of formulas where it is possible to prove satisfiability. If a set of clauses is given whose sets of variables are pairwise disjoint, then it is clear that one can find a satisfying assignment, actually many of them. But suppose that a certain degree of "overlap" between clauses is allowed, in the sense that $\mathit{Var}(C) \cap \mathit{Var}(C') \neq \emptyset$. If these overlaps do not add up to large values then a satisfying assignment is still achievable. This is formulated in the following theorem.

Theorem (Lovász Local Lemma)

Let F be a formula in *CNF*. Suppose all the clauses of F have exactly size k. If for every clause $C \in F$ it is true that there are fewer than $\frac{1}{4} \cdot 2^k = 2^{k-2}$ clauses $C' \in F$ such that $\mathit{Var}(C) \cap \mathit{Var}(C') \neq \emptyset$, then F is satisfiable.

Proof: We will show that the following probabilistic algorithm, given the assumptions formulated in the theorem, will terminate with high probability, and in this case will output a satisfying assignment for F. Let $F = \{C_1, C_2, \ldots, C_m\}$, $\mathit{Var}(F) = \{x_1, \ldots, x_n\}$. On F we perform the following main program:

> Randomly choose an initial assignment α
> **for** $j := 1$ **to** m **do**
>   **if** $C_j \alpha = 0$ **then** Repair (C_j) $(*)$

The procedure Repair modifies the assignment α in such a way that after its termination (if it terminates) we have $C_j \alpha = 1$, and all clauses that were satisfied by α before its modification, are still satisfied afterwards. Therefore, it is clear that after the main program has terminated, a satisfying assignment for F is found. The critical point is the termination of the recursive procedure Repair. This procedure is easy to describe:

> **proc** Repair (C : clause)
> For all the k variables in C choose a random value, and replace it in α
> (and keep the assignments to all other variables in F unchanged)
> **for** $j := 1$ **to** m **do**
>   **if** $\mathit{Var}(C_j) \cap \mathit{Var}(C) \neq \emptyset$ **then**
>   **if** $C_j \alpha = 0$ **then** Repair (C_j)

At first glance it is unclear whether this procedure terminates at all. Indeed, it does, and we argue as follows. The whole computation process, while passing through, say, s instantiations to Repair (either by a call from the main program, or by a recursive call by Repair itself) consumes $s \cdot k$ random bits to give the variables occuring in of a violated clause new values. Additionally, there are n bits needed for producing the initial assignment. Below, a method is presented which shows how these $n + s \cdot k$ bits can be reconstructed from fewer than $n + s \cdot k$ bits if s is sufficiently large. But this is impossible, since random bits cannot be compressed (with high probability). This proves that the whole algorithm stops with high probability after a certain number s of Repair-applications.

In order to reconstruct these $n + s \cdot k$ many bits, the following pieces of information are needed: first, the n bits that describe the status of α *after* these s many Repair-applications. Further, using m bits, one can indicate which for-loop of the main program started a call to Repair. The jth bit is 1 if and only if a call of Repair(C_j) was done in the main program. A recursive call to Repair can only occur if a variable that overlaps with some neighboring clause C_j has been found (i.e. $\mathit{Var}(C) \cap \mathit{Var}(C_j) \neq \emptyset$). Since there are at most $2^{k-2-\varepsilon}$ such neighbors (for some $\varepsilon > 0$), it is possible to describe the sequence of length s of such neighboring clauses, which cause Repair to be called on $(k - 2 - \varepsilon) \cdot s$ many bits. This can be considered as some kind of relative addressing or indexing. Finally, it is possible to describe the tree structure of those recursive calls to Repair on $2s$ bits. Writing a 1 denotes a procedure call, that is, go one level down; whereas writing a 0 means a return from a procedure call, that is, go one level up. For example, the following tree

can be described by the bitstring 10101110010010.

Altogether these descriptions needs $n + m + s \cdot (k - \varepsilon)$ bits. Having this information available, the entire computation can be reconstructed by working backwards. Starting with the final assignment α after the s many calls to Repair, each single call to Repair can be revoked. The crucial point is, if the clause C_j that caused a call to Repair can be identified, the situation before the call can be uniquely determined. This is because there is just one assignment of the k variables occurring in the clause which falsifies it. The k affected variables can be set in such a way that the clause C_j takes the value 0 as in the situation before the call to Repair. In this manner all $n + s \cdot k$ original random bits can be reconstructed. In general, it is not possible to describe a sequence of random bits by a smaller number of bits (only with a negligible probability). This is a so-called incompressibility proof argument which relies on the concept of Kolmogorov complexity, cf. (Li, Vitanyi, 2008).

Therefore, we obtain the inequality

$$n + s \cdot k \leq n + m + s \cdot (k - \varepsilon)$$

which has to hold for "almost all" sequences of random bits. Solving for s yields $s \leq m/\varepsilon$. In other words, if the number s of calls to Repair grows beyond m/ε, with high probability, the computation process will stop and deliver a satisfying assignment. □

The above proof of this particular version of the Lovász Local Lemma goes back to Moser's presentation at the FOCS conference (Moser, 2009). Actually, this is not the strongest form of the lemma. The bound $2^{k-2} = 2^k/4$ can be improved to $2^k/e$, cf. (Moser, Tardos, 2009) and (Moser, 2012).

Similarly, as the observation at the beginning of this chapter was generalized to a theorem by allowing clauses of different sizes, the Lovász Local Lemma can also be generalized, (cf. Moser, 2012).

Theorem

Let F be a formula in *CNF*. If every clause $C \in F$ satisfies the condition

$$\sum_{D \in N(C)} 2^{-|D|} < \frac{1}{4}$$

then F is satisfiable.

Here $N(C)$ is the set of "neighbors" of C, i.e. $N(C) = \{D \in F \mid Var(C) \cap Var(D) \neq \emptyset\}$.

In the following two theorems the number of clauses and the number of variables are compared to each other.

Lemma

Let F be a set of clauses. If for every subset G of F it holds that $|G| \leq |Var(G)|$, then F is satisfiable (here the expression $|G|$ refers to the number of clauses contained in the clause set G).

Proof: Associate with F a bipartite graph (see the appendix about graphs): the set of vertices is split into two disjoint sets. One vertex set (on the left) consists of the set of clauses $C \in F$; the other set of vertices (on the right) corresponds to the set of variables $Var(F)$. An edge (C, x) is present if and only if variable x occurs in C (positively or negatively). The well-known marriage theorem of P. Hall states that a matching with $|F|$ edges exists in this graph if and only if the condition $|G| \leq |Var(G)|$ is satisfied for all $G \subseteq F$. By virtue of this matching every clause $C \in F$ is assigned a (different) variable. This variable can be assigned value 0 or 1 in such a way that C becomes satisfied. Therefore, F is satisfiable. $\square$

Definition

A set of clauses F is called *minimally unsatisfiable*, if F is unsatisfiable, but $F \setminus \{C\}$ is satisfiable, for every clause $C \in F$.

Theorem

If F is minimally unsatisfiable, then $|F| > |Var(F)|$.

Proof: Since F is unsatisfiable, by the previous lemma, there must be a subset $G \subseteq F$ such that $|G| > |Var(G)|$. We choose such a *maximal* subset of G. If $G = F$, the theorem is already proven. So suppose G is a *proper* subset of F.

Let $H \subseteq F \setminus G$ be arbitrary. It is clear that $|H| < |Var(H) \setminus Var(G)|$, because otherwise it follows $|G \cup H| > |Var(G \cup H)|$ contradicting the maximality of G.

Therefore the clause set $F \setminus G$ satisfies the precondition of the previous lemma, and is satisfiable (using an assignment α such that $Var(\alpha) = Var(F) \setminus Var(G)$, which can be established by the proof of the lemma). Since F is minimally unsatisfiable, G must be satisfiable, say, by an assignment β such that $Var(\beta) = Var(G)$. It follows that $\alpha \cup \beta$ satisfies the clause set F. This is a contradiction proving the theorem. $\square$

The theorem just proven is sometimes called *Tarsi's lemma*, cf. (Aharoni, Linial, 1986). There are also some further developments which are discussed in chapter 11 of the handbook, cf. (Biere et al., 2009).

The following theorem also uses the above lemma in its proof, hence the marriage theorem of Hall, and goes back to (Tovey, 1984).

Theorem
Let $k \geq 1$ and let $F \in CNF$ such that each clause in F has at least k literals. Suppose further that each variable occurs (positively or negatively) in at most k clauses. Then F is satisfiable.

Proof: We show that the precondition of the previous lemma is satisfied. Thus it follows that F is satisfiable. Let G be an arbitrary subset of F. By assumption, the $|G|$ many clauses in G consist of at least $k \cdot |G|$ many instances of literals. Each variable can contribute to at most k clauses. Therefore, there are at most $|G|$ many different variables in G, hence $|G| \leq |Var(G)|$. The lemma applies. Therefore, F is satisfiable. $\square$

From this theorem an interesting special case of *SAT* can be seen to be polynomially solvable. Consider a clause set $F \in CNF$, where each variable occurs in at most 2 places. Then satisfiability of F can be decided as follows. By unit propagation (cf. page 18) all unit clauses can be eliminated. If this process produces the empty clause, then F is unsatisfiable. Otherwise, we are left with a clause set satisfying the conditions of the theorem with $k = 2$, and in this case, F is satisfiable.

Notice that the satisfiability problem for *CNF*-formulas containing at most 3 instances of each variable is already NP-complete. This can be seen as follows. Next, it is shown how every formula in *CNF* can be transformed into a sat-equivalent formula where each variable occurs at most 3 times. Suppose that the variable x occurs $(s > 3)$-times. Then substitute each occurrence of x by new variables $x_1, x_2, \ldots, x_s$. Additionally, add the following clauses:

$$(\overline{x_1} \vee x_2), (\overline{x_2} \vee x_3), \ldots, (\overline{x_{s-1}} \vee x_s), (\overline{x_s} \vee x_1)$$

By this circle of implications it can be guaranteed that either all variables receive the value 0, or all take the value 1. This new formula is sat-equivalent to the original one, and it contains each variable at most 3 times.

2 Resolution Calculus

We start with a general discussion about calculi and their relation to the NP vs. co-NP problem. Afterwards we specialize to the resolution calculus and analyze its particular properties. Recall that *SAT* is NP-complete, and therefore, $\overline{SAT}$ as well as *TAUT* (the set of propositional tautologies) are co-NP-complete (see appendix).

2.1 Calculi and NP versus co-NP

A *calculus* is understood as a collection of transformations which manipulate formulas or clause sets. A well-known traditional calculus consists of the usual collection of rules for producing equivalent formulas, like the associative laws, the commutative laws, the distributive laws, the deMorgan laws, etc. If it is possible to transform formula F, using the calculus C, into the formula G, we denote this by $F \vdash_C G$.

In general, given some formula F, there are several possibilities to apply a rule of the underlying calculus to F. Therefore, a calculus can be considered as a *nondeterministic* process (or algorithm). Given an input formula F, the nondeterministic algorithm branches, and each computation branch might yield a different output formula G (such that $F \vdash_C G$).

We say that a calculus C is *correct* if $F \vdash_C G$ implies that $F \to G$ is a tautology. *results in a Truth value*

A calculus C is *complete* if for all F, G such that $F \to G$ is a tautology, it follows that $F \vdash_C G$. For a complete calculus C, this implies that the property that F is a tautology can be proved by showing that $1 \vdash_C F$. The property of F being unsatisfiable is equivalent to the property $F \vdash_C 0$.

A sequence of formulas $F = F_0, F_1, F_2, \ldots, F_t = G$ such that $F_i \vdash_C F_{i+1}$ (for $i = 0, 1, \ldots, t-1$) is a single application of a calculus rule, is called a *proof* (of the fact that $F \to G$ is a tautology) within the calculus C. Furthermore, t is the *length* of this proof.

In the following we will only consider the *resolution calculus* $\mathcal{R}$. This calculus $\mathcal{R}$ is correct, but it is not complete in the sense defined above. However, the resolution calculus is *refutation complete* as we will show below. This means that for every unsatisfiable formula F we have $F \vdash_{\mathcal{R}} 0$. Actually, compared with completeness, this is not a very strong restriction. Suppose, the goal is to show that $F \to G$ is a tautology. Then instead, one can show that $F \wedge \neg G$ is unsatisfiable which is equivalent to $(F \wedge \neg G) \vdash_{\mathcal{R}} 0$.

NESS:38

CHAPTER 2. RESOLUTION CALCULUS

Additionally, notice that the resolution calculus $\mathcal{R}$ can only be applied to formulas in *CNF*, that is, to clause sets. Instead of 0 (for the generic unsatisfiable formula), one obtains the empty clause $\square$, therefore we write $F \vdash_{\mathcal{R}} \square$.

It is an interesting observation that there is a certain way of certification for both, the satisfiability as well as the unsatisfiability of a formula F. Satisfiability can be certified by a satisfying assignment. This can be done by a nondeterministic, polynomial-time algorithm which "guesses" such an assignment. This is the bottom line when showing that $SAT \in$ NP (see appendix about P and NP). [nondeterministic polynomial]

On the other hand, a proof $F \vdash_{\mathcal{C}} 0$ is a certificate for the fact that F is unsatisfiable. Also, such a proof can be found by a nondeterministic algorithm. Put in succinct mathematical terms:

* $F \in SAT \quad iff \quad \exists \alpha : F\alpha = 1$
$$F \in \overline{SAT} \quad iff \quad \exists F_1, F_2, \ldots F_t : F \vdash_{\mathcal{C}} F_1 \vdash_{\mathcal{C}} \cdots \vdash_{\mathcal{C}} F_t = 0$$

The question remains how many proof steps are necessary to prove that a formula F (which is unsatisfiable, or which is a tautology) is indeed unsatisfiable (resp. a tautology). It may be expected that in the worst case (i.e. for some formulas of a given size n) this requires exponentially in n many proof steps. Indeed, for the resolution calculus we will show this in a moment. The expectation is justified by the following theorem.

> **Theorem**
>
> If there is a correct and refutation-complete calculus $\mathcal{C}$, as well as a polynomial p, such that for every unsatisfiable formula (or clause set) F it is possible to show $F \vdash_{\mathcal{C}} 0$ by a proof of length at most $p(n)$ (where n is the length, or the number of variables, of F) then it follows NP = co-NP.

Proof: The set of unsatisfiable formulas, *UNSAT*, as well as the set of tautologies. *TAUT*, is co-NP-complete. Therefore, it follows NP = co-NP, if we could show *UNSAT* $\in$ NP (resp. *TAUT* $\in$ NP). But this is what the assumption of the theorem claims: there is a nondeterministic process (given by the calculus $\mathcal{C}$) which, given an unsatisfiable formula of size n permits a proof of unsatisfiability which has length at most $p(n)$. A nondeterministic Turing machine can "guess" such a proof and verify that all steps are correct, and if so, accept. $\square$

This connection between the question of whether NP = co-NP and the lengths of proofs for unsatisfiability (or the property of being a tautology) was first observed in (Cook, Reckhow, 1979).

2.2 Refutation Completeness

In this section we introduce the resolution calculus in detail, and we prove its refutation completeness.

Definition

Two clauses C_1 and C_2 are said to be *resolvable* if there exists a literal u such that $u \in C_1$ and $\overline{u} \in C_2$. In this case a third clause C_3 can be defined, called the *resolvent* of C_1 and C_2, by

$$C_3 = (C_1 \setminus \{u\}) \cup (C_2 \setminus \{\overline{u}\})$$

If u or $\overline{u}$ is the variable x we say that C_3 was derived from C_1 and C_2 by *resolving on* x. Also, C_1 and C_2 are called the *parent clauses* of C_3.
The following symbolic notation is used to express the situation as described in this definition.

$$\begin{array}{cc} C_1 & C_2 \\ & \\ & C_3 \end{array}$$

When resolving C_3 from C_1 and C_2, the following semantic property can be easily verified. If α is an assignment which satisfies both C_1 and C_2, that is $(C_1 \wedge C_2)\,\alpha = 1$, then α satisfies C_3 too, i.e. $C_3\,\alpha = 1$. This simple observation is the key for the correctness of the resolution calculus (see below).

Producing a resolvent is just a single step in a complete resolution proof, which we define next.

Definition

Let F be a clause set (a formula in *CNF*). A *resolution proof* (or *resolution refutation*) is a sequence of clauses $\mathcal{R} = (C_1, C_2, \ldots, C_t)$ such that the last clause is the empty clause: $C_t = \square$. Furthermore, for $i = 1, 2, \ldots, t$ either C_i is one of the clauses from F, or C_i is a resolvent of two clauses C_j and C_l which appeared earlier in the sequence, i.e. $j, l < i$.

Suppose formula F consists of m clauses. Without loss of generality we may assume in this definition that the first m clauses of the sequence are the clauses of F. As the *length* of the proof $\mathcal{R}$ we count the number of clauses which are resolvents, i.e. $t - m$.

We use this not very suggestive representation of resolution proofs, as a sequence of clauses according to the definition, mainly for proof-technical reasons. A graphic description of a resolution proof can be given as follows. As an example, let

$$F = (x \vee \overline{z}) \wedge (x \vee y \vee z) \wedge (\overline{x} \vee \overline{y} \vee \overline{z}) \wedge (\overline{x} \vee y) \wedge (\overline{y} \vee z)$$

A resolution refutation of F can be represented as in the figure.

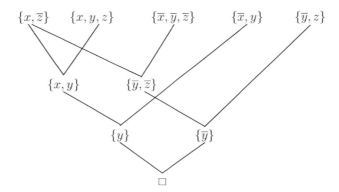

The next two lemmas will be useful when dealing with resolution proofs. The first lemma shows how an existing resolution proof can be restricted by a partial assignment such as $\{u = 1\}$. The second lemma shows how a resolution proof can be extended by adding a literal u into certain clauses.

Resolution Restriction Lemma

Let $\mathcal{R} = (C_1, C_2, \ldots, C_t)$, $C_t = \square$, be a resolution proof for a set of clauses F. Let u be a literal occurring in F. Then there is a resolution proof $\mathcal{R}'$ for $F\{u = 1\}$. This new resolution proof does not contain any clause with literal u or $\overline{u}$. Further, the length of $\mathcal{R}'$ is at most the length of $\mathcal{R}$ minus the number of clauses in R which contain literal u.

Proof for Resolution

Proof: We construct the desired resolution proof $\mathcal{R}'$ iteratively, for $i = 1, \ldots, t$, from the proof $\mathcal{R}$. In every step there are several possibilities: either the clause C_i from $\mathcal{R}$ will be cancelled and does no longer occur in $\mathcal{R}'$. This happens exactly when $u \in C_i$. The second possibility is that a clause $C'_i \subseteq C_i$ is adopted in $\mathcal{R}'$. In logical terms this means that C'_i implies C_i. This clause C'_i is either a clause from $F\{u = 1\}$, or it is a resolvent of two clauses $C'_j \subseteq C_j$ and $C'_l \subseteq C_l$, which have been listed in $\mathcal{R}'$ before, i.e. $j, l < i$. Another possibility is that C'_i is a duplicate of another clause C'_j from $\mathcal{R}'$ that was listed before (i.e. $j < i$, $C'_j = C'_i$).

1. If C_i is a clause from F and does not contain u or $\overline{u}$, then $\mathcal{R}'$ also lists C_i at this point, i.e. $C'_i = C_i$.

2. If C_i is a clause from F and contains $\overline{u}$ then we let $C'_i = C_i \setminus \{\overline{u}\}$.

3. If C_i contains the literal u (whether C_i comes from F or is a resolvent), then we don't have a clause in $\mathcal{R}'$ at this point (i.e. the clause is cancelled).

4. If C_i is the resolvent of two clauses C_j, C_l, and there exist respective clauses C'_j and C'_l in $\mathcal{R}'$, and these clauses contain the variable on which they were resolved, then C'_i is the resolvent of C'_k and C'_l.

5. If C_i is the resolvent of two clauses C_j and C_l, and there exist respective clauses C'_j and C'_l in $\mathcal{R}'$, and one of these clauses, say C'_j, no longer contains the variable on which they were resolved, then we let $C'_i = C'_j$ (i.e. a duplication). Observe that in this case we also have $C'_i \subseteq C_i$, as desired.

6. If C_i is the resolvent of two clauses C_j and C_l, but one of the parent clauses, say C_j, was cancelled (according to rule 3) because it contained u, then C_i does not contain u (otherwise rule 3 would have applied). It was the literal u resp. $\overline{u}$ which was resolved on in this resolution step. Consequently, C'_l does no longer contain $\overline{u}$, and we let $C'_i = C'_l$ (i.e. a duplication). Again, we have $C'_i \subseteq C_i$, as desired.

Since C_t does not contain u, a corresponding clause C'_t exists in $\mathcal{R}'$. From $C'_t \subseteq C_t = \square$ it follows that $C'_t = \square$. By renumbering the non-cancelled clauses in $\mathcal{R}'$, and by listing the duplicate clauses just once, one obtains a resolution refutation for $F\{u = 1\}$. $\square$

As an example, we take the resolution proof of the formula

$$F = (x \vee \overline{z}) \wedge (x \vee y \vee z) \wedge (\overline{x} \vee \overline{y} \vee \overline{z}) \wedge (\overline{x} \vee y) \wedge (\overline{y} \vee z)$$

as presented above. By setting $x = 0$ we obtain

$$F\{x = 0\} = (\overline{z}) \wedge (y \vee z) \wedge (\overline{y} \vee z)$$

The restricted resolution proof, obtained by applying the rules of the lemma, has the following form, where we indicate duplications by a double line.

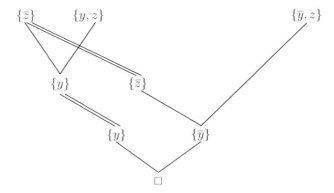

Resolution Expansion Lemma

Let F be a clause set and u be a literal occurring in F. Let $\mathcal{R}'$ be a resolution refutation of $F' = F\{u = 1\}$. Then there exists a sequence $\mathcal{R}$ of resolution steps, based on the clause set F which either ends with $\square$, like $\mathcal{R}'$, or ends with the unit clause $\{\overline{u}\}$.

Proof: For each clause $C \in F$ which contains the literal $\overline{u}$ there exists in $\mathcal{R}'$ a corresponding clause $C' = C \setminus \{\overline{u}\}$. By reinstalling $\overline{u}$ in such clauses – as well as in all subsequent resolvents – this modification can have the effect that the final clause $\square$ becomes the unit clause $\{\overline{u}\}$. $\qquad\square$

Resolution Theorem

The resolution calculus for clause sets is *correct* and *refutation complete*, that is, a clause set F is unsatisfiable *if and only if* there exists a resolution refutation of F.

Proof: (Correctness) If there exists a resolution refutation of F, and if we assume that F is satisfiable with some assignment α, then, by the remark given after the definition of resolution, this assignment also satisfies each resolvent, especially the last clause which is the empty clause. But this is impossible. Therefore, F must be unsatisfiable.

(Refutation completeness) Conversely, let F be unsatisfiable. We show by induction on $n = |\mathrm{Var}(F)|$, the number of variables, that F has a resolution refutation.

If $n = 0$, we have $F = \{\square\}$, and we are done.

If $n > 0$, let x be an arbitrary variable in F. Then both clause sets $F_0 := F\{x = 0\}$ and $F_1 := F\{x = 1\}$ are unsatisfiable, too. These clause sets contain at most $n - 1$ variables. Therefore, F_0 and F_1, by the induction hypothesis, have resolution refutations, say $\mathcal{R}_0$ and $\mathcal{R}_1$.

By reestablishing the original clauses of F in $\mathcal{R}_0$ and $\mathcal{R}_1$, as in the resolution expansion lemma, one obtains two resolution sequences ending in the two unit clauses $\{x\}$ and $\{\overline{x}\}$ (or with $\square$). In a last resolution step

$$\{x\}\ \{\overline{x}\}$$
$$\square$$

the empty clause can be obtained. $\qquad\square$

It can be observed that the length $l(n)$ of the resolution refutation constructed in this proof satisfies

$$l(n) \leq \begin{cases} 0, & n = 0 \\ 2 \cdot l(n-1) + 1, & n > 0 \end{cases}$$

where n is the number of variables in F. This recursion results in $l(n) \leq 2^n - 1$. Furthermore, the resolution proof constructed has a tree structure, a so called *tree resolution*, in the sense that every resolvent is used in at most one further resolution step. In many cases resolution proofs can be much shorter, especially when they do not have a tree structure.

Next, we present an alternative proof for the refutation completeness of resolution (from a personal communication with Volker Diekert). We assume that all potential resolvents derivable from F have been constructed (which form a finite set). Let us denote this set of clauses (i.e. F and all conceivable resolvents) as G. This is, G is the closure of F under resolution. We will show that under the precondition $\square \notin G$, a satisfying assignment for F can be constructed. This assignment naturally also satisfies G since all clauses in G follow from the clauses in F. We start with the empty assignment $\alpha = \emptyset$, and successively add an assignment to each variable. Let $x \in Var(F)$ be an as yet unassigned variable. If the unit clause $\{x\}$ occurs in G (which prevents $\{\overline{x}\}$ from being in G, otherwise also $\square \in G$), then we set $\alpha := \alpha \cup \{x = 1\}$, otherwise, if $\{x\} \notin G$, we set $\alpha := \alpha \cup \{x = 0\}$.

In the next step we set $G := G\{x = a\}$ where $a = 1$ in the former case, and $a = 0$ in the latter case.

Before we continue with the discussion, let us verify that this modification of α and of G satisfies the following invariants:

First, $G\{x = a\}$ is also closed under resolution. Whenever two clauses in $G\{x = a\}$ are resolvable, then the original clauses in G neither contain x nor $\overline{x}$ (otherwise at least one of these clauses will be deleted in $G\{x = a\}$). Therefore, the resolvent is also present in $G\{x = a\}$.

Second, it holds that $\square \notin G\{x = a\}$. The empty clause could only appear if, in the case of $a = 1$, the unit-clause $\{\overline{x}\}$ was present in G. But this is impossible, by the discussion above. The other case $a = 0$ is symmetric.

We continue by fixing assignments for variables and plugging these assignments into the clause set G. Finally, $G = \emptyset$ which corresponds to a tautology. This means that F is satisfied by the determined assignment to the variables.

Example: Consider the given clause set

$$F = \{\, \{x\}, \{\overline{x}, z\}, \{\overline{x}, y, z\}, \{\overline{y}, \overline{z}\} \,\}$$

We construct every possible resolvent, starting out from F, and obtain the following set:

$$G = F \cup \{\, \{z\}, \{y, z\}, \{\overline{x}, \overline{y}\}, \{\overline{x}, z, \overline{z}\}, \{\overline{x}, y, \overline{y}\}, \{\overline{y}\}, \{z, \overline{z}\}, \{y, \overline{y}\}, \{\overline{x}, \overline{y}, \overline{z}\} \,\}$$

Since $\{x\} \in G$ we let the assignment to x be 1, and in the next step we get

$$G\{x = 1\} = \{\, \{z\}, \{y, z\}, \{\overline{y}, \overline{z}\}, \{\overline{y}\}, \{z, \overline{z}\}, \{y, \overline{y}\} \,\}$$

Since $\{y\} \notin G\{x = 1\}$ we set y to 0, and we get

$$G\{x = 1, y = 0\} = \{\, \{z\}, \{z, \overline{z}\} \,\}$$

Since $\{z\} \in G\{x = 1, y = 0\}$ we set z to 1, and we finally get

$$G\{x = 1, y = 0, z = 1\} = \emptyset \quad \text{(tautology)}$$

This means that $\{x = 1, y = 0, z = 1\}$ is a satisfying assignment for F.

We have presented both proofs for refutation completeness since each proof provides a different constructive argument. Under the assumption that F is unsatisfiable, we have constructed a resolution refutation for F in the first proof. Under the assumption that the empty clause cannot be resolved from F, we have constructed a satisfying assignment for F in the second proof.

Finally, observe that there is an interesting connection between resolution refutations and branching programs (see the appendix). If one turns a resolution refutation "upside-down" so that it starts with the empty clause, the resulting graph can be interpreted as a branching program. Each node in this graph is assigned the variable which was used for the respective resolution step. Each path in this graph corresponds to an assignment α, and it ends in a clause from F which is falsified by this particular assignment. This connection between resolution proofs and branching programs can be used to transform lower bound proofs for the size of branching programs to lower bound proofs for the length of resolution refutations, and vice versa.

2.3   Unit Clauses, Subsumption and Pure Literals

Inspecting the proof of the resolution completeness theorem, it should be clear that in general it is not possible to remove the parent clauses once they have been used for a resolution step. It is still possible that such a parent clause needs to be used for another resolution step. In this section several forms of possible simplifications will be discussed, in the sense of an equivalent or a sat-equivalent transformation.

Example: The clause set $F = \{\{x\}, \{\overline{x}, y\}, \{\overline{x}, \overline{y}\}\}$ is unsatisfiable. By resolving the first two clauses one obtains $\{y\}$. After this, it is not possible to remove $\{x\}$ since this clause has to be used for another resolution together with the third clause of F.

In contrast, it is possible to remove the second clause of F since this parent clause $\{\overline{x}, y\}$ is a logical consequence of the resolvent $\{y\}$.

Definition

If we have two clauses C_1, C_2 such that $C_1 \subset C_2$, it is said that the clause C_1 *subsumes* the clause C_2 (in logical terms, this simply means that $C_1 \rightarrow C_2$ is true).

Theorem

If C_1 subsumes C_2, i.e. $C_1 \subset C_2$, and both clauses occur in a clause set F, then F and $F \setminus \{C_2\}$ are equivalent. That is, C_2 can be eliminated from F.

Proof: If $F \setminus \{C_2\}$ is satisfied by some assignment α, then α also satisfies C_1 which occurs in $F \setminus \{C_2\}$, and since $C_1 \subset C_2$, the clause C_2 is also satisfied by α, and therefore also $F\alpha = 1$.   □

So it is possible to remove a clause from a clause set without harm if it is subsumed by another clause. On the other hand, searching for a clause set for pairwise subsumption is relatively expensive. Therefore, often such a test is not implemented. Often it turns out that the fact of one clause subsuming another clause comes about "automatically", as a side effect, for example during a resolution step with a unit clause as resolvent. In this case (as in the example above) the resolvent subsumes one of its parent clauses, and this parent clause can be removed.

Usually we are content with transformations which are sat-equivalent. There are more possibilities to achieve sat-equivalence than to achieve equivalence. The above example contains the unit clause $\{x\}$. Using unit propagation (cf. page 18) it is possible to apply the assignment $x = 1$ and to obtain the sat-equivalent formula $F\{x = 1\} = \{\{y\}, \{\overline{y}\}\}$. Now, $\{y\}$ is also a unit clause (as well as $\{\overline{y}\}$). After another unit propagation one obtains $F\{x = 1, y = 1\} = F\{x = 1, y = 0\} = \{\square\}$, hence F is unsatisfiable. So we could show unsatisfiability by applying unit propagation only, without resolution. Later we will see that unit propagation is always successful in the case of (renamable) Horn formulas.

Another possibility for formula simplification was already mentioned in the section on autark assignments. Suppose we have a *pure literal* u which occurs in F (possibly at several places), but the complementary literal $\overline{u}$ does not occur anywhere in F. In this case the formula F can be simplified to $F\{u = 1\}$. The formulas F and $F\{u = 1\}$ are sat-equivalent.

Finally, to discuss the case in which a resolution step involves a *tautology*, that is, a clause which contains a variable together with its complement. This concerns both a tautology as parent clause, as well as a tautology as resolvent.

Consider the following example: $\{x_1, x_2, \overline{x_3}\}$ and $\{\overline{x_2}, x_3, x_4\}$. It is possible to resolve these two clauses using the variable x_2 producing the resolvent $\{x_1, \overline{x_3}, x_3, x_4\}$. Another possibility is to use the variable x_3 for resolution and obtain the resolvent $\{x_1, x_2, \overline{x_2}, x_4\}$. Note that the resolution rule, as defined, does not allow us to resolve to $\{x_1, x_4\}$. Actually, this would be logically incorrect. Indeed, both resolvents are tautologies. In order to achieve the final goal to derive the empty clause, there is no progress in deriving or using a tautology in the resolution proof. Actually, the number of resolution steps increases unnecessarily. There is no harm, no loss of refutation completeness, if the use of tautologies in resolution proofs is forbidden. This can be considered as a simple form of complete resolution restriction, a notion that is considered in the next section.

Formally, it is not hard to see that "resolution without tautologies" is still a refutation complete calculus. The statement and the proof of the resolution theorem (page 44) can be easily adapted, essentially by changing everywhere "resolution proof" to "resolution proof without tautologies". Another way to see this is by way of the last theorem: a tautology is subsumed by any other clause, and thus, can be eliminated.

2.4 Strategies and Restrictions

Resolution is a *nondeterministic* calculus. By fixing a particular sequential arrangement of the resolution steps one obtains a *deterministic* algorithm. The ordering of resolution steps in a particular way, thereby obtaining a deterministic process, is called a (resolution) *strategy*. Since every possible resolution step is performed sooner or later, a strategy still has the property of being refutation complete. The hope is that doing the resolution steps in a particular order will lead to the empty clause somewhat faster.

An example for a strategy is the *unit preference strategy* whereby resolution steps involving unit clauses are always done whenever possible. Applying this strategy does not lead to a deterministic algorithm since there are still nondeterministic choices if no unit resolution step is available, but still, the amount of nondeterminism is certainly restricted.

The DPLL-type algorithms discussed in chapter 4 can be considered as certain types of resolution strategies since the algorithmic transformations done by these algorithms can be understood as resolution steps.

In contrast, a *resolution restriction* means that certain resolution steps, if they do not satisfy certain criteria, are simply forbidden. The advantage is, again, that the scope of nondeterministic alternatives is restricted. On the negative side, it can be observed that the proof length might increase as compared to the general case.

The following diagram outlines this effect.

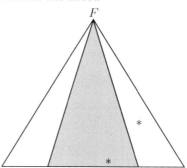

The grey area indicates the restricted nondeterministic search space; the stars indicate solutions (i.e. the possibility of deriving the empty clause).

Even worse than lengthening the proof is possible: a strong restriction of a calculus might result in the loss of the (refutation) completeness. In the above picture this means there is no star at all in the grey area. Later we will see an example of a restriction that makes resolution incomplete.

P-res vs Neg-res vs linear resolution
restriction

Definition

We define several resolution restrictions: *P-resolution* (or, the *positive* resolution restriction) means that in each resolution step it is required that one of the parent clauses has to be positive (i.e. consists of positive literals only).

Similarly, *N-resolution* (or, the *negative* resolution restriction) means that one of the parent clauses must consist of negative literals only.

The *linear resolution restriction* (or, linear resolution, for short) requires that the resolution proof forms a linear chain. First, a so-called *base clause* has to be selected from F. It forms the first element of the chain. From then on each resolution step uses the last element of the chain as one of the parent clauses. After the resolution step the resolvent forms the new last element of the chain.

We show that these resolution restrictions are still refutation complete.

Theorem

P-resolution is refutation complete.

Proof: Let F be an unsatisfiable clause set. We show by induction on $n = |Var(F)|$ that it is possible to obtain the empty clause by P-resolution steps only.

(*Case* $n = 0$): In this case we have $F = \{\square\}$, and there is nothing to prove.

(*Case* $n > 0$): Let $x \in Var(F)$. Since $F\{x = 1\}$ and $F\{x = 0\}$ are unsatisfiable and contain at most $n - 1$ variables, the induction hypothesis can be applied and yields P-resolution proofs starting from $F\{x = 0\}$ as well as from $F\{x = 1\}$. By re-entering the variable x into the P-refutation of $F\{x = 0\}$ we obtain a sequence of resolution steps starting from clauses in F which lead to the unit clause $\{x\}$ (cf. the resolution expansion lemma). Notice that this is still a P-resolution since x is a positive literal. Next we add resolution steps which resolve the resulting unit clause $\{x\}$ with each clause in F that contains $\overline{x}$. Again, these are P-resolution steps. We obtain the clauses in $F\{x = 1\}$. Finally, the P-resolution proof of $F\{x = 1\}$ can be attached which exists by the induction hypothesis. □

Theorem

N-resolution is refutation complete.

Proof: Interchange the roles of positive and negative, x and $\overline{x}$, as well as $F\{x = 0\}$ and $F\{x = 1\}$ in the previous proof. □

Theorem

Linear resolution is refutation complete.

More precisely: for every unsatisfiable clause set F there exists a clause $C \in F$ such that the empty clause can be derived by a linear chain of resolution steps, starting with the base clause C.

Proof: Let F be unsatisfiable and let $F' \subseteq F$ be a minimally unsatisfiable subset (i.e. F' is also unsatisfiable, but for every clause $C \in F'$ the clause set $F' \setminus \{C\}$ is satisfiable). We claim that every clause C in F' can be used as the base clause in a linear resolution proof. The proof of this claim proceeds again by induction on the number n of variables, $n = |\text{Var}(F')|$.

Induction base ($n = 0$):

In this case we have $F' = \{\Box\}$ and $C = \Box$. There is nothing to prove.

Induction step ($n > 0$):

Case 1: $|C| = 1$, hence $C = \{u\}$ for some literal u. The formula F' must have a clause C' with $\overline{u} \in C'$. The clause set $F'\{u = 1\}$ is unsatisfiable and contains at most $n - 1$ variables. Let F'' be a minimally unsatisfiable subset of $F'\{u = 1\}$. In F'' there exists the clause $C' \setminus \{\overline{u}\}$. Consider an assignment α which satisfies all clauses in F' except C'. This assignment exists since F is minimally unsatisfiable. Since $u\alpha = 1$, the assignment α also satisfies all clauses in $F'\{u = 1\}$ except $C' \setminus \{\overline{u}\}$. Therefore, this clause must be contained in F''.

By the induction hypothesis there is a linear resolution refutation of $F'\{u = 1\}$, based on the clause $C' \setminus \{\overline{u}\}$. The desired linear refutation, based on $C = \{u\}$, is now constructed as follows. The first step resolves C with C'. The obtained resolvent is $C' \setminus \{\overline{u}\}$. Afterwards we take the linear resolution based on $C' \setminus \{\overline{u}\}$ given by the induction hypothesis. Each time, in this resolution proof, where in the initial clauses the literal $\overline{u}$ was eliminated, we re-insert this literal in the proof and obtain as the last clause the unit clause $\{\overline{u}\}$ (cf. resolution expansion lemma). In a last step, we resolve $\{\overline{u}\}$ against the base clause $\{u\}$ and obtain the empty clause.

Case 2: $|C| > 1$.

In this case we choose an arbitrary literal $u \in C$ and let $C' = C \setminus \{u\}$. The clause set $F'\{u = 0\}$ is unsatisfiable and it contains C' as a clause. Let α be an assignment which satisfies all clauses in F' except C. This assignment exists since F is minimally unsatisfiable. Since $u\alpha = 0$, the assignment α also satisfies all clauses in $F'\{u = 0\}$ except C'. Therefore, this clause must be contained in a minimally unsatisfiable subset F'' of $F'\{u = 0\}$. Applying the induction hypothesis on F'' gives a linear resolution of $F'\{u = 0\}$ based on the clause C'. By re-inserting the literal u (cf. resolution expansion lemma) we obtain a linear resolution of F based on C which ends with the unit clause $\{u\}$.

Now $(F' \setminus \{C\}) \cup \{\{u\}\}$ is unsatisfiable (observe that $\{u\}$ subsumes C) and $F' \setminus \{C\}$ is satisfiable. Therefore, Case 1 can be used which implies that a linear resolution refutation of $(F' \setminus \{C\}) \cup \{\{u\}\}$ exists based on $\{u\}$. By attaching this refutation to the one obtained earlier which leads to $\{u\}$ we obtain the desired linear resolution refutation for F based on the clause C. □

In the following we define and analyze *Davis-Putnam resolution* (cf. (Davis, Putnam, 1960), *DP-resolution*, for short), which can be used and extended to define an algorithm, called *Davis-Putnam algorithm* or *DP algorithm* for short. The particular use of resolution here has both the character of a strategy and a restriction. It is partly a strategy because one needs to fix a particular order of the variables and apply the basic steps of DP-resolution in this order. The order can be successively fixed during the process.

In a basic step in DP-resolution we first produce all resolvents from a given clause set F which can be derived by a particular fixed variable x (as resolution variable). Afterwards all parent clauses of these resolvents are eliminated resulting in a new clause set which does no longer contain the variable x.

Let us describe this process more formally. Let $F_x \subseteq F$ be those clauses in F which contain x or its complement $\overline{x}$. Let $R_x(F)$ be the set of resolvents which can be obtained from F_x by using variable x for resolution. Observe that no clause in $R_x(F)$ contains x anymore. The set of clauses F from which we started will now be replaced by $(F \cup R_x(F)) \setminus F_x$.

← Davis - Putnam resolution *(handwritten annotation, right margin: "* work one var at a time ↓ once added all resolvents for particular var, may remove all clauses containing that var")*

Theorem (completeness of DP-resolution)
The clause set F is satisfiable if and only if $(F \cup R_x(F)) \setminus F_x$ is satisfiable.

Proof: If F is satisfiable, then so is $F \cup R_x(F)$, by the correctness of the resolution calculus. Therefore, also $(F \cup R_x(F)) \setminus F_x$ is satisfiable.

Conversely, suppose $(F \cup R_x(F)) \setminus F_x$ is satisfiable by some assignment α (which does not involve x). Suppose there is a clause $C \cup \{x\}$ in F_x not being satisfied by α. Let $F' \subseteq F_x$ be the set of clauses in F_x which contain the literal $\overline{x}$. The clause $C \cup \{x\}$ can be resolved with every clause in F' (using variable x) and the resolvent then belongs to $R_x(F)$. By assumption, all these resolvents are satisfied by α. Therefore, *all* clauses in F' are satisfied by α (without an assignment to x – otherwise α would satisfy C). By setting $\beta = \alpha \cup \{x = 1\}$, we obtain an assignment that satisfies F.

An analogous argument holds if there is a clause $C \cup \{\overline{x}\}$ in F_x that is not satisfied by α. □

Let us consider an example. A formula in *3-CNF* has 100 variables and consists of 400 clauses, each with 3 literals. Therefore, there are 1200 occurrences of literals in the formula. On average, a variable occurs in $1200/100 = 12$ clauses. Suppose that x has 6 positive instances and 6 negative instances in the clauses. Then we have $|F_x| = 12$ and

$|R_x(F)| = 6 \cdot 6 = 36$. After a basic DP-step, F is replaced by $(F \cup R_x(F)) \setminus F_x$. This new clause set has 99 variables and $400 + 36 - 12 = 424$ clauses of which at most 36 clauses might be in 4-*CNF*.

It might happen that some of the clauses in $R_x(F)$ coincide with each other or with clauses being already in F, so we do not actually need to add these clauses. Furthermore, it is possible that a clause in $R_x(F)$ contains complementary literals stemming from its two parent clauses. This is a tautology clause and can be eliminated without harm (cf. page 47). Therefore, it might happen (not so seldom) that we obtain a clause set with fewer variables than before *and* with no more clauses than before. Because of this, this procedure has been adapted for *preprocessing* clause sets before they become input to some *SAT* solver.

It remains to present the DP algorithm in pseudo code. Here, it seems advantageous to insert unit propagation (cf. page 18) between each basic DP-step.

> **proc** DavisPutnam (F : clause set) : **bool**
> // yields 1, if F is satisfiable, and 0 otherwise
> **if** $\square \in F$ **then return** 0
> **if** $F = \emptyset$ **then return** 1
> **while** (F contains a unit-clause $\{u\}$) **do** $F := F\{u = 1\}$
> Select a variable $x \in Var(F)$
> **return** DavisPutnam ($(F \cup R_x(F)) \setminus F_x$)   slide 45

Although the number of clauses might decrease during a DP-step, the above example shows that it might also happen that the number of clauses increases dramatically. Therefore, heuristics for deciding which variable to select next play an important role here. On the other hand, once the last variables have to be selected, it is clear that the number of clauses (which can just contain the remaining variables) will decrease again, just as rapidly. It seems very difficult to prove theoretical bounds on the number of clauses which have to be handled during the course of a DP-resolution. Computer experiments show that other approaches like DPLL and its successors are more efficient than Davis-Putnam.

Next we define two resolution restrictions which lose their refutation completeness. Nevertheless they can be useful, especially in the context of Horn formulas as can be seen in the next chapter.

Definition
Input resolution requires that at least one of the parent clauses in a resolution step is an input clause, that is, it comes from the original clause set F.
The *unit resolution* restriction requires that at least one of the parent clauses in a resolution step is a unit clause.

These both resolution restrictions are incomplete as can be seen by the following example.

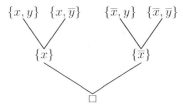

This resolution proof of length 3 is the shortest possible, but it does not satisfy any of the defined restrictions. The following proof

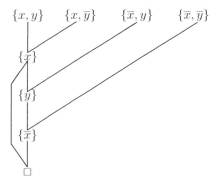

is a P-resolution, as well as a linear resolution, but it requires 4 resolution steps.

It is easy to check that neither a unit resolution nor an input resolution is possible. But we observe the following.

Theorem

A clause set F has a refutation with the unit resolution restriction *if and only if* it has a resolution refutation obeying the input resolution restriction.

Proof: We show by induction on the number of variables in F that every unit resolution proof can be transformed into an input resolution proof, and vice versa. This is obvious for $n = 0$ and $n = 1$.

Let $n > 1$. First we argue from unit to input. We assume that a unit resolution proof exists. Therefore, in the clause set F there must exist a unit clause $\{u\}$. We restrict the clause set and its resolution proof to $F\{u = 1\}$ according to the resolution restriction lemma. The restricted proof is still a unit resolution proof. By the induction hypothesis there is an input resolution proof for $F\{u = 1\}$. By re-inserting the literal $\overline{u}$ which was removed before, into the clauses and their respective resolvents (cf. resolution expanding lemma) we obtain a sequence of input resolution steps (starting from F) which ends with the clause $\{\overline{u}\}$. Finally, a last input resolution step with $\{u\}$ yields the empty clause.

Now, conversely, suppose we have an input resolution proof for F. In the very last resolution step, two unit clauses are resolved producing the empty clause as resolvent. At least one of these, say $\{u\}$, has to stem from the input F. Again, consider $F\{u = 1\}$ and the restricted resolution proof which is still an input resolution. By the induction hypothesis this proof can be transformed to a unit resolution proof for $F\{u = 1\}$. We obtain the desired unit resolution proof for the original formula F as follows. First, we start by resolving each clause in F which contains $\overline{u}$ with the unit-clause $\{u\}$. Now we have all clauses in $F\{u = 1\}$ available and can add the unit resolution proof of $F\{u = 1\}$ which leads to the empty clause. $\square$

2.5 Exponential Lower Bounds for the Length of Resolution Proofs

In this chapter we show that the length of the refutations of certain formulas must be exponential with respect to the formula size. The clause set PH_n is especially difficult to refute for the resolution calculus. This set of clauses encodes the *pigeonhole principle* from Dirichlet as a Boolean formula: if $n + 1$ pigeons are placed in n pigeonholes, then at least one pigeonhole must contain at least two pigeons. We define an unsatisfiable formula when we postulate that the $n + 1$ pigeons can be placed in such a way that each pigeonhole contains at most one pigeon. We use for this the variables $x_{i,j}$ in the formula, interpreting that the variable takes the value 1 when pigeon i is placed in pigeonhole j.

Definition

The pigeonhole set of clauses PH_n is defined for every $n > 0$ as follows: On the one hand for $i = 0, 1, \ldots, n$ the clauses

$$(x_{i,1} \lor x_{i,2} \lor \cdots \lor x_{i,n})$$

indicate that "pigeon i must be placed in pigeonhole 1 or 2 or ...or n."
On the other hand, we have for every $j = 1, 2, \ldots, n$ the set of $\binom{n+1}{2}$ clauses

$$(\overline{x_{0,j}} \lor \overline{x_{1,j}}), (\overline{x_{0,j}} \lor \overline{x_{2,j}}), \ldots, (\overline{x_{n-1,j}} \lor \overline{x_{n,j}})$$

indicating that "in pigeonhole j at most one pigeon can be placed."

It is clear that one cannot place $n + 1$ pigeons in n pigeonholes in this way, and therefore the set of clauses PH_n is unsatisfiable. We observe that PH_n contains $n \cdot (n + 1) = O(n^2)$ Boolean variables and has $(n + 1) + n \cdot \binom{n+1}{2} = O(n^3)$ clauses.

The following is a resolution refutation of PH_2 (that is, 3 pigeons do not fit in 2 pigeonholes):

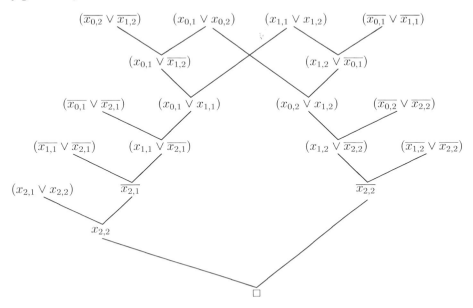

From this example one already can get the feeling that such a refutation is (and has to be) complex. The following theorem proves this.

Theorem
The length of every resolution refutation of PH_n is at least $2^{n/20}$.
Let k be the number of variables and m the number of clauses in PH_n. This result says that the length of a resolution refutation for PH_n is at least $2^{\Omega(\sqrt{k})}$, respectively $2^{\Omega(\sqrt[3]{m})}$.

Proof: Let us suppose that there is a resolution refutation $\mathcal{R} = (K_1, K_2, \ldots, K_s)$, $K_s = \square$, of PH_n with $s < 2^{n/20}$. We associate with every clause K in $\mathcal{R}$ a clause $\widehat{K}$, by substituting in K every negative literal $\overline{x_{i,j}}$ by the set of positive literals $x_{i,k}$ for $k \neq j$. In the following we will call a clause K in $\mathcal{R}$ *large*, if the associated clause $\widehat{K}$ contains at least $n(n+1)/10$ (positive) literals. Let r be the number of large clauses in the resolution refutation $\mathcal{R}$. Of course, $r \leq s$ holds. There must be at least $rn(n+1)/10$ literals in the r many clauses associated with the large clauses. Therefore, there has to be a literal $x_{i,j}$, that appears in at least $r/10$ such clauses. This is also a consequence of the pigeonhole principle. By applying step by step the following partial assignment to $\mathcal{R}$, according to the Resolution Restriction Lemma,

$$\{x_{i,j} = 1\} \cup \{x_{i,k} = 0 \mid k \neq j\} \cup \{x_{l,j} = 0 \mid l \neq i\}$$

we obtain a resolution refutation for PH_{n-1}, since the assignments mentioned above "freeze" the correspondence from pigeon i to pigeonhole j, and only a resolution refutation of a PH_{n-1}-formula remains. Pigeon i and pigeonhole j do no longer appear in this PH_{n-1}-formula. Besides, because of this action, as one can infer from the Resolution Restriction Lemma, at least $r/10$ large clauses K are eliminated from the new resolution refutation for PH_{n-1}. This is because from this assignment either the positive literal $x_{i,j}$ was set to 1 in K, or a negative literal of the form $\overline{x_{i,k}}$, $k \neq j$, was set to 0. After such a restriction step, the obtained resolution refutation for PH_{n-1} contains at most $9r/10 \leq 9s/10$ large clauses. Continuing in this way, eliminate in each step a fraction of at least one tenth of the remaining large clauses, so that after at most $\log_{10/9} s$ many restriction steps, no large clauses are left. At this point we have to deal with a resolution refutation for $PH_{n'}$ satisfying

$$ n' \geq n - \log_{10/9} s > n - \log_{10/9} 2^{n/20} > 0.671 \cdot n. $$

This means that all (associated) clauses $\widehat{K}$ in the resulting resolution refutation for $PH_{n'}$ have fewer than $n(n+1)/10$, and therefore also fewer than $2n'(n'+1)/9$ literals. The following lemma shows that this is a contradiction. This implies that our hypothesis $s < 2^{n/20}$ is wrong, and the theorem is proven.   □

Lemma

In every resolution refutation for PH_m there must be a clause C_0, so that the associated clause $\widehat{C_0}$ contains at least $2m(m+1)/9$ many literals.

Proof: Let $\mathcal{R}$ be a resolution refutation for PH_m.

An assignment α is called *k-critical*, when it assigns to every pigeon except for pigeon k exactly one pigeonhole and no two pigeons are assigned the same hole. More formally: α is k-critical, if there is a bijective function f from $\{0, 1, \ldots, m\} \setminus \{k\}$ to $\{1, 2, \ldots, m\}$, so that we have

$$ \alpha(x_{i,j}) = \begin{cases} 1, & \text{if } f(i) = j \\ 0, & \text{otherwise} \end{cases} $$

We define the *significance* of a clause C in $\mathcal{R}$, abbreviated by $\sigma(C)$, as follows:

$$ \sigma(C) = \sum_{k=0}^{m} [\text{ there is a } k\text{-critical assignment, that falsifies } C] $$

The square brackets express an indicator function: when the proposition between the brackets holds, then its value is 1, otherwise it is 0. It is clear, that the initial clauses in PH_m have significance 1 or 0. The empty clause, at the end of the resolution refutation $\mathcal{R}$, has significance $m + 1$. Moreover, when C is the resolvent of two clauses C_1, C_2, having significance s_1 and s_2, then the significance of C is at most $s_1 + s_2$, since every assignment that falsifies C, falsifies also C_1 or C_2. In other words: there can be no assignment that falsifies C, while satisfying both C_1 and C_2. From this it follows that there must be a clause C_0 in $\mathcal{R}$ with significance $s \in [\frac{m+1}{3}, \frac{2(m+1)}{3}]$. One can choose for C_0 the first clause C in $\mathcal{R}$ with $\sigma(C) \geq \frac{m+1}{3}$. Consider an arbitrary k-critical assignment α, falsifying C_0 (and therefore also the associated clause $\widehat{C_0}$). According to the definition of $\sigma(C)$, one can choose such an assignment in s different ways, or in other words, for s many k's. Let j be such that *all* j-critical assignments satisfy the clause C_0 (and therefore also $\widehat{C_0}$). Such a j can be chosen in $m + 1 - s$ different ways; there are therefore $s \cdot (m + 1 - s)$ many such (k, j) combinations. We modify α in one position, so that it mutates to a j-critical assignment α': instead of not assigning pigeon k any hole and assigning j one pigeonhole, say l, α' assigns the hole l to the pigeon k, while j does not receive any pigeonhole; apart from this modification, there is no other difference between α' and α. As a consequence of the modification, α' satisfies the clause C_0. This implies that the literal $x_{k,l}$ must occur in $\widehat{C_0}$. On can prove in this way the existence of $s \cdot (m + 1 - s)$ many literals in $\widehat{C}$. Observe that for a fixed k-critical assignment α and changing values of j, also the values for l are different. From $s \in [\frac{m+1}{3}, \frac{2(m+1)}{3}]$ it follows, that $s \cdot (m + 1 - s) \geq \frac{2m(m+1)}{9}$, and this proves the lemma. $\square$

This exponential lower bound for the set of clauses PH_n applies, of course, also to all algorithms proceeding in a way that can be interpreted as the implementation of resolution steps (for example the DP algorithm). Such algorithms require exponential running time when the input is PH_n. Because of this, PH_n is frequently used as an input benchmark for testing *SAT* solvers.

The clause set vPH_n contains clauses of size n. One may wonder whether this fact was necessary to derive the exponential proof-length lower bound, or whether the result can still be obtained when the original clause set has only clauses of size at most 3, instead. Notice that clauses of size 2 are certainly not sufficient because the number of potential resolvents is polynomial in this case, cf. page 66.

A clause of size $n > 3$, like $(x_1 \vee x_2 \vee \cdots \vee x_n)$, can be split into several clauses of size 3 by introducing new auxiliary variables y_i:

$$(x_1 \vee x_2 \vee y_1) \wedge (\overline{y_1} \vee x_3 \vee y_2) \wedge (\overline{y_2} \vee x_4 \vee y_3) \wedge \cdots \wedge (\overline{y_{n-4}} \vee x_{n-2} \vee y_{n-3}) \wedge (\overline{y_{n-3}} \vee x_{n-1} \vee x_n)$$

This construction leads to a sat-equivalent formula and it can also be applied in the case of the PH_n clauses. This is nothing else as a reduction from *CNF-SAT* to *3-SAT*. For the above proof still to go through, one needs to redefine the concept of a k-critical assignment. Apart from the assignment of the x-variables which is still defined as before, the assignment of the auxiliary y-variables is chosen such that a maximum number of the *3-CNF* clauses above are satisfied. Notice that the *3-CNF* clauses which can be obtained from the original clause

$$(x_{i,1} \vee x_{i,2} \vee \cdots \vee x_{i,n})$$

are all satisfied by a k-critical assignment, if $i \neq k$. Therefore, the property that $\sigma(C) \leq$ 1 for all initial clauses C is still valid. This property is crucial for the proof.

A different method, based on Craig interpolants, is considered next for obtaining lower bounds for the length of resolution refutations. Craig's Interpolation Theorem says that for every tautology of the kind $F \rightarrow G$ there must be a formula I, containing only the variables common to F and G, so that both $F \rightarrow I$ and $I \rightarrow G$ hold. We show that it is possible to construct a circuit for I from a given resolution refutation $\mathcal{R}$ for $\neg(F \rightarrow G)$, that is, the *CNF* version of this formula. This circuit has approximately the same size as $\mathcal{R}$. From a lower bound for the circuit size of I it follows then a lower bound for the length of a resolution refutation for $\neg(F \rightarrow G)$. The formula $\neg(F \rightarrow G)$ is equivalent to $F \wedge \neg G$. We can interpret an interpolant for $F \rightarrow G$ as a circuit C over the variables $\mathit{Var}(F) \cap \mathit{Var}(G)$, which for every possible input decides whether F or $\neg G$ are falsified (at least one of both formulas must be false). We denote by A and B the *CNF* for F and $\neg G$ respectively. The gates of circuit C are functions from the set $\{0, 1, \vee, \wedge, sel\}$. Recall from the appendix that the selector function $sel : \{0,1\}^3 \rightarrow \{0,1\}$ is defined as

$$sel(x, y, z) = \begin{cases} y & \text{if } x = 0 \\ z & \text{if } x = 1 \end{cases}$$

⌐Theorem

Let $\mathcal{R}$ be a resolution refutation of the set of clauses $A \cup B$ (defined as described above from a tautology $F \rightarrow G$). There is then a Boolean circuit C over the set of variables $\mathit{Var}(A) \cap \mathit{Var}(B)$, which for every assignment α with $\mathit{Var}(\alpha) = \mathit{Var}(A) \cap \mathit{Var}(B)$ satisfies the following conditions:
$C\alpha = 0 \Rightarrow A\alpha$ is unsatisfiable, and
$C\alpha = 1 \Rightarrow B\alpha$ is unsatisfiable.
Moreover, the circuit C has at most $O(|\mathcal{R}|)$ many gates.

Proof: In order to construct the circuit C, we use the structure of the resolution refutation $\mathcal{R} = (K_1, \ldots, K_t)$ for the set of clauses $A \cup B$. Let $\mathit{Var}(A) \cap \mathit{Var}(B) = \{x_1, \ldots, x_p\}$, $\mathit{Var}(A) \setminus \mathit{Var}(B) = \{y_1, \ldots, y_q\}$, and $\mathit{Var}(B) \setminus \mathit{Var}(A) = \{z_1, \ldots, z_r\}$. We call these sets as x-variables, y-variables, and z-variables.

We denote by H the conjunction of the clauses in $A \cup B$. We know as a consequence of the Resolution Restriction Lemma that for each assignment $\alpha = \{ x_1 = a_1, \ldots, x_p = a_p\}$ of the x-variables, there is a resolution refutation $\mathcal{R}_\alpha$ for $H\alpha$. The clauses in $\mathcal{R}_\alpha$ do not contain any x-variables. Moreover, a single clause in $\mathcal{R}_\alpha$ can contain only y-variables or z-variables, but not both. This holds because a clause that contains at the same time both y-variables and z-variables, can only happen after a resolution of an x-variable, and such resolution steps cannot exist in $\mathcal{R}_\alpha$. Considering this, we call a clause $K_i' \in \mathcal{R}_\alpha$ a y-clause, if it only contains y-variables, or if $K_i' = \square$ and K_i' can be reached from a y-clause. The z-clauses are defined in a similar way. The empty clause K_t in $\mathcal{R}$ is transformed into a clause K'_t in $\mathcal{R}_\alpha$: it is either a y-clause or a z-clause. In the first case we have a refutation of $A\alpha$ as part from $\mathcal{R}_\alpha$ and in the second case a refutation of $B\alpha$. In other words, the decision of whether K'_t is a y-clause or a z-clause can be used as an interpolant for $A \cup B$. The circuit C will be constructed based on this idea. The clause C has the x-variables $\{x_1, \ldots, x_p\}$ as inputs, and for each clause K_i in $\mathcal{R}$ a gate g_i in C is defined. The following properties hold for each assignment α of the x-variables:

1. If K'_i is a y-clause in $\mathcal{R}_\alpha$, then g_i gets value 0 in $C\alpha$ and

2. If K'_i is a z-clause in $\mathcal{R}_\alpha$, then g_i gets value 1 in $C\alpha$.

The circuit C then has exactly t gates over the base $\{\vee, \wedge, sel\}$ (see the appendix on circuits) and when these conditions hold and g_t is the output gate, then C computes an interpolant. The gates of C are constructed as follows:

For the initial clauses in $\mathcal{R}$, if $K_i \in A$, then g_i is the constant 0, and if $K_i \in B$ then g_i is the constant 1.

In case K_i is the resolvent of two clauses K_j, K_l, and the variable which is resolved for is an x-variable x_k, then $g_i = sel(x_k, g_j, g_l)$.

In case K_i is the resolvent of two clauses K_j, K_l, and the variable which is resolved for is a y-variable, then $g_i = g_j \wedge g_l$.

In case K_i is the resolvent of two clauses K_j, K_l, and the variable which is resolved for is a z-variable, then $g_i = g_j \vee g_l$.

Let α be an assignment of the x-variables and let K'_i be a y-clause in $\mathcal{R}_\alpha$. We prove by induction over i that g_i takes the value 0. If K_i is an initial clause, then g_i takes the value 0 for each assignment. In case K_i is obtained by resolution of the variable x_k from the parent clauses K_j and K_l $(j, l < i)$ and $x_k \in K_j$, then, depending on whether the assignment α assigns variable x_k with 1 or with 0, so is $K'_i = K'_l$ or $K'_i = K'_j$ (cf. Rule 6 in the Resolution Restriction Lemma). We are dealing in both cases with a y-clause (otherwise K'_j and K'_l were not y-clauses) and because of the induction hypothesis, the value of g_l (respectively g_j) is 0. The sel function computes the correct value for g_i. In case K_i is obtained by resolution of the variable y from the parent clauses K_j and K_l, since K'_i is a y-clause, at least one of the clauses K'_j, K'_l must be a y-clause. The value of $g_i = g_j \wedge g_l$ under the assignment α is then 0. The case for the z-clauses is similar. $\square$

If the x-variables only appear positively in the clauses in A, or only negatively in the clauses in B, then the construction of C in the previous theorem can be modified in such a way, that C is a monotone circuit (that is, it contains only gates from the set $\{0, 1, \wedge, \vee\}$). This is very useful since there exist strong lower bounds for monotone circuits. Such lower bounds can then be transformed into lower bounds for the length of resolution refutations for certain formulas.

─Theorem

Let $\mathcal{R}$ be a resolution refutation of the set of clauses $A \cup B$. If the variables $Var(A) \cap Var(B)$ appear only positively in the clauses of A, respectively only negatively in the clauses of B, then there is a monotone Boolean circuit C over the variables $Var(A) \cap Var(B)$ such that for every assignment α of $Var(C)$ satisfies the following conditions:

$C\alpha = 0 \Rightarrow A\alpha$ is unsatisfiable, or

$C\alpha = 1 \Rightarrow B\alpha$ is unsatisfiable.

Moreover, circuit C has at most $|\mathcal{R}|$ gates from the set $\{\vee, \wedge\}$.

Proof: Assume that the x-variables appear only positively in the clauses of A. When a negated x-variable appears in a clause K_i, then we get for every assignment α that K_i' cannot be a y-clause. The sel gates from the previous proof are not monotone: they are introduced in one of the cases in the construction of C. We transform this case in the following way: if K_i is obtained by resolution of variable x_k from the two clauses K_j, K_l, and x_k is an x-variable and $x_k \in K_j$, then $g_i = x_k \vee g_j$.

Let α be an assignment of the x-variables. Assume that K_i' is a y-clause or a z-clause in $\mathcal{R}_\alpha$ (that is K_i' was not eliminated in $\mathcal{R}_\alpha$). When x_k is assigned value 1, then $K_i' = K_l'$ (cf. Rule 6 in the Resolution Restriction Lemma). Since $\overline{x_k} \in K_l$, K_l' cannot be a y-clause and K_i' is then a z-clause. The value of g_i is defined as $x_k \vee g_j = 1$. When x_k is assigned value 0, then $K_i' = K_j'$. Accordingly we have that g_i equals g_j.

The case in which the x-variables only appear negated in the B clauses, is symmetric.

□

We give as an example two families of formulas F and G, satisfying that $F \to G$ is a tautology, for which there can be only monotone interpolants of exponential size. These formulas are based on the clique function defined next.

We say that an undirected graph G with n vertices is an (n, k)-*clique*, if G contains a single clique with k vertices and does not have any further edges. That is, G has $n - k$ isolated vertices.

We say that G is an $(n, k-1)$-*coloring*, if the vertices of G can be partitioned in $k-1$ disjoint sets, so that no edges join vertices from the same set, but all the edges between the vertices of different sets are present.

It can be easily observed that for every k, if G is an (n, k)-clique, then G cannot be an $(n, k - 1)$-coloring.

Let $Clique_{n,k} : \{0, 1\}^{\binom{n}{2}} \to \{0, 1\}$ be the Boolean function with variables $x_{i,j}$, $1 \leq i < j \leq n$, taking value 1 if the values of the variables encode an undirected graph G containing a clique of size k (and taking value 0 otherwise).

The way in which the input variables encode a graph should be interpreted as $x_{i,j} = 1$ if and only if there is an edge between the vertices i and j in G. We observe that $Clique_{n,k}$ is a monotone function.

In (Razborov, 1985) an exponential lower bound for the size of every monotone circuit for the clique function $Clique_{n,n^{1/4}}$ was proven. The proof of this lower bound can be extended to other functions in the following way: let $Q_{n,k}$ be any monotone Boolean function on the variables $x = (x_{i,j})_{1 \le i < j \le n}$, encoding a graph G_x with n vertices, and satisfying $Q_{n,k}(G_x) = 1$, if G_x is an (n, k)-clique, and $Q_{n,k}(G_x) = 0$, if G_x is an $(n, k-1)$-coloring (the value of the function is irrelevant in all the other cases). It follows then for $k = n^{1/4}$ and some $\varepsilon > 0$, that every monotone Boolean circuit computing $Q_{n,k}$ must have at least $2^{\Omega(n^{\varepsilon})}$ gates.

We consider two types of formulas $F_{n,k}(x, y)$ and $G_{n,k}(x, z)$, respectively, expressing that a graph G_x encoded in the x-variables contains a clique of size k and is $(k-1)$-colorable. The formula $F_{n,k}(x, y) \to \neg G_{n,k}(x, z)$ is a tautology and because of the Interpolation Theorem there must be an interpolant for the formula. The existence of $F_{n,k}$ and $G_{n,k}$ follows from the Cook-Levin Theorem (NP-completeness of *SAT*). We give nevertheless an explicit definition of the formulas in order to be able to estimate its size and that of the interpolant.

The formula $F_{n,k}(x, y)$ contains the variables $x = \{x_{i,j} \mid 1 \le i < j \le n\}$ and $y = \{y_{i,l} \mid 1 \le i \le n, 1 \le l \le k\}$. The x-variables encode the graph and variable $y_{i,l}$ is 1, if vertex i is the l-th vertex in the k-clique. $F_{n,k}$ is the conjunction of the following sub-formulas:

$$\bigvee_{l,m} (y_{i,l} \land y_{j,m}) \to x_{i,j} \quad 1 \le i < j \le n$$

expressing that in case the vertices i and j are both in the clique, then there must be an edge between them:

$$\bigvee_i y_{i,l} \quad 1 \le l \le k$$

$$\neg(y_{i,l} \land y_{j,l}) \quad 1 \le i < j \le n, 1 \le l \le k$$

$$\neg(y_{i,l} \land y_{i,m}) \quad 1 \le i \le n, 1 \le l < m \le k$$

These formulas express that exactly one vertex is the l-th vertex in the clique, and that every vertex appears in the clique at most once.

The formula $G_{n,k}(x, z)$ has the variables $x = \{x_{i,j} \mid 1 \le i < j \le n\}$ in the same way as $F_{n,k}$, and besides $z = \{z_{i,l} \mid 1 \le i \le n, 1 \le l \le k - 1\}$. The x-variables encode the graph and the variable $z_{i,l}$ is 1 if and only if vertex i has color l. $G_{n,k}$ is the conjunction of the following sub-formulas:

$$x_{i,j} \to \bigwedge_l (z_{i,l} \to \neg z_{j,l}) \quad 1 \le i < j \le n$$

expressing that in case there is an edge between i and j, then i and j have different colors, and

$$\bigvee_l z_{i,l} \quad 1 \le i \le n$$

$$\neg(z_{i,l} \wedge z_{i,m}) \quad 1 \le i \le n,\, 1 \le l < m \le k - 1$$
$$\bigvee_i z_{i,l} \quad 1 \le l \le k - 1$$

These formulas express that every vertex has exactly one color, and that there is at least one vertex for each color.

The formula $F_{n,k}(x, y) \wedge G_{n,k}(x, z)$ is unsatisfiable. This formula can be written in CNF, without becoming much larger. Its length can be bounded by $O(n^4)$. Moreover, it can be observed that the x-variables only appear positively in the F formula. This formula satisfies the conditions of the theorem for the construction of monotone interpolants out of resolution refutations.

It follows from the lower bound for monotone circuits, that every monotone circuit computing an interpolant for the formulas $F_{n,k}(x, y)$ and $G_{n,k}(x, z)$ for $k = n^{1/4}$, must have size $2^{\Omega(m^{\varepsilon'})}$ for some $\varepsilon' > 0$. From the previous theorem it follows then, that $2^{\Omega(m^{\varepsilon'})}$ is also a lower bound for the size of a resolution refutation of $F_{n,n^{1/4}}(x, y) \wedge G_{n,n^{1/4}}(x, z)$.

The first exponential size lower bound for resolution refutations was proven by (Haken, 1985). The proof given here is an adaptation of the work of (Beame and Pitassi, 1996). The proof using Craig interpolants follows from the works of (Pudlák, 1997) and (Krajíček, 1994), which rely on a lower bound for the size of monotone circuits from (Razborov, 1985). More constructions for formulas having exponentially long resolution refutations have been given, based for example on expander graphs (Urquhart, 1987), (Schöning, 1997), or on random formulas (as in chapter 7), cf. (Chvátal, Szemerédi, 1988).

3 Special Cases Solvable in Polynomial Time

The satisfiability problem can be solved in polynomial time for certain classes of clause sets. Before using complicated *SAT* algorithms, one should look first if the problem to be solved lies in one of these classes. Moreover, these efficiently solvable special cases define often the situations in which the recursion is brought to an end in the complicated recursive algorithms solving the *SAT* problem in the general case.

At this point, it might be appropriate to introduce the concept of a *backdoor set* of variables.

> **Definition**
> A subset $V \subseteq Var(F)$ of the variables of a formula F is called a *backdoor*, if every assignment $\alpha : V \to \{0, 1\}^{|V|}$ of these variables has the property, that the formula $F\alpha$ belongs to one of the polynomial time solvable special cases (that will be discussed in the following).

A special goal of a *SAT* algorithm could be to try to find such a backdoor (of the smallest possible size). It would follow then that the original formula F is satisfiable if and only if there is an assignment α for the backdoor variables, so that $F\alpha$ is satisfiable, and moreover, the test for the satisfiability of $F\alpha$, for each such α, can be done efficiently. In the case that a set of clauses F has a backdoor set of size k, say, but we do not know which k variables these are, the algorithm could systematically consider all the subsets of size k in $Var(F)$, as well as all the formulas of the type $F\alpha$, with $\alpha : V \to \{0, 1\}^{|V|}$, $|V| = k$, and analyze its satisfiability, as long as they belong to one of the polynomial time solvable classes. The running time of such an algorithm would be $O^*(\binom{n}{k} \cdot 2^k) = O^*(n^k \cdot 2^k)$. For a backdoor of size $k < \log n$ this could be a relatively efficient algorithm.

An idea behind the DPLL algorithms (explained in the corresponding chapter) is to devise a procedure, that without having to systematically explore all the $\binom{n}{k}$ subsets, by using heuristic methods, arrives at a backdoor (as long as it exists).

Experiments have shown that formulas arising from practical applications have often small backdoors, while this is not the case for random formulas chosen close to the threshold value (see the chapter on random formulas).

3.1   2-**CNF**

We show now that the satisfiability problem for formulas in *CNF* with at most two literals in each clause (in short 2-*CNF*) can be efficiently solved. Sometimes these formulas are called *Krom formulas*, referring to the publication (Krom, 1967).

> **Theorem**
> The class of 2-*CNF* formulas can be efficiently tested for satisfiability. In short: 2-*SAT* $\in$ P.

Proof. Let F be a formula in 2-*CNF* with the set of variables $\{x_1, \ldots, x_n\}$. We construct a directed graph $G_F = (V, E)$ with $V = \{x_1, \ldots, x_n\} \cup \{\overline{x_1}, \ldots, \overline{x_n}\}$. For each clause $(u \vee v) \in F$ we include the two directed edges $(\overline{u}, v)$ and $(\overline{v}, u)$ in E. For every clause with a single literal (u) we add the directed edge $(\overline{u}, u)$ to E.

One should observe that $(u \vee v)$ is equivalent to $(\overline{u} \rightarrow v)$ and to $(\overline{v} \rightarrow u)$, and moreover, that (u) is equivalent to $(\overline{u} \rightarrow u)$. Because of this, a directed edge or a directed path in G_F can be understood as a logical chain of implications.

We claim that F is unsatisfiable if and only if there is a cycle in G_F including vertices for a variable x and for its negation $\overline{x}$, as in the sketch:

Suppose there is such a cycle, and F is satisfiable with an assignment α. If $x\alpha = 1$, then the chain of implications $x \rightarrow \cdots \rightarrow \overline{x}$ implies that $\overline{x}\alpha = 1$, respectively, $x\alpha = 0$. Analogously, it follows from $x\alpha = 0$, considering the chain of implications $\overline{x} \rightarrow \cdots \rightarrow x$ that $x\alpha = 1$. Put together, this is a contradiction.

For the other direction we show that if there is no variable with such a cycle in G_F, then we can construct a satisfying assignment for F. For doing so we repeat the following step, until all variables in F are assigned. Choose a variable x that has not been assigned yet and for which there is either a path from x to $\overline{x}$, or there is a path from $\overline{x}$ to x (both situations are not possible, by assumption). In the first case we assign x value 0 and in the second case value 1.

We then assign further literals following the implication chains. For example, if x is assigned value 1, and there is an edge (x, y) in the graph, then y must take value 1. In case there are still unassigned variables, we can then assign any of them in any particular way and follow the implication chains to assign further variables.

The constructed assignment satisfies all the clauses in F. This is clear for clauses (u) with a single literal. Following the described procedure, these literals would receive value 1. Let us suppose that for a clause with two literals $(u \vee v)$, u had been assigned before v, and that the literal had been assigned value 0. The edge $(\overline{u}, v)$ takes care that directly afterwards, v takes value 1 (implying the satisfaction of the clause). It cannot happen that v should take value 0 because of the existence of a path from v to $\overline{v}$. This would imply the existence of the cycle

$$\overline{u} \to v \to \cdots \to \overline{v} \to u \to \cdots \to \overline{u}$$

and would contradict the hypothesis stating that such a cycle does not exist.   □

One should observe that the proof not only shows whether F is satisfiable, but in the positive case it also gives an efficient method to construct such an assignment.

Example: Consider the formula:

$$F \;=\; (x_1) \wedge (\overline{x_1} \vee \overline{x_2}) \wedge (x_2 \vee x_3) \wedge (\overline{x_1} \vee x_2)$$

We associate with this 2-*CNF* formula the following graph G_F:

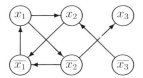

The formula is unsatisfiable. This is witnessed by the cycle $x_1 \to x_2 \to \overline{x_1} \to x_1$.

The algorithmic method to solve 2-*SAT* given in the proof, can be interpreted in a different way: start with any variable, let us say x_1, and set it tentatively to 0. Because of the clauses containing x_1, some further variables will be assigned by unit propagation, and these assignments might imply further assignments, and so on. This can lead to a conflict, in which case we delete the assignments and then set variable x_1 to 1. By following again the assignments implied by unit propagation, this might lead again to a conflict in which case the formula is unsatisfiable. If no conflict occurs, and the produced partial assignment does not satisfy the formula right away, then it is autark. This means that the partial assignment can be applied to the formula, simplifying it, and the same procedure can be repeatedly applied to the rest of the formula.

Sketch:

```
 ┌─────────┐      ╱‾‾‾‾‾‾‾‾‾╲  yes   ┌─────────┐      ╱‾‾‾‾‾‾‾‾‾╲  yes
 │ x₁ = 0  │────▶ ╲ Conflict?╱ ────▶ │ x₁ = 1  │────▶ ╲ Conflict?╱ ────▶  unsatisfiable
 └─────────┘       ╲_____╱          └─────────┘       ╲_____╱
                       │ no                                 │ no
                       └──────────────────────────────────┘
                                     ┌────────────────────────┐
                                     │  autark assignment      │
                                     │  apply it and continue  │
                                     └────────────────────────┘
```

Yet another way to show that 2-*SAT* $\in$ P is to apply resolution to the set of clauses in the 2-*CNF* formula. Whenever two clauses with at most two literals are resolved, the resolvent also contains at most two literals. Therefore, the number of possible clauses that can appear in a refutation is at most $O(n^2)$, where $n = |\text{Var}(F)|$. Because of this, one can generate in polynomial time all possible resolvents which can be derived from the initial clauses and test whether the empty clause has been generated by this process or not. In case the empty clause cannot be generated, then is F satisfiable. A satisfying assignment can be found as is done in the second proof of the refutation completeness of the resolution calculus (cf. page 45).

Another method of a very different kind, based on local search, is the following: We choose an arbitrary (random) initial assignment α for the variables in F. In case this assignment does not satisfy F (which is, of course, very likely), then there is at least one clause $C \in F$ with $C\alpha = 0$. Let $C = (u \vee v)$ be any such clause (in case of a clause with a single literal let $u = v$). We choose now either literal u or v, with probability $1/2$ each, and change α in such a way, that now $u\alpha = 1$ (respectively $v\alpha = 1$) holds. The change of this bit from α results in the clause C being satisfied. Of course, the Boolean value of some other clauses could be made false (or remain false) by this modification of assignment α. We continue changing α in this way for several steps, with the hope to arrive at some point at a satisfying assignment (provided one exists). The question is, how long should we continue with the 1-bit changes in α?

Let us suppose that F is satisfiable and that α_0 is a satisfying assignment. The assignment α used by the described algorithm, can be different from α_0 in some of its bits. We denote by $d(\alpha, \alpha_0)$ the *Hamming distance* between the two assignments, that is, the number of variable assignments that are different in α and α_0. By changing in a clause $C = (u \vee v)$ with $C\alpha = 0$ either the value of u or the value of v, with probability (at least) $1/2$, the Hamming distance between α and α_0 is decreased by 1, since $C\alpha_0 = 1$, and therefore $u\alpha_0 = 1$ or $v\alpha_0 = 1$. On the other side, the Hamming distance can increase by 1 with probability (at most) $1/2$. This randomized algorithm can therefore be understood as a random walk on a Markov chain with states $0, 1, \ldots, n$, where the state number indicates the Hamming distance between the actual assignment α and α_0. The state n is reflecting and the state 0 absorbing.

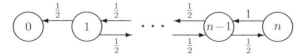

We denote by $S(j)$, $j = 0, 1, \ldots, n$, the expected number of steps until state 0 is visited, in case we start from an initial assignment α with $d(\alpha, \alpha_0) = j$. The following equations hold for the worst case in which the transition probabilities in both directions are exactly $\frac{1}{2}$:

$$
\begin{aligned}
S(0) &= 0, \\
S(j) &= 1 + \tfrac{1}{2} \cdot S(j-1) + \tfrac{1}{2} \cdot S(j+1), \quad \text{for } j = 1, 2, \ldots, n-1, \\
S(n) &= 1 + S(n-1).
\end{aligned}
$$

These are $n+1$ equations with the $n+1$ unknowns $S(0), \ldots, S(n)$. By applying the first equation to the second, writing the last equation as $\tfrac{1}{2} \cdot S(n) = \tfrac{1}{2} + \tfrac{1}{2} \cdot S(n-1)$, and then summing over the remaining n equations, we get $S(1) = 2n - 1$. Plugging this into the second equation one obtains $S(2) = 4n - 4$, and so on. In general the solution for $S(j)$ is $S(j) = 2 \cdot j \cdot n - j^2$. Independently of the initial assignment from which the process started, the expected number of steps until the goal (i.e. state 0) is reached, thereby obtaining a satisfying assignment, is at most $S(n) = n^2$. Using Markov's inequality (see the appendix) it follows that the probability that the algorithm does not reach the goal within $2n^2$ steps is at most $\tfrac{1}{2}$. This argument shows, that the satisfiability problem for 2-*CNF* formulas, i.e. 2-*SAT*, lies in the class RP. This is weaker than the other deterministic algorithms given before, where it was shown that 2-*SAT* is in P, but the algorithm has some nice relationship with the one in chapter 5.4, and even with the proof of the Local Lemma (page 33).

The results in this section are originally from (Aspvall, Plass, Tarjan, 1979) for the graph-theoretic approach, and (Papadimitriou, 1991) for the local search algorithm.

3.2 Horn Formulas

> **Definition**
>
> A *Horn formula* (after Alfred Horn, 1918–2001) is a formula in *CNF* (clause form), with the property that each clause contains at most one positive literal.

Horn formulas play an important role in the programming language Prolog. This has to do with the fact that a Horn clause like $(x \vee \overline{y_1} \vee \cdots \vee \overline{y_k})$ can be rewritten equivalently as an implication:

$$
(x \vee \overline{y_1} \vee \cdots \vee \overline{y_k}) = ((y_1 \wedge \cdots \wedge y_k) \to x)
$$

In words: when the all y-variables are assigned value 1, then x must necessarily also take value 1.

Also, the positive unit clauses as well as the purely negative clauses that appear in Horn formulas, can be written as implications:

$$
\begin{aligned}
(x) &= 1 \to x \\
(\overline{y_1} \vee \cdots \vee \overline{y_k}) &= (y_1 \wedge \cdots \wedge y_k) \to 0
\end{aligned}
$$

This is called the procedural interpretation of Horn clauses. The following algorithms and calculi for Horn clauses are also based on the procedural interpretation that can be understood almost as a list of instructions.

One should observe that a Horn formula that does not contain any positive unit clauses, or does not contain any purely negative clause, is always satisfiable. This follows from the first observation in section 1.7.

Theorem

The (un-)satisfiability of Horn formulas can be tested efficiently (in polynomial time).

Proof: We give an algorithm for the problem. If the formula does not contain any positive clauses, then it can be satisfied just by assigning value 0 to all the variables. Let us suppose that the Horn formula contains the positive clause $\{x\}$. Because of the Horn property this must be a unit clause. By unit propagation we obtain the formula $F\{x = 1\}$. This formula is again a Horn formula, and we can continue applying the described procedure to it in the same way.   □

Here is the procedure again in pseudo code:

> **input** F (a Horn formula)
> **while** $\{x\} \in F$, for a variable x **do** $F := F\{x = 1\}$
> **if** $\square \in F$ **then** "unsatisfiable"
> Set all remaining variables to 0: "satisfiable"

One should observe, that in case of a satisfiable Horn formula, the algorithm actually finds a satisfying assignment that sets as few variables as possible to 1. This is called a *minimal model* (which in this case is even unique).

We go back to the incomplete resolution restrictions introduced in the last chapter and obtain the following theorem.

Theorem

Unit resolution is refutation complete for the class of Horn formulas.

Proof: Since P-resolution is complete for the general case, this restriction is also complete for the case of Horn formulas. In the case of Horn formulas, it holds that a purely positive clause can only be a unit clause. It follows immediately from this that unit resolution is complete for Horn formulas.   □

We can also easily prove this result without having to use the concept of P-Resolution. We must show that there is a unit resolution refutation for every unsatisfiable Horn formula F. This can be shown by induction on the number n of variables in F. The claim is clear for $n = 0$ and $n = 1$. Consider now $n > 1$. Since every set of clauses is satisfiable when it does not contain any purely positive clauses (by the assignment setting all variables in F to 0), there must be in F a positive clause, and because of the Horn property, this must be a unit clause. Let $K = \{x\} \in F$ be this clause. By resolving K with all clauses in F containing the literal $\overline{x}$ (observe that these are indeed unit resolution steps), we obtain the clauses in $F' := F\{x = 1\}$. This clause set F' contains only Horn clauses and has fewer variables than F. By the induction hypothesis, there is a unit resolution refutation for F'. These two refutations put together give a unit resolution refutation for F.

Since the execution of unit resolution steps is essentially the same as the execution of unit propagation (see page 18), we can also formulate the last theorem by saying that the decision of whether a Horn formula is satisfiable can be done just by using unit propagation steps. Since after applying one such step the obtained formula is strictly shorter and contains fewer variables, this is also a polynomial time algorithm for Horn formulas.

Because unit resolution refutations exist exactly in the case when input resolution refutations exist, see page 53, we obtain:

Corollary
Input resolution is refutation complete for the class of Horn formulas.

3.3 Renamable Horn Formulas

There is an interesting and powerful generalization of the class of Horn formulas that will be considered next.

Definition
A formula F in conjunctive normal form is called *renamable Horn* (or also *hidden Horn*) if there is a subset U of the variables $Var(F)$, so that $F[x = \overline{x} \mid x \in U]$ is a Horn formula.
We call such a set U a *renaming*.

Although there are exponentially many potential renamings, in case that there is such a renaming leading to a Horn formula, it is possible to compute it efficiently. For doing this, we associate to a given formula F in conjunctive normal form a new formula F^* in 2-*CNF* in the following way:

$$F^* = \{ (u \vee v) \mid u, v \text{ are literals in the same clause } K \in F \}$$

Theorem

The *CNF* formula F is renamable Horn if and only if the associated 2-*CNF* formula F^* is satisfiable.

Moreover, a satisfying assignment α for F^* (in case it exists) encodes a renaming U in the sense that $x \in U \Leftrightarrow x\alpha = 1$.

This means that renamings can be obtained efficiently, since the satisfiability of 2-*CNF* formulas can be tested efficiently. i.e. 2-*SAT* $\in$ P.

Proof: Let F be a renamable Horn formula and let $U \subseteq \text{Var}(F)$ be the corresponding renaming transforming F into a Horn formula. We consider the assignment

$$\alpha = \{x = 1 \mid x \in U\} \cup \{x = 0 \mid x \in \text{Var}(F) \setminus U\}$$

Let $(u \vee v)$ be an arbitrary clause in F^*. The literals u and v must appear together in a clause K in F. After the renaming there is in $(u \vee v)[x = \overline{x} \mid x \in U]$ at least one negated literal. Expressed in a different way, at least one literal in $(u \vee v)$ is set to 1 by α. This implies that F^* is satisfiable.

The other direction is proven analogously: let α be a satisfying assignment for F^*. In F this means that there is no pair of literals in the same clause being both set to 0 by α. Defining $U = \{x \in \text{Var}(F) \mid x\alpha = 1\}$, one obtains a renaming that does not generate two positive literals in a clause. This implies that the renaming produces a Horn formula. $\square$

Theorem

A minimally unsatisfiable set of clauses F can be refuted using unit resolution if and only if F is renamable Horn.

Proof: Let F be a renamable Horn, unsatisfiable set of clauses. This means that there is a renaming $U \subseteq \text{Var}(F)$, so that $G = F[x = \overline{x} \mid x \in U]$ is a Horn formula. Since unit resolution is complete for the class of Horn formulas, there must be a unit resolution refutation for G of the form $(K_1, K_2, \ldots, K_t)$, $K_t = \square$. By applying the renaming U to all the clauses in the resolution refutation (that is by inverting the renaming used in the clauses in F), all the resolution steps in the refutation are still legal resolution steps. We obtain in this way a unit resolution refutation for F.

For the other direction, let F be minimally unsatisfiable and consider that there is a unit resolution refutation $(K_1, K_2, \ldots, K_t)$, $K_t = \square$, for F. Let us suppose that the first m clauses in the refutation are the clauses in F, $F = \{K_1, \ldots, K_m\}$, $m \leq t$. Using induction on $t - m$ we show that F is renamable Horn. The case $t - m = 0$ is trivial, since in this case, it must hold that $F = \{\square\}$, because F is minimally unsatisfiable.

Let $t - m > 0$. We consider now the first resolvent K_{m+1} in the refutation, with its two parent clauses K_i and K_j, $i, j \leq m$, in F and such that at least one of them, say K_i, is a unit clause. Let $K_i = \{u\}$. No other clause in F can include the literal u, since if there was a clause $K \in F$ with $u \in K$, $|K| \geq 2$, then the clause set $F \setminus \{K\}$ would be satisfiable (because F is minimally unsatisfiable) with some assignment α. Since $K_i = \{u\} \in F \setminus \{K\}$, we have $u\alpha = 1$. It follows that also $K\alpha = 1$, since K contains the literal u. But from this we obtain $F\alpha = 1$, which is a contradiction.

We observe that $K_j \setminus \{\overline{u}\} = K_{m+1}$. By using the notation K' for $K \setminus \{\overline{u}\}$, we can conclude, that

$$(K_1', \ldots, K_{i-1}', K_{i+1}', \ldots, K_m', K_{m+2}', \ldots, K_t')$$

is a unit resolution refutation for the clause set

$$F' := \{K_1', \ldots, K_{i-1}', K_{i+1}', \ldots, K_m'\}.$$

Moreover, we can see that F' is minimally unsatisfiable. For an arbitrary clause K' in F', because F is minimally unsatisfiable, the clause set $F \setminus \{K\}$ is satisfiable with some assignment β. Since $\{u\}$ appears as a unit clause in F, $u\beta = 1$ and $\overline{u}\beta = 0$. It follows that $(F' \setminus \{K\})\beta = 1$.

Using the induction hypothesis, F' is renamable Horn with some renaming V'. We can now extend V' to a renaming V for F, by defining:

$$V = \begin{cases} V' & \text{if } u \text{ is positive} \\ V' \cup \{u\} & \text{if } u \text{ is negative} \end{cases}$$

The clauses in $F[x = \overline{x} \mid x \in V]$ must be all of the Horn type, since after the renaming $\{u\}$ is a positive clause with a single literal while all other clauses are enlarged with a negative literal. $\square$

Since a unit resolution refutation is equivalent to the execution of unit propagation steps, this last result says that unit propagation leads to success exactly in the class of renamable Horn formulas.

The results presented in this section are originally from (Henschen, Wos, 1974), (Lewis, 1978), (Goldberg, 1979), (Mannila, Mehlhorn, 1985), (Schöning, Schuler, 1989), (del Val, 2000).

3.4 Schaefer Classification

A very influential publication (Schaefer, 1978) analyzed the cases in which the satisfiability problem for a class of "*CNF*-like" formulas of the type

$$R_1(x_1, \ldots, x_n) \wedge R_2(x_1, \ldots, x_n) \wedge \cdots \wedge R_m(x_1, \ldots, x_n)$$

is NP-complete and the cases in which the problem can be solved in polynomial time. The R_i symbols in the formula can represent any Boolean function.

Among many other results, on the one hand, it is proved in (Schaefer, 1978), that in this setting only two possibilities exist: NP-complete or solvable in polynomial time (called *Schaefer dichotomy*). These are, of course, two different possibilities only in the case when $P \neq NP$ holds. On the other hand, the publication (Schaefer, 1978) characterizes exactly those R_i's whose corresponding satisfiability problem is solvable in polynomial time.

We will not deal with the technical details in Schaefer's result, since this would bring us far from the actual *SAT* problem and the algorithmic ways to solve it. We will just mention that we have already described (almost) all the cases that can be solved in polynomial time in the last sections on 2-*CNF* and (renamable) Horn formulas. It remains only one polynomially solvable case, namely when the R_i's have one of the following forms:

$$x_{i_1} \oplus x_{i_2} \oplus \cdots \oplus x_{i_k} \quad \text{or} \quad x_{i_1} \oplus x_{i_2} \oplus \cdots \oplus x_{i_k} \oplus 1$$

That is, R_i expresses the condition that in a subset of the variables, the number of them assigned to value 1 must be even or odd.

Example: Let $F = (x_1 \oplus x_3) \wedge (x_2 \oplus x_3 \oplus x_4 \oplus 1) \wedge (x_1 \oplus x_2 \oplus 1) \wedge (x_2 \oplus x_3)$. This formula can be seen as a linear equation system over the field with two elements ($\{0, 1\}, \oplus, \wedge$):

$$\begin{pmatrix} 1 & 0 & 1 & 0 \\ 0 & 1 & 1 & 1 \\ 1 & 1 & 0 & 0 \\ 0 & 1 & 1 & 0 \end{pmatrix} \cdot \begin{pmatrix} x_1 \\ x_2 \\ x_3 \\ x_4 \end{pmatrix} = \begin{pmatrix} 0 \\ 1 \\ 1 \\ 0 \end{pmatrix}$$

Such a system can be solved using Gaussian elimination, and this gives an efficient method for testing the satisfiability of F.

One should observe, that in this case we are no longer dealing with formulas in *CNF* (conjunctions of disjunctions) as it is done almost everywhere else in this book.

4 Backtracking and DPLL Algorithms

Most *SAT* solvers are based on the simple backtracking algorithm:

> **proc** backtracking (F : clause set) : **bool**
> // outputs 1, if F is satisfiable, 0 otherwise
> **if** $\square \in F$ **then return** 0
> **if** $F = \emptyset$ **then return** 1
> choose a variable $x \in Var(F)$
> **if** backtracking ($F\{x = 0\}$) **then return** 1
> **return** backtracking ($F\{x = 1\}$)

The algorithm can be easily modified to produce, besides the yes/no answer, also a satisfying assignment α in the positive case (when F is satisfiable). In principle, the backtracking algorithm is more efficient than simply trying all assignments for F, since in case $\square \in F\alpha$ for some partial assignment α created in the recursive process, it follows that $F\beta = 0$ for all extensions β from α. In this case the algorithm does not need to visit the whole subtree with the extensions of α and the search space becomes smaller.

The backtracking algorithm presented here can be seen as a "meta algorithm." It describes a class of algorithms because the step "choose a variable $x \in Var(F)$" is not completely specified. There can be many possibilities for the choice of the next variable x to be assigned.

A proof for the unsatisfiability of a formula with the backtracking algorithm is closely related to a resolution refutation of the corresponding formula, as shown in the next result.

> **Theorem**
> Let F be an unsatisfiable formula in *CNF*, and let r be the minimal number of recursive calls made by the backtracking algorithm with input F (with any strategy for the variable selection). Then there is a tree resolution refutation for F with at most r clauses.

Proof: We can associate a resolution refutation to the recursion tree defined by the execution of the backtracking algorithm on input F. Every node in the tree is identified with a clause. Each of these clauses is falsified by the assignment leading from the root of the tree to the corresponding node (the assignment applied to the formula F defined by the recursive calls made so far). We identify each leaf in the recursion tree with a clause from F falsified by the assignment leading from the root to this leaf. Such a clause in F must exist since otherwise this assignment would satisfy F. We work now from the leaves of the tree back to the root, indicating the clauses identified with the inner nodes. For an inner node v for which the branching variable x was chosen, and with two descendant nodes, already identified with the clauses K_i and K_j, we consider a new clause K_v. In the case both K_i and K_j contain variable x, then it must occur positively in one of the clauses and negated in the other clause (because the clauses are falsified by the assignments leading from the root to the corresponding nodes). K_v is then defined as the resolvent of K_i and K_j. Otherwise one of the descendant clauses K_i, K_j, not containing variable x, is identified with v. One can see that in both cases K_v is falsified by the assignment leading from the root to v. Moreover, every clause in the tree is either the resolvent of the descendent clauses or a copy of one of the descendant clauses. The root of the tree is identified with the empty clause $\square$ since this is the only clause falsified by the empty assignment. By listing the duplicated clauses only once, one obtains a tree-like resolution refutation for F. $\qquad\square$

One can observe in the proof, that the resolution refutation defined by the backtracking tree, has a special property: each variable appears at most once in every path from a clause in F to the empty clause. This resolution restriction is called *regular resolution*. From our proof of the refutation completeness of the general resolution, it follows also that regular resolution is refutation complete. One can also observe, that the relation between regular tree-like resolution and the backtracking algorithm holds also in the other direction: when there is a tree-like regular resolution refutation of size r for an unsatisfiable formula F, then the backtracking algorithm (with the corresponding variable selection strategy) needs at most r recursive calls.

As we will see, the DPLL algorithms include some deterministic rules to decide which one of the variables should be selected for the next branching step. It follows from the last theorem, that a lower bound on the size of a tree-like resolution refutation for a formula F implies also a lower bound for the backtracking algorithm on F, independently of the strategy used for the selection of variables. This is therefore a lower bound for the following DPLL-type algorithms.

In spite of this, with a simple strategy for the selection of the next variable it is possible to prove an upper bound for a variant of the DPLL algorithm for the k-*SAT* problem that is better than the "brute-force" search on every possible assignment. Let us suppose that the algorithm on input a formula F in k-CNF with n variables chooses first a clause C and then assigns simultaneously all the (at most k) variables in C. For exactly one of the possible 2^k assignments for these k variables that appear in C it holds that $C\alpha = 0$. This means that at least one of the branches in the (original) backtracking structure does not need to be followed. The search structure created by the algorithm can be seen as a recursion tree with branching degree $2^k - 1$, thereby "exhausting" k of the n

variables. In other words, the recursion equation is given by $T(n) = (2^k - 1) \cdot T(n - k)$. The number of recursive calls is therefore bounded by $(2^k - 1)^{n/k}$. For $k = 3$ this yields the upper bound $O(1.913^n) = O(2^{0.936n})$ for the problem, compared to $O(2^n)$ from the naive backtracking or truth table algorithms (see chapter 1).

We will in the following express running times of algorithms in the form a^n for a constant $a \in (1, 2)$. We calculate these, as we just did, also in the form 2^{bn}, where $b = \log_2(a)$, $b \in (0, 1)$, since this form is much more meaningful because it expresses that the corresponding algorithm, instead of having to branch over n variables, as the naive algorithm would do, branches in fact (on average) only over bn variables.

4.1 DPLL and Heuristic Functions

In (Davis, Putnam, 1960) as well as in (Davis, Logemann, Loveland, 1982) a version of backtracking is proposed, equipped with a simple heuristic strategy to decide which is the next variable to be selected. This algorithm (and sometimes refinements of it) goes by the name DPLL, after the first letters of the authors.

> **proc** DPLL (F : clause set) : **bool**
> // outputs 1, if F is satisfiable, 0 otherwise
> **if** $\square \in F$ **then return** 0
> **if** $F = \emptyset$ **then return** 1
> **if** F contains a unit clause $\{u\}$ **then return** DPLL($F\{u = 1\}$)
> **if** F contains a pure literal u **then return** DPLL($F\{u = 1\}$)
> choose with the adequate strategy a variable $x \in \mathit{Var}(F)$ $(*)$
> **if** DPLL($F\{x = 0\}$) **then return** 1
> **return** DPLL($F\{x = 1\}$)

The possibility to simplify the formula, if it includes a unit clause, plays an important role. When F includes the clause $\{u\}$ and the algorithm chooses u as branching variable, then the recursive call DPLL($F\{u = 0\}$) would immediately stop at the next step. Therefore, one can save the branching and just set $\{u = 1\}$. Since this step is very easy to implement and can simplify the formula considerably, the unit clause rule is executed first in most *SAT* solvers. The successive use of this simplification rule is called *unit propagation*.

A similar role is played by the pure literal rule, although this one is harder to implement (and therefore it is often left out). We recall that a literal u in F is called *pure* when $\overline{u}$ does not appear in F. If u in pure in F, then the algorithm does not need to consider the assignment $\{u = 0\}$ since F and $F\{u = 1\}$ are sat-equivalent.

The running time of DPLL depends in practice crucially on the selection of variables for the branching steps. This should be done in a way such that many unit propagation steps (or other simplification possibilities like pure literals) are produced. The more branching steps one can save, the better.

Because of this, many different "heuristic functions" for selecting the next branching variable in the DPLL algorithm have been proposed. Such functions are applied to the simplified formulas obtained by the subsequent substitution of some of the variables in order to provide at line $(*)$ in the algorithm a good selection of one of the remaining variables. For the formulation of the heuristic functions we define for every formula in CNF and for every literal u in the formula the values:

$$
\begin{aligned}
f_k(u) &= \text{number of occurrences of } u \text{ in clauses of size } k \\
f(u) &= \textstyle\sum_{k=2}^{n} f_k(u), \quad \text{number of occurrences of } u \text{ in } F
\end{aligned}
$$

We mention here some of the most popular heuristic functions:

DLIS (Dynamic Largest Individual Sum): The algorithm chooses a literal u with maximal $f(u)$ and assigns first $u = 1$.

DLCS (Dynamic Largest Clause Sum): The algorithm chooses a variable x with maximal $f(x) + f(\overline{x})$ and assigns first $\{x = 1\}$, if $f(x) \geq f(\overline{x})$ and $\{x = 0\}$ otherwise.

MOM (Maximum Occurrence in Minimal Size Clauses): Let k be the shortest size of a clause in the formula. The algorithm chooses a variable x with maximal value

$$
(f_k(x) + f_k(\overline{x})) \cdot p + f_k(x) \cdot f_k(\overline{x})
$$

Here p is a parameter that should be big enough so that the first term dominates over the second one. The variable that appears more often in the shortest clauses is selected, and when there is more than one with this property, the algorithm chooses the one with the highest balance in the distribution of positive and negative occurrences.

Böhm Heuristic: For every variable x, the vector $H(x) = (H_2(x), \ldots, H_n(x))$ is defined, with

$$
H_i(x) = p_1 \cdot \max(f_i(x), f_i(\overline{x})) + p_2 \cdot \min(f_i(x), f_i(\overline{x})).
$$

Here are p_1 and p_2 free parameters. The algorithm chooses the variable x for which the vector $H(x)$ is maximal (according to the lexicographical ordering).

Jeroslaw-Wang: Let jw be the function defined for a literal u as

$$
jw(u) = \sum_{i=2}^{n} f_i(u) 2^{-i} = \sum_{u \in K} 2^{-|K|}.
$$

In a one sided version of this heuristic, a literal u with maximal value $jw(u)$ is chosen and the literal is first set to 1. For a two sided version the algorithm, an x with maximal value $jw(x) + jx(\overline{x})$ is selected, and then $\{x = 1\}$, if $jw(x) \geq jw(\overline{x})$ is set first, otherwise $\{x = 0\}$ is set first.

Shortest Clause: The algorithm chooses first an arbitrary literal from one of the shortest clauses. DPLL with this heuristic function is the basis for the Monien-Speckenmeyer algorithm, which will be presented in the next section.

VSIDS (Variable State Independent Decaying Sum): This heuristic function is similar to DLIS. The difference is that when a conflict occurs, producing a backtracking step in the DPLL algorithm, the f values of the variables causing the conflict are increased by 1 (for the concept of "conflict clause" see Section 4.4.1). It pays off to concentrate on such variables responsible for conflicts in order to eliminate them early on in the execution of the algorithm. This means that the computation of the (now modified) function f is (as opposed to DLIS) also dependent on the previous history. In order not to let these f values grow arbitrarily during the execution of the algorithm they are divided by 2 in regular intervals, which causes a certain kind of "oblivion" regarding the conflicts that happened long ago.

The heuristic functions described here are not the only possibilities. More about this kind of functions can be found in chapter 7 in the handbook (Biere et al., 2009). One can interpret these heuristics in connection with the backdoor concept (see page 63). One hopes that the variables selected according to a heuristic process are in fact backdoor variables. As long as the right backdoor variables are selected (and correctly assigned) the remaining formula can be solved in polynomial time by using unit propagation.

4.2 Monien-Speckenmeyer Algorithm

This algorithm for k-*SAT* appears originally in (Monien, Speckenmeyer, 1985). It can be seen as a particular case of DPLL with a concrete selection heuristic. One can also understand the algorithm as a kind of look-ahead solver (cf. chapter 5 in the handbook (Biere et al., 2009)).

We consider first a simplified version of the algorithm that will be improved afterwards. The shortest clause heuristic would select the first literal u_1 in the first of the shortest clauses $C = \{u_1 \vee u_2 \vee \cdots \vee u_m\}$ in the input formula F, and assign $\{u_1 = 1\}$. In case that a satisfying assignment is not found, $C \setminus \{u_1\}$ is still one of the shortest clauses in $F\{u_1 = 0\}$ and u_2 will be selected as the new branching variable. The algorithm continues then with the assignment $\{u_1 = 0, u_2 = 1\}$, and so on. The selection and successive assignment of these literals from a (shortest) clause is done within the same incarnation of the following recursive prcedure MS.

proc MS (F : clause set) : **bool**
// outputs 1, if F is satisfiable, 0 otherwise
if $\square \in F$ **then return** 0
if $F = \emptyset$ **then return** 1
choose a shortest clause C in F
let $C = (u_1 \vee u_2 \vee \cdots \vee u_m)$
for $i := 1$ **to** m **do**
    if MS ($F\{u_1 = 0, \ldots, u_{i-1} = 0, u_i = 1\}$) **then return** 1
return 0

Let $T(n)$ be the number of recursive calls in the MS procedure on an input formula with n variables. When a clause of size m is selected, m branching steps are produced. In the i-th branching step i variables are assigned and $n - i$ variables remain in the formula. The recursive calls refer to a formula with $n - i$ variables. This produces the recursive inequality $T(n) \leq T(n - 1) + T(n - 2) + \cdots + T(n - m)$.

For formulas in k-*CNF* it holds that $m \leq k$. Under the hypothesis that MS has an exponential worst case complexity, that is, $T(n) = a^n$ for some number a, we obtain the equality $a^k = a^{k-1} + \cdots + a^1 + 1$. With the formula $a^{k-1} + \cdots + a^1 + 1 = \frac{1-a^k}{1-a}$ (for $a \neq 1$) we obtain the equivalent equation $a^{k+1} + 1 = 2a^k$. The solutions for the equation for small values of k are listed in the table. We have also listed the values b with $a = 2^b$ (respectively $b = \log_2(a)$).

k	3	4	5	6	7	8
a	1.839	1.928	1.966	1.984	1.992	1.996
b	0.879	0.947	0.975	0.988	0.994	0.997

The running time of the previous algorithm can be improved by using the concept of autark assignment (cf. section 1.5). We recall that an assignment α is autark for a formula F in CNF if, for all clauses $C \in F$ with $\mathit{Var}(\alpha) \cap \mathit{Var}(C) \neq \emptyset$ it holds that $C\alpha = 1$. One can efficiently test whether an assignment α is autark for F. In Section 1.5 we showed, that if α is autark for F, then F and $F\alpha$ are sat-equivalent. The Monien-Speckenmeyer algorithm is now modified in such a way that, before the recursive calls are made, it is tested as to whether the constructed partial assignments are autark for the corresponding formula.

In the positive case, one can directly assign the variables and obtain (without further recursion) a reduced sat-equivalent formula.

proc MS2 (F : clause set) : **bool**

// outputs 1, if F satisfiable, otherwise 0

if $\square \in F$ **then return** 0

if $F = \emptyset$ **then return** 1

choose a shortest clause C in F

let $C = (u_1 \vee u_2 \vee \cdots \vee u_m)$

for $i := 1$ **to** m **do**

 begin

  $\alpha_i := \{u_1 = 0, \ldots, u_{i-1} = 0, u_i = 1\}$

  if α_i is autark for F **then return** MS2$(F\alpha_i)$

 end

for $i := 1$ **to** m **do**

 if MS2 ($F\alpha_i$) **then return** 1

return 0

For the complexity analysis for k-*SAT* we have to distinguish two cases depending on whether at least one of the partial assignments α_i is autark or not. In the first case (at least one assignment is autark) we obtain the recursion $T(n) \leq T(n-1)$, since at least one of the variables is assigned by the algorithm.

In the second case, all the assignments produced by the recursive calls of the algorithm are not autark. This implies that in the following recursive call, after applying a non-autark assignment, the shortest clause then has size at most $k-1$. This is so because for each non-autark assignment α_i there must be a clause C, that is not satisfied by α_i but is "touched" by the assignment. This means $\mathit{Var}(C) \cap \mathit{Var}(\alpha_i) \neq \emptyset$. At least one literal in C must then be assigned 0 and this makes the clause shorter. Since $F\alpha_i$ contains a clause with at most $k-1$ variables, there will be at most a $(k-1)$ branching in the next call of the recursive procedure. Let us denote by $T'(n)$ the number of recursive calls in the algorithm with formulas with n variables and under the hypothesis that there is a clause with at most $k-1$ literals. We have in the first case $T(n) \leq T(n-1)$. In the second case we obtain $T(n) = T'(n-1) + \cdots + T'(n-k)$. There are analogous case distinctions for $T'(n)$, and we obtain the following recursion equalities:

$$\begin{aligned} T(n) &= \max\{T(n-1), T'(n-1) + \cdots + T'(n-k)\} \\ T'(n) &= \max\{T(n-1), T'(n-1) + \cdots + T'(n-k+1)\} \end{aligned}$$

Using induction one can observe that the maximum of both functions corresponds to the second case hence $T(n-1) \leq T'(n-1) + \cdots + T'(n-k+1)$. This allows the simplification of the equalities to

$$\begin{aligned} T(n) &= T'(n-1) + \cdots + T'(n-k) \\ T'(n) &= T'(n-1) + \cdots + T'(n-k+1) \end{aligned}$$

Using the hypothesis that $T'(n)$ is an exponential function, that is, $T'(n) = a^n$, the second recursion equality produces the characteristic equation $a^{k-1} = a^{k-2} + \cdots + a^1 + 1$. From the first recursion it follows $T(n) = O(T'(n))$. Again with the formula $a^{k-1} + \cdots + a^1 + 1 = \frac{1-a^k}{1-a}$ (for $a \neq 1$) we obtain the equivalent equation $a^k + 1 = 2a^{k-1}$. For the case $k = 3$ we get $a = \frac{\sqrt{5}+1}{2} \approx 1.6181$, the golden ratio. For small values of k, the values for a and for $b = \log_2(a)$ are listed in the following table.

k	3	4	5	6	7	8
a	1.618	1.839	1.928	1.966	1.984	1.992
b	0.694	0.879	0.947	0.975	0.988	0.994

We summarize the results:

Theorem

The deterministic Monien-Speckenmeyer algorithm for k-SAT (under the consideration of autark assignments) has a running time of $O^*(a^n)$, where $a > 1$ is the solution of the equation $a^k + 1 = 2a^{k-1}$.

4.3   Paturi-Pudlák-Zane Algorithm

We describe now a probabilistic algorithm for the k-SAT problem from (Paturi, Pudlák, Zane, 1997). One can understand this algorithm as a probabilistic version of DPLL, in which the order for assigning the variables as well as part of the assignment itself is randomly chosen. Instead of branching with backtracking as in DPLL, the algorithm has to be repeated a sufficient number of times since for a single iteration the probability of "guessing" the right values for the variables is quite small. This is discussed in more detail in the appendix about probabilistic algorithms.

Let S_n be the set of permutations over n elements. In order to find a satisfying assignment for the input formula, the algorithm randomly chooses a permutation $\pi \in S_n$ and uses it as the ordering for the variable assignment. In doing this, *unit propagation* can be used, when the variable to be assigned next according to π, is the only one in a clause. When the unit propagation rule cannot be used, then the variable will be randomly assigned value 0 or 1 (as mentioned above, this substitutes the backtracking).

input F (let $n = |\text{Var}(F)|$)

$\alpha := \emptyset$

randomly choose a permutation $\pi \in S_n$

for $i := 1$ **to** n **do**

    if $\{x_{\pi(i)}\}$ is a unit clause in F

        then $\alpha := \alpha \cup \{x_{\pi(i)} = 1\}$

    else if $\{\overline{x_{\pi(i)}}\}$ is a unit clause in F

        then $\alpha := \alpha \cup \{x_{\pi(i)} = 0\}$

        else randomly choose $a \in \{0, 1\}$

            $\alpha := \alpha \cup \{x_{\pi(i)} = a\}$

return α

Let p be the probability that the algorithm finds a satisfying assignment, in case the formula is satisfiable. Repeating the algorithm t times with independent random numbers, the probability that in none of the t trials a satisfying assignment is found is then $(1 - p)^t \leq e^{-tp}$. It suffices to repeat the algorithm $\frac{c}{p}$ times in order to obtain an error probability of at most e^{-c} (see the appendix on probabilistic algorithms). We prove the following result:

Theorem

The probabilistic version of the DPLL algorithm from Paturi-Pudlák-Zane described above finds, with probability $p \geq 2^{-n(1-1/k)}$ a satisfying assignment for an input formula in k-SAT with n variables. The complexity of the whole procedure for a constant error probability is therefore $O^*(2^{n(1-1/k)})$.

The following table shows for some values of k the basis number $a = 2^{1-1/k}$, as well as the value $b = 1 - \frac{1}{k}$. The last one gives an indication about the fraction of the variables that have to be "guessed" on average (this corresponds to the backtracking steps in the deterministic algorithm).

k	3	4	5	6	7	8
a	1.587	1.682	1.741	1.782	1.811	1.834
b	0.667	0.75	0.8	0.833	0.857	0.875

One can observe that the basis number a for increasing values of k does not converge towards 2 as fast as in other k-SAT algorithms.

We give now a proof of the result.

Let F be satisfiable and $\alpha = \{x_1 = a_1, \ldots, x_n = a_n\}$ be a satisfying assignment for F, thus $F\alpha = 1$. The i-th bit a_i in the assignment α is called *critical* in case the flipping of a_i produces a non satisfying assignment, that is $F\alpha[x_i = \overline{a_i}] = 0$. In case the i-th bit in the assignment α is critical, then there must be a clause $C \in F$ so that exactly one literal in C is assigned 1 in α. Let x_i be the variable in this literal. Both the clause C and the variable in the literal are said to be *critical*. A critical clause can contain at most one critical variable for a satisfying assignment α since only one literal is assigned 1. Let $j(\alpha)$ be the number of critical bits in α ($0 \leq j(\alpha) \leq n$), and let $s(\alpha) = n - j(\alpha)$. This means that $s(\alpha)$ is the number of bits that can be flipped in α obtaining in this way a new satisfying assignment for F. Our estimation for the success probability p will depend on these functions $j(\alpha)$ and $s(\alpha)$.

Lemma

Let F be a satisfiable formula and let $S \subseteq \{0,1\}^n$, $S \neq \emptyset$, be the set of satisfying assignments of F. Then we have:

$$\sum_{\alpha \in S} 2^{-s(\alpha)} \geq 1$$

Proof: By induction on n. The case $n = 0$ is trivial. For $n > 0$ define the sets $S_0 = \{\beta \in \{0,1\}^{n-1} \mid \beta 0 \in S\}$ and $S_1 = \{\beta \in \{0,1\}^{n-1} \mid \beta 1 \in S\}$. Associate with these sets the functions s_0, s_1, defined like s but on the formulas $F\{x_n = 0\}$, respectively $F\{x_n = 1\}$. By the induction hypothesis we have $\sum_{\beta \in S_i} 2^{-s_i(\beta)} \geq 1$. Since $1 \leq |S| = |S_0| + |S_1|$, both sets cannot be empty. If both sets are non-empty, then

$$\begin{aligned} \sum_{\alpha \in S} 2^{-s(\alpha)} &= \sum_{\beta \in S_0} 2^{-s(\beta 0)} + \sum_{\beta \in S_1} 2^{-s(\beta 1)} \\ &\geq \sum_{\beta \in S_0} 2^{-s_0(\beta)-1} + \sum_{\beta \in S_1} 2^{-s_1(\beta)-1} \\ &\geq \tfrac{1}{2} + \tfrac{1}{2} = 1 \,. \end{aligned}$$

In case (w.l.o.g) S_0 is empty, it holds that

$$\sum_{\alpha \in S} 2^{-s(\alpha)} = \sum_{\beta \in S_1} 2^{-s(\beta 1)} = \sum_{\beta \in S_1} 2^{-s_1(\beta)} \geq 1 \,.$$

$\square$

The next task is to estimate the probability that the algorithm finds a concrete satisfying assignment $\alpha \in S$. When in the algorithm the variables are being assigned as in α and a critical variable x_i is the last one to be assigned in its critical clause, then the algorithm finds the correct value for x_i deterministically by using unit propagation. This increases the probability to find α. For a permutation σ denote by $r(\alpha, \sigma)$ the number of critical variables under α that are the last ones being assigned in their critical clauses, under the ordering defined by $\sigma \in S_n$. Then it holds that $0 \leq r(\alpha, \sigma) \leq j(\alpha)$. When the program variable π gets value σ, then the number of saved random bits in the search for α is exactly $r(\alpha, \sigma)$. Therefore,

$$P(\text{ the algorithm finds } \alpha \mid \pi = \sigma) = 2^{-n+r(\alpha,\sigma)}$$

Since the permutation π is chosen under the uniform distribution (in symbols $\pi \sim U(S_n)$; see the appendix on random variables for the explanation of this notation), each one of the k variables in a clause can be the last one in π with probability $\frac{1}{k}$. This holds for each one of the $j(\alpha)$ critical variables, and the expectation for $r(\alpha, \pi)$ is therefore at least $\frac{j(\alpha)}{k}$. Expressed in a formula:

$$\mathbb{E}[r(\alpha, \pi)] = \frac{1}{n!} \cdot \sum_{\sigma \in S_n} r(\alpha, \sigma) \geq \frac{j(\alpha)}{k} \qquad (*)$$

One can now estimate the probability for finding a particular satisfying assignment α:

$$
\begin{aligned}
P(\text{the algorithm finds } \alpha) &= \sum_{\sigma \in S_n} P(\text{the algorithm finds } \alpha \mid \pi = \sigma) \cdot P(\pi = \sigma) \\
&= \sum_{\sigma \in S_n} 2^{-n+r(\alpha,\sigma)} \cdot \frac{1}{n!} \\
&= 2^{-n} \cdot \Big(\frac{1}{n!} \sum_{\sigma \in S_n} 2^{r(\alpha,\sigma)}\Big) = 2^{-n} E[2^{r(\alpha,\pi)}] \\
&\geq 2^{-n} 2^{E[r(\alpha,\pi)]} \qquad \text{(Jensen inequality)} \\
&= 2^{-n} 2^{\frac{1}{n!} \sum_{\sigma \in S_n} r(\alpha,\sigma)} \geq 2^{-n} 2^{j(\alpha)/k} \qquad \text{(by } (*))
\end{aligned}
$$

Let S be the set of satisfying assignments for F. The probability that the algorithm finds *some* assignment in S, is then:

$$
\begin{aligned}
\sum_{\alpha \in S} P(\text{the algorithm finds } \alpha) &\geq \sum_{\alpha \in S} 2^{-n} 2^{j(\alpha)/k} = 2^{-(n-n/k)} \sum_{\alpha \in S} 2^{-(n-j(\alpha))/k} \\
&\geq 2^{-n(1-1/k)} \sum_{\alpha \in S} 2^{-s(\alpha)} \geq 2^{-n(1-1/k)}
\end{aligned}
$$

The last inequality follows from the lemma. $\square$

The algorithm was improved in (Paturi, Pudlák, Saks, Zane, 1998 and 2005) with the development of a preprocessing phase. In this phase all the possible resolvents up to length about $\log n$ resulting from the initial clauses are derived, and this extended clause set is then used as input for the algorithm. This has the advantage that the "unit propagation effect" (which causes fewer variables to be randomly guessed) takes place more often. The authors prove an upper bound of $O(1.36^n)$ for 3-*SAT*. With a minor change of the algorithm, but with a more precise analysis the bound of $O(1.308^n)$ is proven in (Hertli, 2011). This is up until now the best upper bound for 3-*SAT* (for probabilistic algorithms).

4.4 DPLL in Practice

The original DPLL algorithm is the basis for many of the modern *SAT* solver used in practice. However, the algorithm has been modified in several important ways that allow the search process to be sped up drastically. A problem arising with the backtracking in the original algorithm is that some of the information about a formula gained during the search process in a recursive call is not kept in memory and cannot be used later when the algorithm returns to the stage where the call was made. This information is lost. In order to avoid this, some additional clauses encoding the information are added to the original formula. When, in a later execution of the search algorithm, a partial assignment α falsifies one of these clauses, the algorithm does not need to search the subtree with all the α extensions and computation time is saved. This concept is called *clause learning*. This technique is often used together with another idea. We have seen that one can associate a resolution refutation with the recursion tree obtained by an execution of the DPLL algorithm by identifying every node in the tree with a clause. This clause is falsified by the assignment leading from the root of the tree to the corresponding node. For a node v with branching variable x there are two recursive calls represented by two successor nodes, identified with two clauses C_1 and C_2. The resolvent of these two clauses is the clause for v. However, when C_1 does not contain variable x, one can spare the second call and identify instead v with the clause C_1. In other words, when x is not responsible for the current conflict in the search tree, then it is possible to jump over x and the algorithm can return back to a variable lying further up in the backtracking tree. This method is called *non-chronological backtracking*.

4.4.1 Clause Learning

When a conflict occurs while a partial assignment α is being generated in an execution of the DPLL algorithm (that is, a clause is falsified by α), then a new clause (the so called conflict clause) is added to the original formula F. This clause is a logical consequence of F. For the choice of the conflict clause, the variables assigned by α are divided in two groups: those that are assigned in a recursive call from the DPLL algorithm (*decision variables*) and those that are assigned in a unit propagation step (*propagation variables*). The *level* of an assigned variable x is defined as the number of decision variables that have been assigned before x by the DPLL algorithm. The variables assigned by unit propagation at the beginning of the algorithm execution are at level zero. The level in which a conflict (a logical contradiction) takes place, because an already assigned variable has to be assigned a different value (0 instead of 1 or 1 instead of 0), is called *a conflict level*. One stores also for each propagation variable the "reason" for its assigned value. This is the index of the clause which became a unit clause with the assignment, and thereby forcing the value of the propagation variable.

The choice of the conflict clause is described with the help of the so called *implication graph*. This graph is constructed during the course of the DPLL algorithm in stages. The vertices in this graph are the literals that have been assigned the value 1 by α. There is a directed edge from u to v in case the variable of literal v is a propagation variable and $\overline{u}$ occurs in the clause that is the *reason* for this variable. The vertices corresponding to literals of decision variables have in-degree 0; they do not have any predecessors. In the case of a conflict, there is a literal w that is assigned 0, and it is the last assigned literal in a clause C. Therefore, it should be assigned 1. We include then the corresponding vertices for w as well as for $\overline{w}$, and C is in this case the reason for w. The literals w and $\overline{w}$ are called *conflict literals*. As an example, we consider the formula F with the following set of clauses:

$$\{\overline{x_1}, x_2\}, \{\overline{x_2}, x_3, x_4\}, \{\overline{x_2}, \overline{x_5}\}, \{\overline{x_4}, x_5, x_6\}, \{\overline{x_7}, x_8\}, \{\overline{x_8}, \overline{x_9}\}, \{x_9, \overline{x_{10}}\}, \{x_3, \overline{x_8}, x_{10}\}$$

Let us suppose that the DPLL backtracking algorithm decides to assign $x_1 = 1$. By unit propagation it follows that $x_2 = 1$ and $x_5 = 0$ are assigned. If the algorithm chooses now the assignment 0 for the decision variable x_3, by unit propagation $x_4 = 1$ and $x_6 = 1$ are assigned. In case the variable x_7 is set to 1, then, again by unit propagation, it follows $x_8 = 1, x_9 = 0, x_{10} = 1$ and also $x_{10} = 0$. Here, a conflict happens since the variable x_{10} has to be set to 0 and 1 at the same time. The implication graph for this example assignment is given in the next figure. The decision variables in this case are x_1, x_3 and x_7 (the corresponding vertices are black). All other vertices correspond to propagation variables. The conflict vertices are x_{10} and $\overline{x_{10}}$.

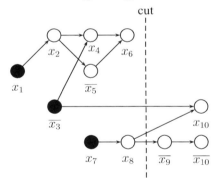

The vertices $x_1, x_2, \overline{x_5}$ have been created at level 1, the vertices $\overline{x_3}, x_4, x_6$ at level 2, and the vertices $x_7, x_8, \overline{x_9}, x_{10}, \overline{x_{10}}$ at the conflict level 3. Let u be the literal assigned the value 1 from a decision variable assigned at the conflict level (here it is x_7). A vertex v is called a UIP (*unique implication point*), if all paths from u to the conflict literals run through v. Note that the literal u itself is also a UIP. The UIP closest to the conflict literals is called the *first* UIP. There are two UIP's in our example, marked with the literals x_7 and x_8, and x_8 is the first UIP.

Let us consider now a cut in the implication graph with the conflict literals on one side (the conflict side), with all the decision literals on the other side (the decision side), and with the property that all the vertices on the conflict side can reach a conflict literal. There are several possible cuts here, one of them is drawn in the figure. This way all the edges between the decision side and the conflict side are cut through. These edges are in some sense responsible for the conflict, since the assignment for the start vertices of these edges produces a contradiction. Therefore, the conjunction of these literals that are the starting points imply the contradiction. In the above example this is $\overline{x_3} \wedge x_8$. The negation of this, that is, the clause C defined as the disjunction of the negation of these start vertices, is therefore a logical consequence of the initial formula F. This clause C can be added as an additional clause to F. In the example, this is the clause $\neg(\overline{x_3} \wedge x_8) = (x_3 \vee \overline{x_8})$. From a logical point of view, C is redundant since it is implied by F, however when later on in the execution of the DPLL algorithm, C is falsified by a partial assignment α', one can conclude that no extension from α' can satisfy F. The clause C is called the learned clause and this prevents, in the future, the partial assignments producing the conflict from being considered again. Actually, a DPLL algorithm augmented with the described clause learning feature is often referred to as CDCL (*conflict driven clause learning*).

4.4.2 Non-Chronological Backtracking

There can be many possibilities for a cut separating decision variables from conflict variables in the implication graph. These different cuts produce different conflict clauses. As we will see, the choice of the conflict clause can influence the backtracking. Some *SAT* solvers select as conflict clause the so called first UIP conflict clause. This is the clause produced from the cut having the first UIP and all the vertices corresponding to literals assigned before the conflict level on the decision side, and having all the literals assigned after the UIP on the conflict side. In the previous example, this is the clause $\{x_3, \overline{x_8}\}$.

Let C be the conflict clause under a partial assignment α and let x be the only variable in C assigned at the conflict level. Let y be the last variable in C being assigned before x and let l be the level of y. Since clause C is learned, one can update α in the backtracking process by deleting all the assignments made in levels greater than l. That is, the algorithm goes back to level l. The new partial assignment α' falsifies all literals in C except for x. Then the algorithm assigns x using unit propagation in order to satisfy C.

Since x does not need to be the last variable being assigned, one can save backtracking steps with this idea. This method is known as *non-chronological backtracking*. There are three assignment levels in our example. In the conflict clause $\{x_3, \overline{x_8}\}$, x_8 is the variable assigned at the conflict level. The algorithm would then jump back to the level of variable x_3. Using unit propagation, variable x_8 would be assigned value 0.

The exposition in this chapter is mainly based on (Kroening, Strichman, 2008) and (Mitchell, 2005). See also chapter 3 and 4 in the handbook (Biere et al., 2009).

5   Local Search and Hamming Balls

Local search is in principle a very simple algorithmic method. Combined with advanced heuristics, however, it can be very efficient: one starts with a solution candidate (randomly produced, for example); in our case this is an assignment. It is, of course, very unlikely that such an arbitrary assignment satisfies the formula we are testing for satisfiability. In general this will not happen. This means that some clauses will be falsified by the initial assignment. These clauses contain several variables. It seems natural to change the truth values of these variables (either again randomly or following some systematic strategy). The hope is that by doing these local changes in the initial assignment, the situation would become better; this could be measured for example in the number of falsified clauses, or in the Hamming distance to the next satisfying assignment. Recall that the *Hamming distance*, named after Richard Hamming (1915–1998), denotes the number of positions whose symbols are different in two given strings of the same length (when considering an assignment as a bitstring).

Both measures should be minimized, and both take value 0 when a satisfying assignment is found. The problem is that the number of falsified clauses does not correlate very well with the Hamming distance. It is like "fishing in murky waters." The number of falsified clauses can be counted efficiently. The much more interesting information about the Hamming distance can only be obtained indirectly and the way to do this remains rather nebulous.

Initially, with a randomly selected assignment, the expected Hamming distance to a fixed satisfying assignment is $\frac{n}{2}$. By randomly choosing a variable and changing its truth value, the Hamming distance is decreased with probability $\frac{1}{2}$. This resembles the method of Papadimitriou, cf. page 66. The problem is that as soon as we come closer to the solution (for example when the Hamming distance is only $\frac{n}{10}$), the probability that with such "blind" guessing of variables the right one is chosen becomes smaller and smaller, in this case $\frac{1}{10}$.

The search for a good variable to flip can only work out by considering and interpreting all the possible "signals" coming from the formula with some assignment α. We consider in the following several algorithms based on the principle of local search. Some of them are deterministic and some are probabilistic.

The deterministic algorithms will output at the end (like the DPLL algorithms) the correct result, "satisfiable" or "unsatisfiable." Such algorithms are known (in the "SAT scene") as *complete* algorithms. In the case of probabilistic algorithms based on local search, after a number of unsuccessful attempts one cannot be sure of whether there is no solution (for an unsatisfiable formula) or one is dealing with a especially hard (but satisfiable) instance of a formula, or one has been very unlucky with the randomized search steps. These algorithms are called *incomplete*.

We do not completely agree with this point of view. It does make a difference when there is a theoretical analysis stating, for example, that after a certain number of randomized search steps a possible solution can exist only with probability 2^{-30}. In this case the search can finish with the output "unsatisfiable" and the denomination of "complete" algorithm is in our opinion as justified as in the deterministic case (especially, when one can make the error probability arbitrarily small). The theoretical analysis is, so to speak, part of the algorithm because the halting conditions or the reasonable number of restarts depend on this analysis.

The situation is different when the algorithm has not been successfully analyzed. This is especially the case in the really practical algorithms using all kinds of heuristic functions (see chapter 5.6). But also deterministic algorithms can include a counter that, when overrun, forces the algorithm to stop unsuccessfully. Therefore, a deterministic algorithm can be an incomplete algorithm as well.

5.1   Deterministic Local Search

A deterministic local search is designed in such a way that for a given set of clauses F with $|\mathit{Var}(F)| = n$ and a given initial assignment α (with $\mathit{Var}(\alpha) = \mathit{Var}(F)$) it should find out whether there exists an assignment α_0 (also with $\mathit{Var}(\alpha_0) = \mathit{Var}(F)$) with $F\alpha_0 = 1$ whose Hamming distance from α does not exceed a maximal given bound.

An assignment α for the n variables present in F can be considered as a sequence of n bits (zeroes and ones). We denote by $d(\alpha, \alpha_0)$ the Hamming distance between the two assignments α and α_0.

Let us suppose that δn, $\delta \leq \frac{1}{2}$, is the given maximal Hamming distance to be evaluated. The constant δ denotes the maximum fraction of the variables of the formula which can be flipped to convert α to a (hopefully) satisfying assignment α_0: $d(\alpha, \alpha_0) \leq \delta n$. The number of assignments differing from α in at most δn bits is $\sum_{i=0}^{\delta n} \binom{n}{i}$ and this number behaves asymptotically like $2^{h(\delta) \cdot n}$ (here h is the entropy function, see the appendix on binomial coefficients). With the help of the clause structure in F, the seemingly necessary computational cost for the search of α_0 will be drastically reduced (in a first attempt to $3^{\delta \cdot n}$, and in a later chapter even to $2^{\delta \cdot n}$, as shown in the next diagram). At this point we are considering formulas $F \in 3\text{-}CNF$:

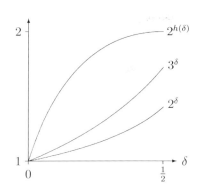

The essential observation is the following: when $C\alpha = 0$ for a clause $C \in F$, $|C| = 3$, thus $C = \{u, v, w\}$ for three literals u, v and w, with α being the current assignment, and if α_0 is a satisfying assignment for F, then $C\alpha_0 = 1$. This means, the assignments α and α_0 must differ in at least one of the 3 bits corresponding to the literals u, v and w. By changing systematically each one of the 3 bits, thus making $\alpha[u = 1]$, $\alpha[v = 1]$, and $\alpha[w = 1]$, at least for one of the three new assignments, the Hamming distance to α_0 decreases by 1.

We can translate this idea directly into the corresponding algorithm:

proc localsearch (F : clause set, α : assignment, p : **nat**) : **bool**
// outputs 1, if there is some satisfying assignment α_0 for F with $d(\alpha, \alpha_0) \leq p$
if $F\alpha = 1$ **then return** 1
if $p = 0$ **then return** 0
let $C \in F$ be a clause with $C\alpha = 0$, $C = \{u_1, u_2, u_3\}$
for $i := 1$ **to** 3 **do**
    if localsearch ($F, \alpha[u_i = 1], p - 1$) **then return** 1   (∗)
return 0

The following picture sketches the idea that this procedure, when called with an assignment α and a given Hamming distance $p = \delta n$, looks in a concrete area of the whole search space, and outputs 1 if a satisfying assignment is found in this region. The area for potential assignments around α,

$$H_p(\alpha) = \{\alpha' \mid d(\alpha, \alpha') \leq p\}$$

is called the *Hamming ball around the assignment α with radius p*.

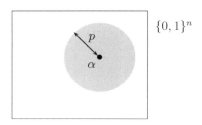

The running time of the localsearch procedure is given (up to a negligible polynomial factor) by the recursion $T(p) = 3 \cdot T(p-1)$, with solution 3^p. For general k-SAT we obtain accordingly k^p.

Here is a little calculation example: let $p = \frac{n}{2}$ and start the procedure localsearch one time with $\alpha_1 = \{x_1 = 0, \ldots, x_n = 0\}$ (in short: $\alpha_1 = 0^n$) and one time with $\alpha_2 = \{x_1 = 1, \ldots, x_n = 1\}$ (in short: $\alpha_2 = 1^n$). Every assignment has a Hamming distance of at most $\frac{n}{2}$ to α_1 or to α_2. We obtain in this way an algorithm for 3-SAT with a running time of $O^*(3^{n/2}) = O(1.733^n) = O(2^{0.793n})$.

Unfortunately, this special selection for the starting assignments cannot be meaningfully extended for $k > 3$: the running time for 4-SAT is already $4^{n/2} = 2^n$, the same as for the naive algorithm.

In the way the algorithm has been described it is possible that a bit that has already been "flipped" is "flipped back" later in a deeper recursion level. This does not affect the correctness of the procedure, but if one wants to avoid this, the recursive call in line $(*)$ could be formulated as localsearch ($F\{u_i = 1\}, \alpha[u_i = 1], p - 1$) instead. In this way, the bit flip $u_i = 1$ becomes "frozen" for all later recursive calls.

In the current formulation, the algorithm can select *every possible* clause $C \in F$ with $C\alpha = 0$. In practice it is for sure advantageous to select a *shortest* clause of this kind. Sometimes, in certain recursion steps, the shortest clause then has size 2 or 1 which shortens the computation time. A theoretical analysis of these cases is however quite difficult. In chapter 5.5 we will deal again with this variant of the procedure localsearch.

5.2   Random Initial Assignments

We combine now the deterministic procedure localsearch with a probabilistic element; we randomly choose several times the initial assignment α. The questions here are how many such random assignments should be produced in order to cover the whole search space, and at the same time, how large should the Hamming radius be.

Let $p = \delta n$ be the Hamming radius, and let t be the number of independent random choices for the initial assignment α. The optimal choices for p and and t are closely connected to each other and will be determined later. We are considering the following algorithm:

```
input F
for i := 1 to t do
   begin
      choose a random assignment α
      if localsearch ( F, α, p ) then return "satisfiable"
   end
return "unsatisfiable"
```

Let us suppose that F is satisfiable and let α_0 be a satisfying assignment for F. We want to estimate now the probability that the algorithm "misses" the assignment α_0, producing the wrong output "unsatisfiable." This happens when in all t calls of localsearch the Hamming distance $d(\alpha, \alpha_0)$ is larger than δn.

$$
\begin{aligned}
P(\,\forall i \leq t \,:\, d(\alpha_0, \alpha_i) > \delta n\,) \;&=\; \prod_{i=1}^{t} P(\,d(\alpha_0, \alpha_i) > \delta n\,) \\
&=\; \prod_{i=1}^{t} (1 - P(\,d(\alpha_0, \alpha_i) \leq \delta n\,)) \\
&=\; \prod_{i=1}^{t} \left(1 - \frac{\sum_{j=0}^{\delta n} \binom{n}{j}}{2^n}\right) \\
&=\; \left(1 - \frac{\sum_{j=0}^{\delta n} \binom{n}{j}}{2^n}\right)^{t} \\
&\leq\; e^{-t \cdot \frac{\sum_{j=0}^{\delta n} \binom{n}{j}}{2^n}} \quad \Big| \quad t = \frac{c \cdot 2^n}{\sum_{j=0}^{\delta n} \binom{n}{j}} \\
&=\; e^{-c}
\end{aligned}
$$

We have used here the estimation $1 - x \leq e^{-x}$. This calculation shows that when we choose the number of trials to be $t = \frac{c \cdot 2^n}{\sum_{i=0}^{\delta n} \binom{n}{i}}$ then, with very small probability (namely e^{-c} for a c that can be fixed arbitrarily), a satisfying assignment can be missed (see the appendix on probabilistic algorithms).

The running time for the algorithm above is then $t \cdot 3^{\delta n}$ (the term $3^{\delta n}$ comes from the algorithm on page 89); up to a polynomial factor this is equal to $[2^{1-h(\delta)} \cdot 3^{\delta}]^n$ (see the appendix on binomial coefficients). The real number in brackets is the base of this exponential function. It behaves with respect to the variation of δ as follows:

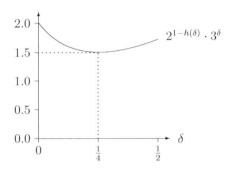

By differentiating with respect to δ and setting the result to zero, one can see that the optimal value of δ is $\frac{1}{4}$. Plugging in $\delta = \frac{1}{4}$ in the above algorithm implies a running time of $O^*(1.5^n)$. This result is originally from (Schöning, 1998).

Theorem

The probabilistic algorithm given above for 3-*SAT* has the (worst-case) running time $O^*(1.5^n)$.

Generalizing this for k-*SAT* $(k \geq 3)$ this means: for every $k \geq 3$ there is a probabilistic algorithm for k-*SAT* with running time $O^*((\frac{2k}{k+1})^n)$.

The error probability e^{-c} can be made arbitrarily small by the choice of c.

As in the previous chapter, we list for small values of k the corresponding a and b values (where $a = 2^b$):

k	3	4	5	6	7	8
a	1.5	1.6	1.667	1.714	1.75	1.778
b	0.585	0.678	0.737	0.778	0.807	0.83

5.3   Covering Codes

It would be better, of course, to design a deterministic algorithm instead of a probabilistic one (if possible with the same running time). In order to do so, the randomly chosen initial assignments $\alpha_1, \ldots, \alpha_t$ from the previous algorithm, should be generated in a systematic deterministic way. We need for this the concept of *covering code*, see (Cohen et al., 1997). The easy example given above with the two initial assignments $\alpha_1 = 0^n$ and $\alpha_2 = 1^n$, in combination with the Hamming radius $\frac{n}{2}$, was such a code.

Definition

A set of words $\{\alpha_1, \alpha_2, \ldots, \alpha_t\}$ over an alphabet Σ (for the moment $\Sigma = \{0,1\}$) of length n is called a *covering code with Hamming radius p*, if

$$\bigcup_{i=1}^{t} H_p(\alpha_i) = \Sigma^n$$

In addition, if the Hamming balls $H_p(\alpha_i)$ are pairwise disjoint, this is called a *perfect code*.

We recall that $H_p(\alpha) = \{\beta \in \Sigma^n \mid d(\alpha, \beta) \leq p\}$ and $|H_p(\alpha)| = \sum_{i=0}^{p} \binom{n}{i}$ for a binary alphabet $\Sigma = \{0,1\}$. For a general alphabet Σ, which we will also need later in chapter 5.5, it holds that $|H_p(\alpha)| = \sum_{i=0}^{p} (|\Sigma| - 1)^i \binom{n}{i}$. Unfortunately, there are no perfect codes with the parameters needed here. Because of this, we have to restrict ourselves to covering codes coming as close as possible (from above) to the ideal number of code words expressed by the so called *Hamming bound*:

$$\frac{|\Sigma|^n}{|H_p(\alpha)|} = \frac{|\Sigma|^n}{\displaystyle\sum_{i=0}^{p} (|\Sigma| - 1)^i \cdot \binom{n}{i}}$$

The Hamming bound is obtained when the Hamming balls are all disjoint but at the same time they cover the complete search space Σ^n. We have included the additional c factor for the choice of a good value for t in the last section because of this fact. For $\Sigma = \{0,1\}$ the Hamming bound behaves asymptotically as $2^{(1-h(\delta))n}$, for $\delta = \frac{p}{n}$, $\delta \leq \frac{1}{2}$.

Lemma

For every $\varepsilon > 0$ and $\delta \in (0, \frac{1}{2})$, there is an n_0, so that there is a covering code $C_0 = \{\alpha_1, \ldots, \alpha_t\}$ (over $\Sigma = \{0,1\}$) with word length n_0 and Hamming radius δn_0, with $t \leq 2^{(1-h(\delta)+\varepsilon)n_0}$.

Proof: Let ε and δ be given. We choose randomly t code words, and estimate then, similar as in the last chapter, the probability that there is an assignment that does not fall into any of the t Hamming balls (the code word length n is arbitrary at this point).

$$
\begin{aligned}
P(\,\exists \alpha_0 \, \forall i \le t \,:\, d(\alpha_0, \alpha_i) > \delta n\,) \;&\le\; \sum_{\alpha_0} \prod_{i=1}^{t} P(\,d(\alpha_0, \alpha_i) > \delta n\,) \\[2mm]
&=\; \sum_{\alpha_0} \prod_{i=1}^{t} (1 - P(\,d(\alpha_0, \alpha_i) \le \delta n\,)) \\[2mm]
&=\; \sum_{\alpha_0} \prod_{i=1}^{t} \left(1 - \frac{\sum_{j=0}^{\delta n} \binom{n}{j}}{2^n}\right) \\[2mm]
&=\; 2^n \cdot \left(1 - \frac{\sum_{j=0}^{\delta n} \binom{n}{j}}{2^n}\right)^{t} \\[2mm]
&\le\; 2^n \cdot e^{-t \cdot \frac{\sum_{j=0}^{\delta n} \binom{n}{j}}{2^n}} \quad\Big|\quad t = \frac{n \cdot 2^n}{\sum_{i=0}^{\delta n} \binom{n}{i}} \\[2mm]
&=\; (\tfrac{2}{e})^n \;\to\; 0 \quad (n \to \infty)
\end{aligned}
$$

It then holds for some n_0:

$$
t = \frac{n_0 \cdot 2^{n_0}}{\displaystyle\sum_{i=0}^{\delta n_0} \binom{n_0}{i}} \;\le\; 2^{(1-h(\delta)+\varepsilon)n_0}
$$

For further explanation see the appendix on binomial coefficients.

This proves the result (a probabilistic existence proof): since the probability esti-mated above – for the adequate choice of t – converges towards 0 (it would have sufficed to show that this probability is smaller than 1), it follows that such codes satisfying the covering condition must exist. Because of the last estimation there exists such a code already for a concrete length n_0 (depending on ε and δ). □

The existence of code C_0 was proven using a probabilistic argument. The code C_0, however, is a concrete finite code that can be "hardwired" in a deterministic algorithm. Of course, it might take quite some "preprocessing" time to find such a C_0, but this has to be done just once, and is not part of the algorithm here. For an arbitrary n we can then obtain the covering code $C \subseteq \{0,1\}^n$ with Hamming radius δn and $|C| \le 2^{(1-h(\delta)+\varepsilon)n}$, by putting together code words from C_0, as if they were building blocks forming words of size n.

$$
C = \{\, w_1 w_2 \ldots w_{n/n_0} \mid w_i \in C_0 \,\}
$$

In other words: $C = C_0 \times C_0 \times \cdots \times C_0$ ($\frac{n}{n_0}$ - times). We obtain in this way (we have supposed here that n_0 divides n):

$$
|C| \;\le\; \left(2^{(1-h(\delta)+\varepsilon)n_0}\right)^{n/n_0} = 2^{(1-h(\delta)+\varepsilon)n}
$$

Moreover, code C of length n, as desired, is also a covering code: let w be an arbi-trary word of length n (representing an assignment of length n) and partition w into $\frac{n}{n_0}$

subwords, $w_1 w_2 \ldots w_{n/n_0}$, each of length n_0. Each subword is within Hamming distance of at most δn_0 from a suitable code word w_i' from C_0. Then $w_1' w_2' \ldots w_{n/n_0}'$ is a code word in C, with Hamming distance at most $\left(\frac{n}{n_0}\right) \cdot \delta n_0 = \delta n$ from w.

The construction of a covering code of length n works only for lengths $n \geq n_0$. Since there are only finitely many 3-*CNF* formulas with fewer than n_0 variables, these can also be "hardwired" in an algorithm. Disregarding this detail, the deterministic version of the 3-*SAT* algorithm from the last section looks as follows:

> **input** F (let $n = |\text{Var}(F)|$, $n \geq n_0$)
> **for** all $w_1 w_2 \ldots w_{n/n_0} \in C_0 \times \cdots \times C_0$ **do**
> > **begin**
> > > interpret $w_1 w_2 \ldots w_{n/n_0}$ as an assignment α
> > > **if** localsearch ($F, \alpha, \delta n$) **then return** "satisfiable"
> > **end**
> **return** "unsatisfiable"

Theorem

For every $\varepsilon > 0$ there is a deterministic algorithm for 3-*SAT* (given above) with running time $O((1.5 + \varepsilon)^n) = O(2^{0.586n})$.

Generalizing to k-*SAT* ($k \geq 3$) this means: for every $\varepsilon > 0$ there is a deterministic algorithm for k-*SAT* with running time $O((\frac{2k}{k+1} + \varepsilon)^n)$.

The results in this section are originally from (Dantsin et al., 2000 and 2002). Based on the construction given here, several authors have obtained improvements for the running time of the algorithm. Most of these improvements rely on different ways to select the clause C after several successive recursive calls to localsearch, obtaining in this way an average branching factor smaller than 3. The constructions and necessary case distinctions are quite involved. The proven upper bounds (for deterministic 3-*SAT* algorithms) are: 1.481^n (Dantsin et al., 2000 and 2002), 1.476^n (Rodošek, 1996), 1.473^n (Brüggemann, Kern, 2004), 1.465^n (Scheder, 2008), 1.439^n (Kutzkov, Scheder, 2010). We will describe in chapter 5.5 a further (and comparably easier to prove) improvement from (Moser, Scheder, 2010), bringing the upper bound down to 1.334^n. In (Makino, Tamaki, Yamamoto, 2011) an upper bound of 1.3303^n has been shown.

5.4 A Random Walk Algorithm

After combining in chapter 5.2 the deterministic local search procedure (from chapter 5.1) with the probabilistic choice of the initial assignment, we described in chapter 5.3 a deterministic algorithm to select the initial assignments (using covering codes) combined with the deterministic local search in a Hamming ball.

We go now back to the probabilistic choice of the initial assignment and substitute also the deterministic local search by a probabilistic search: namely, a random walk in the search space. The algorithm that we will analyze (formulated for *3-SAT*) is the following.

```
input F  (let n = | Var(F)| )
for i := 1 to t do
  begin
    Choose a random initial assignment α
    for j := 1 to n do
      begin
        if Fα = 1 then return "satisfiable"
        Choose a C ∈ F with Cα = 0, C = {u₁, u₂, u₃}
        Choose randomly l ∈ {1, 2, 3}
        α := α[uₗ = 1]
      end
  end
return "unsatisfiable"
```

We have searched until now for a satisfying assignment in a Hamming ball with radius p in 3^p steps. If there is only one single satisfying assignment α_0 with Hamming distance p from the initial assignment, then a random walk over p steps would find it with probability 3^{-p}. That is, every random choice of an assignment to a literal u_l should hit the correct bit in the assigment α_0. What is then the advantage of using this random walk method? By allowing the random walk to be a little longer, say $3p$ steps, something that would increase the running time only by a constant factor, the probability of finding α_0 would increase dramatically. Within the $3p$ steps, p literal choices can be wrong, as long as $2p$ steps are correct. The "success probability" is then $\binom{3p}{2p} \cdot (\frac{1}{3})^{2p} \cdot (\frac{2}{3})^p$, which is close to 2^{-p}.

We will see later that the optimal choice for p is $\frac{n}{3}$. This means that the number n of repetitions in the inner j loop of the above algorithm is exactly $3p$. Observe that the number of random walk steps n coincides in this case with the number of variables. In the original papers (Schöning, 1999 and 2002) the value $3n$ was used for this purpose, but we will show that n suffices.

If we call a pass through the i-loop a *run*, the estimation of the success probability boils down to calculating the probability $q = q(n)$ of finding a satisfying assignment in such a run. The repetition number t for the number of runs can then be bounded by $O(\frac{1}{q(n)})$, in order to have a large enough evidence that an existing satisfying assignment has not been "overlooked" (see also the appendix on probabilistic algorithms).

Let F be a satisfiable formula. We will fix for the following analysis a satisfying assignment α_0, and we will concentrate on the probability of finding exactly this α_0 in a run. There is in every clause $C = \{u_1, u_2, u_3\}$ in F at least a literal u_l, that receives truth value 1 under the assignment α_0. We fix arbitrarily *exactly one* such literal in each clause and call it the "right literal" in clause C. The probability that the algorithm randomly chooses the right literal is exactly $\frac{1}{3}$. When the right u_l is chosen, the Hamming distance between α and α_0 after the bit flip $\alpha := \alpha[u_l = 1]$ decreases by 1.

We can simulate the behavior of the algorithm with the following Markov chain:

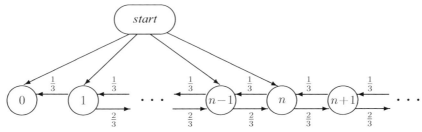

The choice of the initial assignment determines the initial Hamming distance to α_0. It can lie between 0 and n according to a symmetric binomial distribution. This means that (a run of) the algorithm will start in state j with probability $\binom{n}{j}2^{-n}$.

After the probabilistic choice for the initial assignment, n random walk steps take place. As mentioned above, the "right" literal is chosen each time with probability $\frac{1}{3}$, which would bring us from state j to state $j-1$. The selection of a wrong literal happens then exactly with probability $\frac{2}{3}$ and takes us from state j to state $j+1$ (even in the case when the Hamming distance in fact decreases). The real Hamming distance between α and α_0 is then always smaller than or equal to the state number in the Markov chain. By proceeding in this way, the state numbers can now be larger than n.

We restrict the analysis of the probability that a random walk leads to success (to state 0) to certain special cases. We define two events for this, E_1 and E_2:

E_1 : The chosen initial assignment has Hamming distance exactly $\frac{n}{3}$ to α_0.

E_2 : Starting at state $\frac{n}{3}$, n random steps lead to state 0 in such a way that within the n steps in exactly $\frac{n}{3}$ of them a wrong literal choice is made and in $\frac{2n}{3}$ choices a right literal is selected.

Since the Hamming distance from the initial assignment to the satisfying assignment α_0 is distributed according to a binomial distribution, in symbols: $d(\alpha, \alpha_0) \sim Bin(n, \frac{1}{2})$, we get $P(E_1) = \binom{n}{n/3}2^{-n}$ and $P(E_2) = \binom{n}{n/3}(\frac{1}{3})^{2n/3}(\frac{2}{3})^{n/3}$. This implies:

$$
\begin{aligned}
P(\text{ success in a single run }) \quad &\geq \quad P(E_1 \wedge E_2) = P(E_1) \cdot P(E_2) \\
&= \quad \binom{n}{n/3} \cdot 2^{-n} \cdot \binom{n}{n/3} \cdot (\tfrac{1}{3})^{2n/3} \cdot (\tfrac{2}{3})^{n/3} \\
&\overset{poly}{=} \quad 2^{h(1/3)n} \cdot 2^{-n} \cdot 2^{h(1/3)n} \cdot (\tfrac{1}{3})^{2n/3} \cdot (\tfrac{2}{3})^{n/3} = (\tfrac{3}{4})^n
\end{aligned}
$$

See also the appendix on binomial coefficients.

By fixing t, for example to $t = 20 \cdot (\frac{4}{3})^n$, the probability of not obtaining a satisfying assignment in case the input formula is satisfiable is at most e^{-20}.

Theorem

There is a probabilistic algorithm for 3-*SAT* (given above) with running time $O^*((\frac{4}{3})^n)$.

This can be generalized to k-*SAT* ($k \geq 3$) in the following way: there is a probabilistic algorithm for k-*SAT* with running time $O^*((2(1 - \frac{1}{k}))^n)$.

The error probability e^{-c} can be made arbitrarily small by adapting the algorithm's repetition number by a factor of c.

As in the previous chapter, we list the corresponding a and b values for small values of k (recall $a = 2^b$):

k	3	4	5	6	7	8
a	1.333	1.5	1.6	1.667	1.714	1.75
b	0.415	0.585	0.678	0.737	0.778	0.807

The results in this section are from (Schöning, 1999 and 2002). This probabilistic algorithm and the respective bounds were improved in several ways (some of the improvements are quite involved): 1.3302^n (Hofmeister et al., 2002 and 2007), 1.328^n (Baumer, Schuler, 2004), 1.3278^n (Rolf, 2003), 1.324^n (Iwama, Tamaki, 2003), 1.3222^n (Iwama, Seto, Takai, Tamaki, 2010), 1.322^n (Hertli, Moser, Scheder, 2010), 1.308^n (Hertli, 2011).

It is interesting to compare the previous random walk algorithm for 3-*SAT* with the one from Papadimitriou (page 66) for 2-*SAT*. While in the 2-*SAT* algorithm the probability of reaching the absorbing state after j steps tends to 1 (for $j \to \infty$), this is not the case for the 3-*SAT* algorithm (at least in the given mathematical model which admits more than n states): the probability to reach the 0 state grows from $(\frac{1}{2})^n$ at the beginning (for $j = 0$) to the above given value of $(\frac{3}{4})^n$ after $j = n$ random walk steps and decreases again for larger values of j. One can define a threshold value, executing a restart in the algorithm as soon as the probability to find a solution falls under this value. The program variable t sets the number of restarts.

The following diagram illustrates this. In case the Hamming distance from the initial assignment to a satisfying assignment is d, the satisfying assignment cannot be reached in fewer than d random walk steps. The probability of this happening increases then considerably, decreasing again afterwards.

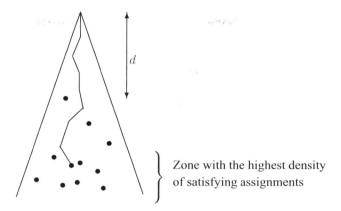

Zone with the highest density
of satisfying assignments

This means that the probability of finding a satisfying assignment is very small immediately after a restart and it increases then. The next restart step should happen before the probability decreases significantly again. This "restart" paradigm is advantageous when the underlying probabilistic algorithm follows a *heavy tail* distribution, see (Moore, Mertens, 2011; page 493), (Wu, 2006). In (Brassard, Bratley, 1996, page 355ff) a similar positive effect from restarts to new initial configurations in connection to the n-queens problem is reported. Similar questions related to the random walk algorithm (or more broadly, to a general Las Vegas algorithm) have been discussed in (Schöning, 2007), (Luby et al., 1993), (van Moorsel, Wolter, 2004) and (Balint, Schöning, 2012). Chapter 8 in this book deals also with this question.

We want to mention a further observation. The random walk algorithm can be understood as an algorithmic simulation of a Markov chain (see the appendix). When the input is a satisfiable set of clauses, the expected running time until an arbitrary satisfying assignment is found is about $(4/3)^n$. Therefore, there cannot be an initial assignment α and a satisfying assignment α^*, so that the probability $P($ starting with α, a run of the algorithm reaches the satisfying assignment α^*) is equal to 0. In the Markov chain terminology this is a form of irreducibility (with respect to satisfying assignments), and in logical terms this is a kind of (probabilistic) completeness: for each possible initial assignment it is possible (with probability greater than 0) to reach some satisfying assignment.

The random walk algorithm mentioned here uses the transition probabilities $(\frac{1}{3}, \frac{1}{3}, \frac{1}{3})$ for the selection of one of the three literals appearing in the zero clause (meaning a clause being falsified by the current assignment). The algorithm ProbSAT (cf. page 106) differs from the random walk algorithm only in the fact that the transition probabilities (p, q, r) with $p + q + r = 1$ and $p, q, r > 0$ are updated before each flip step. The above observation about the completeness of the algorithm is therefore also true for ProbSAT.

5.5   Moser-Scheder-Algorithm

We come back once more to the area of deterministic algorithms as in chapter 5.3, asking ourselves whether it is possible to reach a running time of $(\frac{4}{3})^n$ in a deterministic algorithm for 3-*SAT*. In fact this is possible with an additional trick, based once more on covering codes. We will give a method that allows the procedure localsearch (adapted accordingly) to explore a Hamming ball of radius $p = \delta n$ within running time $O^*(2^p)$, instead of $O^*(3^p)$ as in chapter 5.3. The new calculation for the optimal value for δ in the expression $[2^{1-h(\delta)} \cdot 2^{\delta}]^n$ leads to the following diagram:

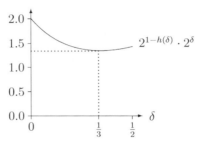

The optimal δ value equals $\frac{1}{3}$ and leads to the running time $(\frac{4}{3})^n$. This will be explained more precisely in the theorem at the end of this section.

The procedure must be modified in several places in order to reduce the running time of localsearch (F, α, p) (defined in page 89) with $p = \frac{n}{3}$, to $O^*(2^p)$. We recall that a variation of the procedure has been already discussed on page 90. The intended variation of 1 bit in the assignment for the subsequent recursive calls will be "frozen" here. This is done by substituting the corresponding 1 bit assignment in the formula. This implies that some clauses in F can disappear (because they are set to 1) and also some clauses can become shorter. Moreover, one chooses in every procedure call always the *shortest* clause. It turns out (see next lemma) that one can guarantee in certain situations, that the shortest clause always has length at most 2.

Here is one of the procedures that we will use:

proc localsearch&freeze (F : clause set, α : assignment, p : **nat**) : **bool**

if $F\alpha = 1$ **then return** 1

if $p = 0$ **then return** 0

Let $C \in F$ be a shortest clause with $C\alpha = 0$, $C = \{u_1, u_2\}$

// Clause C has (at most) 2 literals. Justification: see the text.

for $i := 1$ **to** 2 **do**

    if localsearch&freeze ($F\{u_i = 1\}, \alpha[u_i = 1], p - 1$) **then return** 1

return 0

Lemma

Consider an execution of localsearch&freeze (F, α, p) together with all the recursive calls that are triggered by this. If *all* the clauses in F receiving value 0 under the current assignment α contain at most two literals then the shortest clause C in all further recursive calls from localsearch&freeze (F, α, p) will also have at most 2 literals. This implies that the running time of the procedure is bounded by $O^*(2^p)$.

Proof: As long as a clause with at most two literals is chosen by the procedure, it is clear that only 2 recursive calls will be produced. But in the situation of the lemma statement, also all of the later recursive calls will be based on a falsified clause of size at most 2. This is because when a clause is selected, it is falsified by the current assignment and it is either already falsified by the initial assignment α or it contained initially at least one literal that has been set to 0 and frozen. Because of this, every later call to localsearch&freeze can produce at most 2 recursive calls.   □

The situation in which all the clauses set to 0 by α lie in 2-*CNF* does not happen very often, but we can force this situation in the following way. Let $F_0 \subseteq F$ be the set of clauses in F that are falsified by α. We construct a new subset $F' \subseteq F_0$, made only from clauses in 3-*CNF* with pairwise disjoint sets of variables. Let F' be a maximal subset with this property. This can be obtained by using a simple greedy algorithm: start with the first clause in F_0 in 3-*CNF*, and add successively new variable disjoint clauses until this is no longer possible.

Suppose we have $|F'| < n_0$ for some constant n_0 that will be fixed later. In this case there are $7^{|F'|} < 7^{n_0} = O(1)$ many assignments of the $3|F'|$ variables appearing in F' satisfying all the clauses. We can go through all these $7^{|F'|}$ assignments in a loop, applying each such assignment β in F and calling localsearch&freeze ($F\beta, \alpha[\beta], p - |F'|$). These recursive calls satisfy the hypothesis in the lemma above (because of the maximality of F'). In this way the number of recursive calls can be bounded from above by $7^{|F'|} \cdot 2^{p-|F'|} = O(2^p)$.

Next we indicate where the constant n_0 comes from, and further, what can be done in case $|F'| \geq n_0$.

In each recursive call from localsearch (chapter 5.1) a clause C falsified by the current assignment was chosen, and then one of the (in general) 3 literals u_i was selected for the next bit flip.

We are now in the situation in which there are $\geq n_0$ many variable disjoint clauses in F'. This implies that the Hamming distance between α and α_0 is at least n_0. We fix now exactly n_0 many such clauses in a concrete order: $C_1, C_2, \ldots, C_{n_0} \in F'$. Let $l_1, l_2, \ldots, l_{n_0}$ with $l_i \in \{1, 2, 3\}$, be the selected literals (more accurately, their indices in the corresponding clause C_i). We denote by $\alpha[l_1 l_2 \ldots l_{n_0}]$ the assignment α after having flipped the n_0 many bit positions corresponding to the literals u_{l_i}.

The ingenious idea from (Moser, Scheder, 2010) was to consider a suitable covering code C_0 over the set $\{1,2,3\}^{n_0}$. It turns out that the optimal choice for the Hamming radius of this code is $\frac{n_0}{3}$. The Hamming radius is given by the statement of the next lemma.

Lemma

For every $\varepsilon > 0$ there is a constant n_0 and a covering code $C_0 \subseteq \{1,2,3\}^{n_0}$, with Hamming radius $\frac{n_0}{3}$, whose size is close to that of a perfect code, namely

$$|C_0| \leq \frac{n_0^2 \cdot 3^{n_0}}{\displaystyle\sum_{i=0}^{n_0/3} 2^i \cdot \binom{n_0}{i}} \leq \left(\frac{3}{2^{1/3+h(1/3)}} + \varepsilon\right)^{n_0} = (2^{1/3} + \varepsilon)^{n_0}$$

Proof: Analogous to the one given in section 5.3. □

This explains where the constant n_0 comes from: it depends on ε and it is defined in a way to allow a covering code of dimension n_0 to come sufficiently close to the Hamming bound.

Instead of going through all the assignments of the form $\alpha[l_1 l_2 \ldots l_{n_0}]$, $l_1 l_2 \ldots l_{n_0} \in \{1,2,3\}^{n_0}$, while searching for a satisfying assignment, as done until now, we consider only the assignments of the form $\alpha[k_1 k_2 \ldots k_{n_0}]$, $k_1 k_2 \ldots k_{n_0} \in C_0$.

If there is a satisfying assignment for the formula F, then there is a sequence of bit flips $l_1 l_2 \ldots l_{n_0}$, so that the Hamming distance between the assignment $\alpha[l_1 l_2 \ldots l_{n_0}]$ and the assignment satisfying F is n_0 bits smaller than the distance between α and the satisfying assignment. Since C_0 is a covering code, there is a code word $k_1 k_2 \ldots k_{n_0} \in C_0$, disagreeing with $l_1 l_2 \ldots l_{n_0}$ in at most $\frac{n_0}{3}$ positions (the Hamming radius). This implies that the distance between $\alpha[l_1 l_2 \ldots l_{n_0}]$ and $\alpha[k_1 k_2 \ldots k_{n_0}]$ cannot be too large.

Observation

$d\left(\alpha[l_1 l_2 \ldots l_{n_0}], \alpha[k_1 k_2 \ldots k_{n_0}]\right) \leq 2 \cdot d\left(l_1 l_2 \ldots l_{n_0}, k_1 k_2 \ldots k_{n_0}\right).$

This can be seen in the following way: in order to bridge the Hamming distance between $\alpha[l_1 l_2 \ldots l_{n_0}]$ and $\alpha[k_1 k_2 \ldots k_{n_0}]$ one has to reverse the flips for the wrongly chosen literals, and then in addition perform the correct bit flips. One can also see here that at this point it is important *not* to "freeze" the performed bit flips.

This means that the Hamming distance between $\alpha[l_1 l_2 \ldots l_{n_0}]$ and $\alpha[k_1 k_2 \ldots k_{n_0}]$ is at most $\frac{2n_0}{3}$. Because of this, it is possible to start from $\alpha[k_1 k_2 \ldots k_{n_0}]$ a recursive call of the localsearch procedure with modified Hamming distance parameter $d - n_0 + \frac{2n_0}{3} = d - \frac{n_0}{3}$. The following procedure achieves this.

proc localsearch_MoserScheder (F : clause set, α : assignment, p : **nat**) : **bool**

if $F\alpha = 1$ **then return** 1

if $p = 0$ **then return** 0

Compute a maximal subset F' of falsified, variable disjoint clauses with 3 literals each, as described in the text

if $|F'| < n_0$ **then**

  begin

    for each of the $7^{|F'|}$ assignments β, satisfying the clauses in F' **do**

      if localsearch&freeze ($F\beta, \alpha[\beta], p - |F'|$) **then return** 1

    return 0

  end else

  begin

    for each codeword $k_1 k_2 \ldots k_{n_0} \in C_0$ **do**

      if localsearch_MoserScheder ($F, \alpha[k_1 k_2 \ldots k_{n_0}], p - n_0/3$) **then return** 1

    return 0

  end

We still have to verify that the running time of this algorithm is bounded by 2^p. We consider for this the following recursion: $T(p) = |C_0| \cdot T(p - \frac{n_0}{3})$. It has the solution $|C_0|^{\frac{3p}{n_0}}$. Essentially (up to polynomial factors and up to the ε) this is

$$\left((2^{1/3})^{n_0} \right)^{3p/n_0} = (2^{1/3})^{3p} = 2^p$$

We summarize:

Theorem

For every $\varepsilon > 0$ there is a deterministic algorithm for 3-*SAT* (given above) with running time $O((\frac{4}{3} + \varepsilon)^n) = O(2^{0.416n})$.

Generalizing to k-*SAT* ($k \geq 3$) this means: for every $\varepsilon > 0$ there is a deterministic algorithm for k-*SAT* with running time $O((2(1 - \frac{1}{k}) + \varepsilon)^n)$.

The results from this section are from (Moser, Scheder, 2010). This upper bound was improved (for deterministic 3-*SAT* algorithms) in (Makino, Tamaki, Yamamoto, 2011) where the bound $O(1.3303^n) = O(2^{0.413n})$ was proven.

5.6 GSAT, WalkSAT, Novelty, ProbSAT

The algorithms using the local search principle, that we have described until now, are not very "goal oriented" with respect to the way next variable flips are selected. By this we mean that the only action in order to reach a satisfying assignment was to select a clause falsified by the current assignment and then to choose a variable within this clause to perform a bit flip. But by doing this, it happens with probability $\frac{1}{3}$ (when regarding 3-*SAT*), that the "right" literal is chosen, implying a decrease in the Hamming distance to a satisfying assignment. One refers to this as "focused local search."

Practical algorithms using the local search principle try to improve the "goal orientation" by adapting the probability distribution for the selection of the next variable according to various "scores" based on the number of occurrences of the variables in the satisfied and falsified clauses, the size of these clauses, and sometimes other information.

A direct way to implement this idea is GSAT (Selman, Levesque, Mitchell, 1992), where the G stays for "greedy." After an initial assignment α is chosen, a loop is started in which the variable x with minimal value for

$$score_\alpha(x) \ = \ \text{number of falsified clauses under the assignment } \alpha[x]$$

is selected. Such a variable is flipped then, $\alpha := \alpha[x]$. The algorithm halts as soon as a satisfying assignment in found. When the algorithm gets stuck because, by the selection of a variable flip, no improvement can be achieved any more (but no satisfying assignment has been found), or because a fixed maximal number of flips has been reached, a restart with a new initial assignment is performed. There are, in principle, two probabilistic components in this algorithms. One is the choice of the initial assignment. The other one lies in the fact that there can be more than one variable with minimal score and, in this case, one of them is chosen randomly.

Altogether these measures are not enough to avoid local minima (different from satisfying assignments). Because of this, several improvements have been proposed and tested experimentally. A significant efficiency improvement with respect to GSAT was achieved by the algorithm WalkSAT (Selman, Kautz, Cohen, 1994). The WalkSAT algorithm is, similarly to GSAT, embedded in a loop that chooses first an initial assignment and then executes a maximal number of bit flips. We describe the algorithm for the selection of the next variable flip:

> Select randomly a clause C falsified by α.
> If there is a variable in C, whose value can be flipped,
> without falsifying another clause, then flip this variable.
> Else choose randomly:
> with probability p
> > choose under the uniform distribution a variable in C and flip it.
> with probability $1 - p$
> > find as in GSAT a variable x, with minimal $score_\alpha(x)$ and flip it.

A good value for the probability p has been obtained experimentally on 3-*CNF* random formulas close to the threshold value (see chapter 7); that value is $p = 0.57$ (Seitz, Alava, Orponen, 2005).

Further improvements based on clever ways to select the new flip variables are possible. An algorithm of this kind is called Novelty (McAllester, Selman, Kautz, 1997) and its newer version Novelty+ (Hoos, 1998). Until now the selection of the variables was only based on the formula F and on the the current assignment α, and did not depend on the variables that have been flipped so far: that is, on previous history. This changes now (and with this change we leave the possibility of analyzing the process with the help of homogeneous Markov chains). Each variable is assigned an *age*: this is the number of steps in the local search strategy since the variable was flipped for the last time. The selection of the next variable to flip is done in Novelty as follows. First a falsified clause is chosen randomly. Inside the clause, the variable with the lowest score is taken, and when this variable does not have minimal age (that is, when this variable has not been just flipped) then this is the variable selected for the next flip. Otherwise a random experiment with 2 possible outcomes having probabilities p and $1 - p$ is carried out. In the first case, the variable with the second lowest score will be selected. In the other case the algorithm stays with the variable with the lowest score. This prevents the same variable from being flipped back and forth continuously. Except for this, the method is still quite "greedy," with the effect that Novelty can still get stuck in local optima. What is missing is a little more randomness (or "noise"). In the literature this is called balance between diversification and determinism (Li, Huang, 2005). The latter refers to the greedy focus of the algorithm, with its danger of not being able to get away from a local optimum, as sketched in the figure.

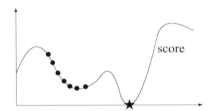

The points indicate the sequence of tested assignments and their scores. The position of a satisfying assignment is represented by a star.

In the improved version, Novelty+, an additional random experiment in the selection of the variables is performed. With probability $1 - q$ the algorithms works as Novelty, but with probability q a randomly chosen variable from a falsified clause is selected, as in the random walk algorithm from chapter 5.4. The value of q is not very large (for example $q = 0.01$), however this small change improves considerably the performance of the algorithm compared to Novelty.

These algorithms have been further improved (measuring this with respect to randomly chosen test formulas, mostly of the kind described in chapter 7). For this, new measures for the selector of the next flip variables have been considered. These can be new score functions, applied to clauses or to variables, indicating how often they have been involved in the previous flip steps. One obtains in this way a certain degree of importance of the clause or variable in question. Similarly, as it is done with the concept of age of a variable as mentioned before, a *tabu list* is considered. A tabu list is a finite list of the last flipped variables. As long as the variables are still in the list, they cannot be flipped again.

It was experimentally shown in (Balint, Schöning, 2012) that a restriction of the measure functions, as done in the following algorithm called ProbSAT, can achieve very good results. Here, the measure functions rely on a simple principle based on probability distributions (without the many "if - then - else" statements contained in the previous algorithms). The algorithm is formulated for the case of 3-*SAT*.

> **for** $i := 1$ **to** maxtries **do**
>   Choose randomly an initial assignment α
>   **for** $j := 1$ **to** maxflips **do**
>   **if** $F\alpha = 1$ **then return** "satisfiable"
>   Choose a clause $C = (u_1 \vee u_2 \vee u_3)$ with $C\alpha = 0$
>   Choose $k \in \{1, 2, 3\}$ with probability $\dfrac{f(u_k, \alpha)}{f(u_1, \alpha) + f(u_2, \alpha) + f(u_3, \alpha)}$
> $\alpha := \alpha[u_k]$

Here, $f(u, \alpha)$ is a function, whose value increases with the evidence that in the current assignment the literal u has to be flipped. If f is a constant function, then this is nothing else than the random walk algorithm from chapter 5.4 since every literal is flipped with probability $\frac{1}{3}$. A very good choice for f is

$$f(u, \alpha) = (1 + break(u, \alpha))^{-3}$$

where $break(u, \alpha)$ (as in WalkSAT) is the number of clauses that change from *true* to *false* by flipping literal u in the assignment α.

We present a little example. Suppose $C = (u_1 \vee u_2 \vee u_3)$ is a clause that is not satisfied by the current assignment, and let the $break$ values for the literals u_1, u_2, u_3 be 0, 1 and 2. This implies the following flip probabilities $\frac{1^{-3}}{1^{-3}+2^{-3}+3^{-3}} \approx 0.86$ for u_1, $\frac{2^{-3}}{1^{-3}+2^{-3}+3^{-3}} \approx 0.11$ for u_2, and $\frac{3^{-3}}{1^{-3}+2^{-3}+3^{-3}} \approx 0.03$ for u_3.

The topic of *restarts* mentioned already at the end of chapter 5.4 (and treated more deeply in chapter 8) also plays a role in the previous algorithm. This is expressed in the fact that after a relatively small number (maxflip) of flips, for example $20n$, the algorithm starts from the beginning with the choice of a new initial assignment.

5.7 Hard Formulas for Local Search

Many algorithms, in particular those using the local search principle, as well as the physical algorithms (section 7.3), are optimized in such a way, that (on average) they perform especially well on randomly chosen formulas. It is possible, however, to consider specific formulas that prove to be hard to solve for most local search procedures: see (Papadimitriou, 1994, Problem 11.5.6), (Hirsch, 2000) and (Knuth, 2013).

We construct a formula F by including *all* the different clauses with 3 different variables so that exactly one of them occurs negated and the other two are positive in the clause. That is, these clauses have the form $(\overline{x_i} \lor x_j \lor x_k)$ and there are exactly $\binom{n}{3} \cdot 3 \approx \frac{n^3}{2}$ clauses of this type. Apart from these clauses, we add two further clauses to F, namely, $(\overline{x_1} \lor \overline{x_2} \lor \overline{x_3})$ and $(\overline{x_4} \lor \overline{x_5} \lor \overline{x_6})$. These last two clauses force the property that in a potential satisfying assignment for F at least two variables must be set to 0. Let us suppose, for example, that the satisfying assignment includes $x_2 = 0$ and $x_4 = 0$. Then the existence of the clauses $(\overline{x_i} \lor x_2 \lor x_4)$, for $i \in \{1, \ldots, n\} \setminus \{2, 4\}$, implies that *all* variables have to be set to 0, and this is in fact the only assignment satisfying F.

The choice of the first group of clauses has the purpose to "confuse" the local search procedure. Since these clauses contain one negative and two positive literals, they tend to influence a local search-type algorithm to change more often the assignment of a variable from 0 to 1 than the other way around.

As an aside remark, this example also shows that the analysis of the random walk algorithm from chapter 5.4 cannot be improved because, for the only satisfying assignment $\{x_1 = 0, x_2 = 0, \ldots, x_n = 0\}$, it is the case that all (but 2) of the clauses just have one literal that is satisfied. Therefore, the Markov chain defined in the analysis of the algorithm (see page 97) indeed achieves the worst-case transition probability $1/3$ for moving from state $j + 1$ to state j.

Consider an arbitrary assignment α, setting dn variables to 1 and $(1 - d)n$ variables to 0, with $0 \leq d \leq 1$. Consider now a variable x that is set to 0 by α. By flipping x to receive value 1 (the wrong action), the score change (= *make* – *break*) of this action would look as follows (we restrict ourselves to count the number of clauses in the first group, which are a clear majority).

- The clauses changing from 0 to 1 have the form $(x \lor y \lor \overline{z})$, where α sets variable y to 0 and variable z to 1. There are $((1 - d)n - 1)dn \approx (1 - d)d \cdot n^2$ clauses of this kind. This is the *make*-value.

- The clauses changing from 1 to 0 have the form $(\overline{x} \lor y \lor z)$, where α sets variable y and z to 0. There are $\binom{(1-d)n-1}{2} \approx \frac{(1-d)^2}{2} \cdot n^2$ clauses of this kind. This is the *break*-value.

The "change in score" produced by flipping variable x from $x = 0$ to $x = 1$, is the difference between both quantities:

$$make - break = \left[(1 - d)d - \frac{(1 - d)^2}{2} \right] \cdot n^2 = \left[2d - \frac{3}{2}d^2 - \frac{1}{2} \right] \cdot n^2$$

Consider now a variable x with value 1 in α. Flipping the value of x to 0 (which would be the correct flip) brings the following score change:

- The clauses changing from 0 to 1, have the form $(\overline{x} \vee y \vee z)$, where the variables y and z are set to 0 by α. There are $\binom{(1-d)n}{2} \approx \frac{(1-d)^2}{2} \cdot n^2$ many clauses of this kind. This is the *make*-value.

- The clauses changing from 1 to 0, have the form $(x \vee y \vee \overline{z})$, where variable y is set to 0 and variable z is set to 1 by α. There are $(1-d)n(dn-1) \approx (1-d)d \cdot n^2$ many clauses of this kind. This is the *break*-value.

The "change in score" produced by the variable flip from $x = 1$ to $x = 0$, is the difference of these quantities:

$$make - break = [\frac{(1-d)^2}{2} - (1-d)d] \cdot n^2 = [-2d + \frac{3}{2}d^2 + \frac{1}{2}] \cdot n^2$$

The progress in the scores, as a function of d, looks as in the figure:

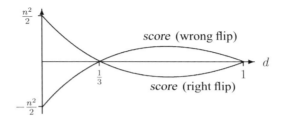

One can see that a greedy variable flip procedure runs in the wrong direction because the advantage in score for the wrong flip is larger than that for a correct one. This happens as long as one starts with an initial assignment setting more than $n/3$ variables to 1. This is something that is very likely in the case of a randomly chosen initial assignment and even in the case of initialization via a greedy local search procedure such as GSAT.

The algorithms WalkSAT and ProbSAT (see section 5.6) base their decision only on the *break*-value and ignore the *make*-value. The *break*-value should be as small as possible in this case. Recalculating the above curves for this particular case, it turns out that the point where the correct flip decision turns into the wrong flip decision is again at $d = 1/3$. Actually, this holds no matter what linear combination of the *make* and *break* value we set up.

Here is a somewhat different discussion about the hardness of the given formula. The intuition behind all local search type algorithms is that the number of falsified clauses (under the actually considered assignment) should be positively correlated with the Hamming distance to a satisfying assignment (provided one exists). The number of falsified clauses is an easily accessible information whereas the Hamming distance is not. In the example formula that was defined in the beginning of this chapter which has the only satisfying assignment $\alpha = 0^n$ the Hamming distance δn means the number of ones in the respective assignments, and δ is the relative Hamming distance, where $\delta \in [0, 1]$. It is easy to see that the number of falsified clauses for an assignment which sets δn variables to 1 is about $\delta(1 - \delta)^2 \cdot n^3/2$. The relative ratio of falsified clauses as compared to the total number of clauses is therefore $\delta(1 - \delta)^2$. The following diagram shows the relationship between the relative Hamming distance δ and the relative ratio of falsified clauses.

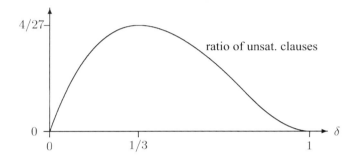

It can be seen that there is only a positive correlation between Hamming distance and the number of falsified clauses if $\delta \leq 1/3$, otherwise both quantities are even negatively correlated.

6 More SAT Algorithms

In the previous chapters we have considered the main algorithmic methods for *SAT*, that is, DPLL-type algorithms, and its successors (like CDCL), on the one hand, and local search, on the other hand. We will show now that other approaches which do not fit in any of these two categories are possible.

6.1 A Divide and Conquer Algorithm

The approach considered next is especially tailored for 3-*SAT* and goes back to (Pudlák, 1998).

Let F be a formula in 3-*CNF*. The variable set is $V = \{x_1, \ldots, x_n\}$. We may assume that n is even. The algorithm divides the variable set into two equally large sets $V_1 = \{x_1, \ldots, x_{n/2}\}$ and $V_2 = \{x_{n/2+1}, \ldots, x_n\}$, each having $\frac{n}{2}$ many variables. The clauses are categorized in 4 different types. Let K_1 be those clauses having solely variables from V_1, and let K_2 be those clauses having solely variables from V_2. Since F is in 3-*CNF* the remaining clauses can be divided again in two classes: K_3-clauses have two variables from V_1 and one variable from V_2, and K_4-clauses have two variables from V_2 and one variable from V_1.

Now the algorithm constructs two lists A and B. The list A consists of all assignments of the V_1-variables which satisfy all K_1 clauses, and the list B consists of all assignments of the V_2-variables which satisfy all K_2 clauses. Since there are up to $2^{n/2}$ such assignments, the algorithm spends $O^*(2^{n/2})$ time up to this point.

After this, every assignment α in A is tested as to whether it can be extended to an assignment α^* that also assigns (some) variables in V_2 such that the clauses in K_3 are satisfied too. Either a K_3-clause is already satisfied by α, or the two literals in a K_3-clause which stem from V_1-variables are set to 0 such that the assignment has to be extended to set the third literal (stemming from V_2) to 1. Should it ever happen that a V_2-variable needs to be set to 1, and also to 0, then it is not possible to extend α in the described way, so we drop α. It is eliminated from the list in this case.

In an analogous way we can consider the assignments β in B one by one to test whether we can extend them to a satisfying assignment β^* for K_2 and K_4.

Let A^* and B^* be the resulting partial assignments. The remaining problem is to determine whether there is a suitable pair $(\alpha^*, \beta^*) \in A^* \times B^*$ such that the variable assignment α^* is consistent with the variable assignment β^*.

Example: Let $n = 8$. The assignment $\alpha = 0\,1\,0\,1 * 1 * *$ from A^* is consistent (non-conflicting) with the assignment $\beta = 0 * * 1\,1\,1\,0\,0$ from B^*. The stars indicate that the respective variable has no assigned value.

The formula F is satisfiable if and only if there exists such a consistent pair. The naive approach would be to check each element of A^* with each element of B^* for consistency. But this would cost us $O^*(2^{n/2} \cdot 2^{n/2}) = O^*(2^n)$ time steps in the worst case. This is not better than the approach of testing all 2^n assignments directly (truth-table method).

The search for a consistent pair of assignments can be done more efficiently by dividing assignments into two groups. Let $|\alpha| = |Var(\alpha)|$ denote the number of variables which are assigned a value in α. Call an assignment α *sparse* if $|\alpha| \leq (1 + c) \cdot \frac{n}{2}$, otherwise it is *non-sparse*. The constant c will be determined later.

Next we describe two different algorithms which search for a consistent pair. The first algorithm is applied for all α which are non-sparse and β is arbitrary. By symmetry, an analogous algorithm exists in the cases where β is non-sparse and α is arbitrary. The second algorithm deals with the remaining case when both, α and β, are sparse.

The first algorithm cycles through all non-sparse $\alpha \in A^*$ and completes α to a total assignment in every possible way. There are $2^{(1-c)n/2}$ ways of completing α to a total assignment. For each of these total assignments it is tested whether there is a consistent $\beta \in B^*$. This test can be done efficiently when the assignments in B^* are organized in a search tree based on the V_2-variables. This search tree has depth $\frac{n}{2}$. In its leaves the remaining assignment of the V_1-variables in β is stored. The test whether there is a $\beta \in B^*$ which is consistent with one of the total completions of α can be done then in time $O(n)$. Altogether, the complexity of this first algorithm is bounded by $O^*(2^{n/2} \cdot 2^{(1-c)n/2}) = O^*(2^{(1-c/2)n})$.

As mentioned above, there is a dual algorithm which does the same for all non-sparse $\beta \in B^*$ and arbitrary $\alpha \in A^*$.

The second algorithm compares those pairs in $A^* \times B^*$ where both assignments are sparse. Let $A' \subseteq A^*$ and $B' \subseteq B^*$ be the corresponding subsets of sparse assignments. We transform the sets A', B' into new sets $\hat{A}$, $\hat{B}$ as follows. Every $\alpha \in A'$ (which consists of $\frac{n}{2}$ assignments of the V_1-variables and some additional assignments of the V_2-variables) is restricted to every possible subset of size $\leq c \cdot \frac{n}{2}$ of the V_1-variables. Only the variables of the respective subset – as well as all existing assignments to V_2-variables – are kept. That is, from 1 assignment $\alpha \in A'$ we produce $\sum_{i \leq cn/2} \binom{n/2}{i}$ many assignments in the set $\hat{A}$. It is possible that the set of assignments coming about from different assignments in A' overlap. In an analogous way, the set B' is transformed to $\hat{B}$ (this time all subsets of size $c \cdot \frac{n}{2}$ of the V_2-variables are constructed).

Now we have that a consistent pair $(\alpha, \beta) \in A' \times B'$ exists if and only if there is an assignment γ (which is a suitable restriction from α and from β) that occurs both in $\hat{A}$ and $\hat{B}$. It is possible to test whether such an assignment γ exists by first sorting the sets

$\hat{A}$ and $\hat{B}$ and then scanning them elementwise. If we use an efficient sorting algorithm we obtain the following running time for the second algorithm:

$$O^*\left(2^{\frac{n}{2}} \cdot \sum_{i \leq c\frac{n}{2}} \binom{n/2}{i}\right) = O^*\left(2^{\frac{n}{2}+h(c)\frac{n}{2}}\right)$$

This holds for $c \leq \frac{1}{2}$. Here h is the binary entropy function (cf. appendix about binomial coefficients).

Now we determine the best value for c by requiring that the running times of the first and the second algorithm should be the same: $2^{(1-\frac{c}{2})n} = 2^{\frac{n}{2}+h(c)\frac{n}{2}}$. This holds if and only if $h(c) = 1 - c$. Therefore, from the following diagram, $c \approx 0.22707$.

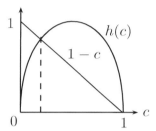

Plugging in this value for c we obtain the complexity $O(1.8487^n)$ for the entire algorithm.

Theorem
There is a deterministic algorithm for 3-*SAT* (as described above) with complexity $O(1.8487^n)$.

It is an interesting observation that, unlike other divide-and-conquer algorithms, here the divide action is just done once, and not repeated in a recursive manner. It is not clear how such a recursive technique might be applied here. Furthermore, the division into two sets of variables is done in an arbitrary fashion; it might be interesting to see if the efficiency can be improved by performing the division in a particularly chosen way.

6.2 Stålmarck Algorithm

Stålmarck's algorithm tests whether a given formula is a tautology. The formula is not necessarily given as a *CNF*. Actually, the first step is to transform the formula into a special form, a list of "triplets." It seems that Stålmarck's algorithm is most successful in industrial applications. Formulas which occur in this context seem best suited for this algorithm. We describe here a version based on (Sheeran, Stålmarck, 1998).

During execution of the algorithm, the test that F is a tautology is accomplished by negating F.

As mentioned above, the first step is to transform the formula into a special form. We start by producing a negation normal form: that is, all negation signs are moved in front of variables. This can be achieved by applying deMorgan's rules. Then, the formula F is rewritten over the complete basis $\{\rightarrow, \neg\}$. After that, in the same manner as in Tseitin's transformation, each subformula of the form $(F \rightarrow G)$ is substituted by $(v_i \leftrightarrow (F \rightarrow G))$ where v_i is a new variable. In the case when F and G are not yet literals, but consist of subformulas themselves, they are substituted by additional variables v_j, v_k. Finally all the resulting formulas are connected by a conjunction:

$$T_1 \wedge T_2 \wedge \cdots \wedge T_m$$

This looks like conjunctive normal form, but it is not quite the same since the T_i have the form $T_i = (a \leftrightarrow (b \rightarrow c))$ where a, b, c can be literals (variables or negated variables) or a constant 0 or 1. We simply denote such a triplet by (a, b, c), and we list the whole formula as a sequence of triplets:

$$(a_1, b_1, c_1)$$
$$(a_2, b_2, c_2)$$
$$\vdots$$
$$(a_m, b_m, c_m)$$

Let us consider an example:

$$F = ((\overline{x} \vee y) \wedge z) \vee (x \wedge \overline{y}) \vee \overline{x} \vee \overline{z}$$

We want to show that F is a tautology. This formula is already in negation normal form as the negation signs are only in front of variables. We transform F into the equivalent formula F' over the basis $\{\rightarrow, \neg\}$:

$$F' = ((x \rightarrow y) \rightarrow \overline{z}) \rightarrow ((x \rightarrow y) \rightarrow (x \rightarrow \overline{z}))$$

Next we introduce new variables v_i, each associated with an implication $F_1 \rightarrow F_2$ in the sense that v_i should be assigned exactly the value of $F_1 \rightarrow F_2$. In our example we get the new variables $v_1, \ldots, v_5$, and the triplets are:

$$(v_1, x, \overline{z})$$
$$(v_2, x, y)$$
$$(v_3, v_2, v_1)$$
$$(v_4, v_2, \overline{z})$$
$$(v_5, v_4, v_3)$$

The variable v_5 is the one associated with the root of the formula. If we set $v_5 = 0$ and plug this assignment into the set of triplets, this corresponds to negating the whole formula. From now on, it suffices to show that the resulting set of triplets is unsatisfiable.

By using a list of rules, the set of triplets can then be transformed and simplified until eventually a contradiction occurs.

The following simple transformation rules are always applied first. Whenever a triplet of some special form occurs, it might force certain assignments for some variables, which again produces further assignments, and so on. Only if a simple rule can no longer be applied, the dilemma rule is used (see below). Here is a list of the simple rules where a, b and c are literals or constants.

$$R1: \quad (0, b, c) \Rightarrow \{b = 1, c = 0\}$$
$$R2: \quad (a, b, 1) \Rightarrow \{a = 1\}$$
$$R3: \quad (a, 0, c) \Rightarrow \{a = 1\}$$
$$R4: \quad (a, 1, c) \Rightarrow \{a = c\}$$
$$R5: \quad (a, b, 0) \Rightarrow \{a = \bar{b}\}$$
$$R6: \quad (a, a, c) \Rightarrow \{a = 1, c = 1\}$$
$$R7: \quad (a, b, b) \Rightarrow \{a = 1\}$$

It should be clear that these rules constitute sat-equivalent transformations of the formula. Each time, some triplet was used as precondition of some rule and has led to some assignments, this triplet can be eliminated from the formula afterwards. Applying these rules has some similarity with the unit propagation process applied to a set of clauses.

In the example above, after v_5 has been set to 0, rule $R1$ is applicable to the triplet $(0, v_4, v_3)$ producing the next assignment $v_4 = 1, v_3 = 0$. Now we have the situation:

$$(v_1, x, \bar{z})$$
$$(v_2, x, y)$$
$$(0, v_2, v_1)$$
$$(1, v_2, \bar{z})$$

Again, by applying $R1$ to the third triplet we get $v_2 = 1, v_1 = 0$ and the new conjunction:

$$(0, x, \bar{z})$$
$$(1, x, y)$$
$$(1, 1, \bar{z})$$

Now rule $R4$ can be applied to the last triplet yielding the assignment $\bar{z} = 1$ and the first triplet turns to $(0, x, 1)$. This triplet represents the unsatisfiable formula $(0 \leftrightarrow (x \rightarrow 1))$. Therefore, it follows that the formula $F'\{v_5 = 0\}$ is unsatisfiable which is equivalent to F being a tautology.

An unsatisfiable triplet like $(0, x, 1)$ is called a *terminal triplet*. There are two further terminal triplets $(1, 1, 0)$ and $(0, 0, x)$. Terminal triplets play the same role as the empty clause in the resolution calculus.

It should be clear that the transformation rules $R1$–$R7$ are correct in the sense of correctness of a calculus (see page 39). But the rules $R1$–$R7$ alone are not refutation complete. We need an additional rule, the *dilemma rule*:

Dilemma rule

Let T be a conjunction of triplets and let x be a variable in T. By setting $x = 0$ and $x = 1$ one obtains the new set of triplets U_0 and U_1, respectively (using the rules $R1$–$R7$ for simplification). If U_0 or U_1 contains a terminal triplet, then U_1, or rather U_0 is the result of the dilemma rule. If neither U_0 nor U_1 contain a terminal triplet, then the set intersection $U_0 \cap U_1$ is the result of the dilemma rule, applied to T.

Intersecting U_0 and U_1 is justified by the observation that a logical consequence of T should be independent of the specific value of x. There is some similarity with the branching operation in DPLL-type algorithms but, unlike DPLL the partial proofs, by intersecting, are put together to a single proof. Also, there is some similarity with the DP-procedure where from one set of clauses, after selecting a variable, we proceed to a new set of clauses (that does not contain x any more).

By the dilemma rule, the underlying calculus becomes refutation complete. If T is unsatisfiable, in the worst case, after the dilemma rule has been applied to all occurring variables, terminal triplets will occur.

As an example we prove the pigeonhole principle from page 54 for 3 pigeons and 2 holes: $\neg PH_2 = (\overline{x_{0,1}} \wedge \overline{x_{0,2}}) \vee (\overline{x_{1,1}} \wedge \overline{x_{1,2}}) \vee (\overline{x_{2,1}} \wedge \overline{x_{2,2}}) \vee (x_{0,2} \wedge x_{1,2}) \vee (x_{0,2} \wedge x_{2,2}) \vee (x_{1,1} \wedge x_{2,2}) \vee (x_{0,1} \wedge x_{1,1}) \vee (x_{0,1} \wedge x_{2,1}) \vee (x_{1,1} \wedge x_{2,1})$. After transforming into triplets, and fixing the root variable $v = 0$, and applying the rules $R1$–$R7$, we obtain:

$$(1, \overline{x_{0,1}}, x_{0,2})$$
$$(1, \overline{x_{1,1}}, x_{1,2})$$
$$(1, \overline{x_{2,1}}, x_{2,2})$$
$$(1, x_{0,1}, \overline{x_{1,1}})$$
$$(1, x_{0,1}, \overline{x_{2,1}})$$
$$(1, x_{1,1}, \overline{x_{2,1}})$$
$$(1, x_{0,2}, \overline{x_{1,2}})$$
$$(1, x_{0,2}, \overline{x_{2,2}})$$
$$(1, x_{1,2}, \overline{x_{2,2}}).$$

In this state, none of the rules $R1$–$R7$ can be applied, and no terminal triplet has occured yet. If we use the dilemma rule with variable $x_{0,1}$, in the case of setting $x_{0,1} = 0$ the first triplet becomes $(1, 1, x_{0,2})$. Now $R4$ can be applied, and after several more simple rule applications we get the terminal triplet $(1, 1, 0)$. In the other case (i.e. $x_{0,1} = 1$) we obtain the triplets $(1, 1, \overline{x_{1,1}})$ and $(1, 1, \overline{x_{2,1}})$ Again $R4$ can be applied and after some further steps we get the terminal triplet $(1, 1, 0)$. Since both cases lead to a terminal triplet, it follows that PH_2 is unsatisfiable, and $\neg PH_2$ is a tautology. Only one application of the dilemma rule was necessary.

In concrete implementations of Stålmarck's algorithm one needs to specify heuristics which determine which variable is selected for the dilemma rule. It seems that formulas stemming from practical, industrial applications need the dilemma rule quite seldom so that Stålmarck's algorithm is quite efficient in these cases.

Nevertheless, the result from page 40 is still valid for Stålmarck's calculus (at least for certain worst-case formulas): unless NP = co-NP, no calculus is able to prove the property of being a tautology (or of being unsatisfiable) within polynomially many steps.

Generalizations and improvements to Stålmarck's algorithm have been investigated in (Kullmann, 1999 and 2004).

6.3 SAT Algorithms with Binary Decision Diagrams

For the basics on branching programs and BDD's see the appendix. There, some remarks can be found about how a *SAT* solver based on BDD's could work.

Each clause of a given *CNF* formula can be represented as a BDD. An example can be found on page 162.

Using the synthesis operation, it is possible to build up, step by step, a BDD that realizes the *and*-connection of the clauses. Having obtained a BDD realizing the total formula, it is trivial to figure out whether the formula is satisfiable. There should exist a path from the start node to the 1-endnode.

The synthesis operation for *and* (and similarly for other binary Boolean operations) takes two BDD's (where the variable order has to agree in both BDD's) and merges them into a single BDD as follows. For simplicity, we assume the order is $1 < 2 < \cdots < n$.

Let u be an arbitrary node in the first BDD, and suppose its associated variable is x_i. The two successor nodes are a and b. Similarly, let v be a node in the second BDD, and suppose its associated variable is x_j. The two successor nodes are c and d.

Then, the new BDD to be constructed, has a node (u, v). If $i = j$ then this node is associated with variable x_i and the two successor nodes are (a, c) and (b, d).

If $i < j$ (the other case $j < i$ is symmetric), then the resulting BDD has node (u, v) being associated with variable x_i, and the two successor nodes are (a, v) and (b, v). The construction of this "cross product-BDD" starts from the initial node and can be restricted to those nodes (u, v) which can be reached from the initial node.

If u_0 and u_1 are the final 0-node and the final 1-node in the first BDD, and if v_0

and v_1 are the final 0-node and the final 1-node in the second BDD, then the resulting BDD should have the 4 final nodes (u_0, v_0), (u_0, v_1), (u_1, v_0), (u_1, v_1). Depending on the binary Boolean operation to be realized by the resulting BDD, one can define which of those nodes should be a 0-node and which should be a 1-node. Here, the *and* operation should be synthesized. Therefore, the nodes (u_0, v_0), (u_0, v_1), (u_1, v_0) can be melted to a single 0-node, and (u_1, v_1) becomes a 1-node of the resulting BDD.

We show the construction with an example. Given are the following two BDD's which represent the clauses $(x_1 \vee x_3)$ and $(x_2 \vee \overline{x_3})$.

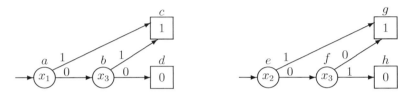

The above algorithm for synthesizing the *and* of both BDD's produces the BDD in the next figure. Notice that not every node in the cross product set $\{a, b, c, d\} \times \{e, f, g, h\}$ needs to be constructed if it is not reachable from the initial node (a, e).

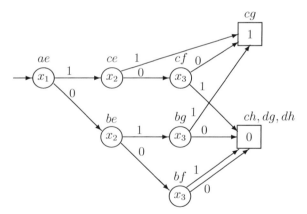

By applying the elimination rule (see appendix) the node bf can be eliminated and substituted by a direct connection.

There is potential for improvement. It is possible to join the synthesis-process and the elimination rule. Heuristic rules might produce a good order of the clauses, as well as a good order of the variables so that the necessary storage for the BDD does not explode too much. It is also possible to change the variable order during the algorithm dynamically. But still, the huge amount of storage needed for the BDD is the problem. It seems that other methods like DPLL (CDCL) have better performance.

6.4 Randomized Rounding and the Cross-Entropy Method

Next we present another unusual type of algorithm. It is an incomplete *SAT* solver in the sense that, only if the input formula is satisfiable, the algorithm will find a satisfying assignment – with a certain probability. One cannot say it is a local search algorithm because the jumps in the search space can be quite large (regarding Hamming distance), at least in the beginning.

The basic principle underlying this algorithm is *randomized rounding*. For every Boolean variable x_i we keep track of a real-valued $r_i \in [0, 1]$. Initially these r_i are all set to $\frac{1}{2}$. At the end of the algorithm these values should be (hopefully) close to 0 or 1 and indicate a respective satisfying assignment (or a set of assignments among which there are satisfying ones). In each round of the algorithm a Boolean value (an assignment α) for x_i is chosen in a random fashion according to the following algorithm.

> $\alpha := \emptyset$
> **for** $i := 1$ **to** n **do**
>   **if** *random* $\leq r_i$ **then** $\alpha := \alpha \cup \{x_i = 1\}$ **else** $\alpha := \alpha \cup \{x_i = 0\}$

Here, *random* is a real-valued random variable being uniformly distributed in $[0, 1]$. This means, with probability r_i, the variable x_i will be assigned the value 1, and with probability $1 - r_i$ the value 0. Expressed differently, the x_i can be considered as random variables distributed according to a Bernoulli distribution: $X_i \sim \begin{pmatrix} 0 & 1 \\ 1 - r_i & r_i \end{pmatrix}$.

Each round of this algorithm starts with such a randomized rounding process. Next it is checked whether the produced assignment α is actually a satisfying assignment. If not, then there are clauses not being satisfied by α (we call them "zero clauses"). For each variable x_i which occurs in a zero clause, its r_i value is modified. If x_i occurs positive, then the r_i value is shifted closer to 1; if x_i occurs negated, then the r_i value is shifted closer to 0. Notice that it is not possible that a variable occurs in zero clauses both positive and negative.

Computer experiments have shown that it is advantageous when these update operations regarding the value of r_i are done in a quite rigorous way. For the update operation which moves an r_i value closer to 0 we used $r_i := (r_i)^3$, and, analogously, for the shift to a value closer to 1 we used $r_i := 1 - (1 - r_1)^3$. After several such updates it might happen, because of the computer real arithmetic, that the value *exactly* 0 or *exactly* 1 is obtained. To avoid this undesired behavior we modified the update operations slightly to $r_i := (r_i)^3 + \varepsilon$ resp. $r_i := 1 - \varepsilon - (1 - r_i)^3$ using, for example, $\varepsilon = 0.0001$.

After a certain number of rounds (involving randomized rounding and updates) have been performed (some thousands) without having found a satisfying assignment, it is reasonable to perform a *restart*, i.e. to set all r_i values to $\frac{1}{2}$ again. For the concept of restarts see chapter 8.

A full theoretical analysis of this algorithm would be most desirable.

It is interesting to see that the above defined update operations show some hysteresis behavior. Such behavior can be observed in physical processes like magnetization and de-magnetization of iron. It means that once the value has reached almost 0 or almost 1, it tends to "stick" there for a while even if several update operations are performed which aim in the other direction. The following diagram shows a typical hysteresis curve.

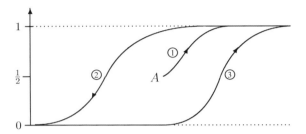

This curve can be interpreted as follows. The process starts at point A when the initial r_i value is $\frac{1}{2}$. Then, during phase 1, the update operation is applied several times and moves the value close to 1. During phase 2 we perform updates which move towards 0, but it can be observed that the value "sticks" for some time at value 1 before it starts to move. Finally, in phase 3, it is moved back to 1 again.

It is interesting that this hysteresis effect seems to be crucial for the good algorithm behavior. As mentioned above, a theoretical analysis has still to be found.

This algorithm has a certain similarity with algorithms that can be subsumed under the generic term "cross entropy method" (Rubinstein, 1999; DeBeur et al., 2005; Wu, Chung, 2007; Kroese, Taimre, Botev, 2011).

Here the task is to find a probability distribution $\mathcal{P}(\Theta)$ of a random variable X, where the probability distribution is controlled by some parameter Θ. More formally, we search for the parameter Θ such that, for some given objective function f, we have

$$\mathop{\mathbb{E}}_{X \sim \mathcal{P}(\Theta)} \Big(f(X) \Big) \;\to\; \max$$

Notice that both X and Θ can be vectors (of random variables, resp. of parameters).

An algorithm according to the cross entropy method initializes the parameter Θ with some neutral value. Then, a large number of rounds are performed. Each round starts by sampling several values a for X according to probability distribution $\mathcal{P}(\Theta)$. For each such sample a the objective function $f(a)$ is evaluated. The samples are sorted according to their f-values and the best, say 10 percent, of them are identified. Call them the "elite" set $\mathcal{E}$. Finally, a round ends by updating the parameter Θ to Θ' in such a way that Θ' maximizes the probability that distribution $\mathcal{P}(\Theta')$ will generate the elite set $\mathcal{E}$. This is called the *maximum likelihood method* in statistics.

Applied to the *SAT* problem the cross entropy method might look like this. The parameter is a vector $\Theta = (r_1, r_2, \dots, r_n)$, $r_i \in [0, 1]$, and the underlying probability distribution $\mathcal{P}(\Theta)$ is given by the randomized rounding process as described in the beginning of this chapter. In each round a couple of samples $(a_1, a_2, \dots, a_n) \in \{0, 1\}^n$ are drawn, say 1000 of them. The objective function f counts the number of satisfied clauses. We select those 100 samples (assignments) which have the highest f-values. These form the elite set $\mathcal{E}$. The update operation substitutes Θ by $\Theta' = (r'_1, \dots, r'_n)$ where

$$r'_i = \frac{\displaystyle\sum_{(a_1,\dots,a_n)\in\mathcal{E}} a_i}{|\mathcal{E}|}$$

That is, r_i is the ratio of 1-assignments of variable x_i among all elite assignments.

For the methods discussed in this section it might be advantageous to combine them with the decimation method that is described on page 133. Another interesting aspect is that the algorithm is well suited for parallelization: producing samples and evaluating them can be done on separate processors in parallel.

7   Random Clauses and Physical Approaches

For testing *SAT* algorithms, if no theoretical analysis is available, it is possible to generate random formulas (in clause form) and test the algorithms on these formulas. Next we discuss the most frequently used model for generating random formulas.

7.1   Threshold and Phase Transition

Suppose a formula with n variables needs to be generated. Also, the clause number m is fixed beforehand, as well as k, the number of literals in a clause. In the following the ratio m/n will play a crucial role; it will be denoted as γ. The following algorithm generates a random formula in k-*CNF* with these parameters $n, m = \gamma n$, and k:

> **for** $i := 1$ **to** m **do**
> > **begin**
> > > In order to generate the i-th clause C_i choose a
> > > random k-element subset T of $\{x_1, x_2, \ldots, x_n\}$
> > > (there exist $\binom{n}{k}$ many possibilities for this choice).
> > > For each of the variables $x_j \in T$ decide at random
> > > (with probability $1/2$), whether x_j should be negated or not.
> > **end**
> > **output** $(C_1 \wedge C_2 \wedge \cdots \wedge C_m)$

We write $F \sim Z(n, \gamma, k)$ when F is randomly generated by this probabilistic algorithm. Here $Z(n, \gamma, k)$ is the notation for the underlying probability distribution on formulas. Let $V = \{x_1, \ldots, x_n\}$ be the set of variables. In the terminology explained in the appendix about random variables, we have:

$$Z(n, \gamma, k) = U\left(\left(\binom{V}{k} \times \{+, -\}^k \right)^{\gamma n} \right)$$

If a probability for some event E, like "F is satisfiable," should be expressed, then this can be denoted by $\underset{F \sim Z(n,\gamma,k)}{P}(E)$.

We start by studying some simple properties of these random formulas. Let α be some fixed assignment of the n variables. Whenever a random clause C_i is generated by the above algorithm, we have

$$P(C_i\alpha = 1) = \frac{2^k - 1}{2^k} = 1 - \frac{1}{2^k} \quad \text{resp.} \quad P(C_i\alpha = 0) = \frac{1}{2^k}$$

This means each choice of some C_i constitutes a Bernoulli experiment with "success probability" $1 - \frac{1}{2^k}$ (resp. $\frac{1}{2^k}$).

Suppose we introduce the random variables

$$X_1 = |\{\, i \mid i \le m,\ C_i\alpha = 1 \,\}| \quad \text{resp.} \quad X_0 = |\{\, i \mid i \le m,\ C_i\alpha = 0 \,\}|$$

Then these random variables are binomially distributed (cf. Fournier, 2007), as symbolized by

$$X_1 \sim Bin(m, 1 - \frac{1}{2^k}) \quad \text{resp.} \quad X_0 \sim Bin(m, \frac{1}{2^k})$$

It follows, for example, that the probability of the random formula F being satisfied by the assignment α is

$$\underset{F \sim Z(n,\gamma,k)}{P} \left(F\alpha = 1 \right) = (1 - \frac{1}{2^k})^m = (1 - \frac{1}{2^k})^{\gamma n} \le e^{-\gamma n/2^k}$$

Further, for the expectations, we get:

$$\mathbb{E}(X_1) = (1 - \frac{1}{2^k}) \cdot m \quad \text{resp.} \quad \mathbb{E}(X_0) = \frac{1}{2^k} \cdot m$$

An interesting threshold or phase transition phenomenon can be observed. For every k there seems to exist a specific constant γ_k, the threshold, where $\gamma_2 < \gamma_3 < \gamma_4 < \ldots$, so that the probability $\underset{F \sim Z(n,\gamma,k)}{P} (F \in SAT)$ is close to 1 for values of γ being strictly below γ_k, and is close to 0 for values of γ being strictly larger than γ_k.

For $k = 3$ this threshold (or median of the distribution) lies at about 4.27 (cf. Biroli, Cocco, Monasson, 2002), see the next figure.

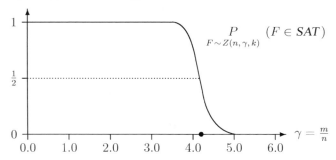

This diagram shows the situation for the case $k = 3$ and some fixed n (maybe $n = 50$). For growing values of n it can be observed that the curve becomes steeper and steeper. This can be formally expressed as:

$$\gamma < \gamma_k \quad \Rightarrow \quad \lim_{n \to \infty} \, P_{F \sim Z(n,\gamma,k)} \, (F \in SAT) \, = \, 1$$

$$\gamma > \gamma_k \quad \Rightarrow \quad \lim_{n \to \infty} \, P_{F \sim Z(n,\gamma,k)} \, (F \in SAT) \, = \, 0$$

At the time of writing this is actually just a conjecture, being confirmed by computer experiments, but not yet by a formal proof. The strongest theoretical result so far is (Friedgut, 1999). There it is shown that the curve indeed becomes steeper with growing n, but it does not rule out the possibility that the phase transition point (where satisfiable turns to unsatisfiable) "moves around" with growing n. The only case where a complete analysis was successful is $k = 2$. The phase transition occurs here at $\gamma_2 = 1.0$, see (Goerdt, 1996), (Chvátal, Reed, 1992). For larger values of k we have only experimental results: $\gamma_3 \approx 4.27$ as already mentioned above, $\gamma_4 \approx 9.93$, $\gamma_5 \approx 21.12$, $\gamma_6 \approx 43.37$, $\gamma_7 \approx 87.79$. Roughly, increasing k by 1 corresponds to doubling the γ_k value.

It is possible to prove lower and upper bounds for the (potential) threshold. A simple upper bound can be obtained by modifying the calculation from above.

$$
\begin{aligned}
P_{F \sim Z(n,\gamma,k)} \, (F \in SAT) \, &= \, P_{F \sim Z(n,\gamma,k)} \, (\exists \alpha \, F\alpha = 1) \\
&\leq \, \sum_{\alpha} P_{F \sim Z(n,\gamma,k)} \, (F\alpha = 1) \\
&\leq \, 2^n \cdot \left(\frac{2^k - 1}{2^k}\right)^{\gamma n} \, = \, \left[2 \cdot \left(\frac{2^k - 1}{2^k}\right)^{\gamma}\right]^n
\end{aligned}
$$

This means, if $2 \cdot \left(\frac{2^k-1}{2^k}\right)^{\gamma} < 1$, then the probability for obtaining a satisfiable random formula goes to 0 as $n \to \infty$. Equivalently, the probability of obtaining an unsatisfiable formula goes to 1. From this we get the estimation $\gamma_k \leq \frac{\ln(2)}{\ln(2^k/(2^k-1))}$. This value is 5.191 for $k = 3$, and is 10.74 for $k = 4$, and overestimates the "real" threshold γ_k. Using the estimation $1 - x \leq e^{-x}$ we obtain $\frac{\ln(2)}{\ln(2^k/(2^k-1))} \leq \ln(2) \cdot 2^k$. This last estimation gives some "explanation" about why the γ_k value roughly doubles when k increases.

Somewhat more difficult is to prove a *lower bound* for the threshold. A possible method to prove a lower bound is to show that some (simple enough) algorithm will almost surely (as $n \to \infty$) find a satisfying assignment on random formulas, as long as the clause-to-variable ratio stays below some appropriate value. Another method for lower bounds involves second moment methods from probability theory.

The best known lower bounds for 3-*SAT* are around 3.5, and the best known upper bounds are around 4.5.

There is another interesting observation regarding the threshold behavior of k-*SAT* (but we concentrate on 3-*SAT* here). Moving from satisfiable to unsatisfiable formulas, which happens around the threshold $\gamma_3 \approx 4.27$, is just one aspect of a random formula. One might also look into the structure of the satisfying assignments (as long as we are below this threshold). It turns out that the structure of satisfiying assignment also shows a sudden phase transition around the point $\gamma = m/n = 3.92$. Below this point the satisfying assignments form a huge connected subset within $\{0, 1\}^n$. Above this point (but below 4.27) the set of satisfying assignments falls apart in many isolated "islands." The following figure illustrates this.

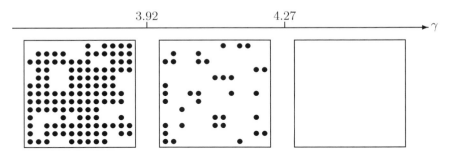

Regarding the situation from an algorithm's point of view, it turns out that the running time of complete (DPLL-type) algorithms typically reach a maximum around the satisfiability threshold. Since verifying unsatisfiability seems to be harder than verifying satisfiability (cf. page 40) the maximum peek is somewhat to the right of the sat/unsat threshold. The next figure indicates this.

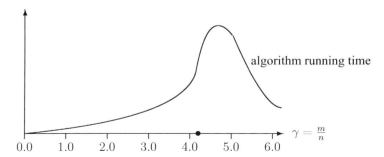

Another interesting aspect occurs when we randomly produce a mixture of 2-*CNF* and 3-*CNF* clauses. This is controlled by a parameter $\varrho \in [0, 1]$. Among the $m = \gamma \cdot n$ clauses we produce a ϱ fraction of clauses of size 3, and a $(1 - \varrho)$ fraction of clauses of size 2. We call this a random $(2 + \varrho)$-*SAT* problem. For $\varrho = 0$ we get a pure 2-*SAT* problem, and for $\varrho = 1$ we get a pure 3-*SAT* problem. Observe that 2-*SAT* is located in P whereas 3-*SAT* is NP-complete. Further observe that the satisfiability threshold for 2-*SAT* is 1.0, and for 3-*SAT* it is 4.27. It can be expected that the threshold moves from 1.0 to 4.27 as we shift ϱ from 0 to 1. The following diagram confirms this.

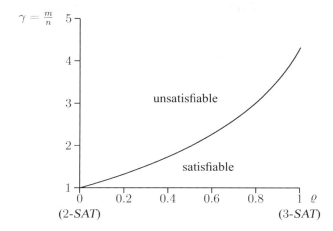

It is an interesting question, at which point along the curve in the above diagram it happens that the "easy" 2-*SAT* problem turns into a "hard" 3-*SAT* problem. Empirical results, and calculations by "physical methods," indicate that the "turn-over point" is reached at $\varrho \approx 0.4$, cf. (Saitta et al., 2011), (Hartmann, Rieger, 2004), (Hartmann, Weigt, 2005).

7.2   Random Satisfiable Formulas

Some applications require random formulas which are guaranteed to be satisfiable, for example benchmark formulas for testing incomplete *SAT* solvers (cf. page 87). One possible approach is to generate random formulas, as discussed above, and to stay reasonably under the threshold so that the resulting formulas will be most likely satisfiable. The problem is that if the gap between the clause/variable density used and the threshold value is too large (to ensure that one gets satisfiable formulas), then the formulas tend to be too "easy" for being appropriate as a benchmark.

Therefore, another generation process has been suggested to obtain formulas which are satisfiable under guarantee. The idea is to "plant" a (randomly selected) satisfying assignment into the random process of generating the formula. The following algorithm achieves this where the parameters $n = |\mathit{Var}(F)|$, $m = \gamma n = |F|$, and k (the clause size) are fixed beforehand.

> Randomly select an assignment α of the n variables
> **for** $i := 1$ **to** m **do**
> > **begin**
> > > Randomly select a k-element subset T of $\{x_1, x_2, \ldots, x_n\}$
> > > (there are $\binom{n}{k}$ equally likely possibilities).
> > > These k variables can form 2^k many potential clauses,
> > > exactly one of them being falsified by α.
> > > Among the $2^k - 1$ remaining clauses choose one
> > > uniformly at random; this gives the clause K_i.
> > **end**
> **output** $(K_1 \wedge K_2 \wedge \cdots \wedge K_m)$

A random formula produced by this algorithm is satisfiable under guarantee. At least α is a satisfying assignment. We write $F \sim S(n, \gamma, k)$ if F was produced by this algorithm randomly. That is, $S(n, \gamma, k)$ is the underlying probability distribution.

But there is a problem with this probability distribution. If α sets the variable x_i to 1, then x_i occurs within a fraction of $4/7$ of all clauses (which contain the variable x_i), and $\overline{x_i}$ occurs within a fraction of $3/7$ (letting $k = 3$). It is the other way around if α sets x_i to 0. This means, among the n_i many occurrences of variable x_i in the clauses, the number of positive occurrences is a $Bin(n_i, \frac{4}{7})$ distributed random variable if $x_i\alpha = 1$, and it is a $Bin(n_i, \frac{3}{7})$ distributed random variable if $x_i\alpha = 0$. Additionally it holds that $\sum_{i=1}^{n} n_i = mk = \gamma nk$.

If we have enough sample clauses drawn under the distribution $S(n, \gamma, k)$, in other words if F is long enough (γ is large enough), then a "majority vote" regarding the number of positive and negative occurrences of x_i is likely to be successful in guessing the correct assignment. This is exactly what the following algorithm does which we call the "democratic algorithm" since it determines an assignment α according to a "majority vote."

> **input** F (being randomly generated according to $S(n, \gamma, k)$)
> $\alpha := \emptyset$
> **for** $i := 1$ **to** n **do**
> > **if** number of positive occurrences of $x_i >$
> > number of negative occurrences of x_i in F
> > > **then** $\alpha := \alpha \cup \{x_i = 1\}$
> > > **else** $\alpha := \alpha \cup \{x_i = 0\}$
> **output** α

Let p_i be the probability that the i-th bit of α was *not* determined correctly by the democratic algorithm. Then this means that a $Bin(n_i, \frac{3}{7})$ distributed random variable takes a value greater than $n_i/2$, or by symmetry, that a $Bin(n_i, \frac{4}{7})$ distributed random variable takes a value smaller than $n/2$. Using the Chernoff inequality (see appendix about random variables) we obtain: $p_i = P(X > n_i/2) < 0.99473^{n_i}$. If p_i should to be around $1/n$, then n_i should be $c \log(n)$, for a constant c. In this case we get as probability that the whole assignment α is determined correctly $(1 - 1/n)^n \approx e^{-1}$, a constant value. Since n_i is about 3γ, we obtain that γ should be $\Omega(\log(n))$. Therefore, one needs to produce a formula with $\gamma n = \Omega(n \log(n))$ random clauses.

We describe now a way of escaping the problem with the biased occurrences of x_i and $\overline{x_i}$ which betrays the assignment of x_i – at least in a statistical sense. The material of this paragraph is based on chapter 7 in (Hartmann, Rieger, 2004). We need to assign appropriate probabilities to the 7 potential clauses that can be built from 3 variables (where the 8-th clause is still forbidden, as above). This probability distribution should be such that an occurrence of x_i in the formula is exactly as likely as an occurrence of $\overline{x_i}$. We distinguish the 7 allowed clauses which can be set up with the variables x_i, x_j, x_k ($1 \leq i < j < k \leq n$) into 3 categories. The *type 1* clauses are those 3 clauses which have exactly one true literal when the planted assignment α is applied. The *type 2* clauses are those where α sets two literals to true. There are 3 such *type 2* clauses; and there is one *type 3* clause where all 3 literals become true. Assign the probabilities p_1, p_2, p_3 for the occurrence of a clause of type 1, 2, 3. The idea is that the algorithm producing random formulas (which are guaranteed to be satisfiable) is modified such that after selecting the 3 variables x_i, x_j, x_k at random which will be part of the clause, one of the 7 possibilities for the clause is no longer selected under uniform distribution $(1/7, 1/7, \ldots, 1/7)$, but under the distribution $(p_1, p_1, p_1, p_2, p_2, p_2, p_3)$. By probability normalization it should hold: $3p_1 + 3p_2 + p_3 = 1$. From the condition that a positive occurrence of a variable should be exactly as likely as a negative occurrence, we get the equation: $p_1 + 2p_2 + p_3 = 2p_1 + p_2$. Put together, this means that (p_1, p_2, p_3) should have the special form $((1 + 2p_3)/6, (1 - 4p_3)/6, p_3), p_3 \leq 1/4$.

In (Jia, Moore, Strain, 2007) it is suggested to choose p_i to be proportional to q^i where $q \in (0, 1]$ is some constant. By this, one can obtain a drastic descent of probabilities: $p_1 > p_2 > p_3$ (in the case of 3-*SAT*). This has the effect that local search algorithms tend to drift away from the planted satisfying assignment, just in the same vein, as for the explicitly constructed formula from chapter 5.7. By combining this suggestion to have p_i proportional to q^i, for some q, i.e. $(p_2/p_1) = (p_3/p_2) = q$, with the special form of (p_1, p_2, p_3) which was calculated above, one obtains as just one admissible choice for q the value $q = (\sqrt{5} - 1)/2 \approx 0.618$, the golden ratio. Using this value for q, we obtain: $(p_1, p_2, p_3) = (0.191, 0.118, 0.073)$.

7.3   Ising Model and Physically Motivated Algorithms

In statistical physics the *Ising model* plays a major role. It goes back to the doctoral dissertation of Ernst Ising in the year 1925. It deals with a special case of a more general theory, called spinglass theory. Imagine some material that can be magnetized. It consists of many particles that can have a spin which is either "up" or "down," see the following figure.

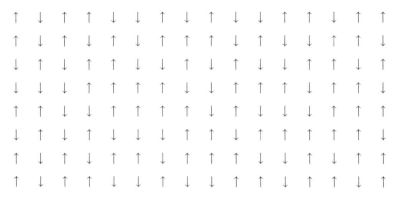

We model the particles by variables x_i that can take the values $+1$ or -1. Each variable is influenced by its neighbors (in the 2-dimensional model there are 4 of them: above, below, left, right). Every configuration K, like the example above, can be associated with an *energy* value (sometimes called *Hamiltonian*) given by the following function

$$H(K) = -\sum_{i \sim j} x_i x_j$$

Here $i \sim j$ means that the particles x_i and x_j are neighbors. This function $H(K)$ takes on its minimum value if all neighboring particles have the same spin, either both are $+1$, or both are -1. Physically this means that the material is completely magnetized, either all spins point upwards, or all spins point downwards. A configuration K which corresponds to a minimum $H(K)$ value is said to be in a *ground state*.

There is an obvious analogy to the *SAT* problem: imagine the particle variables as Boolean variables taking values 0 and 1. Neighbored variables x_i, x_j (i.e. $i \sim j$) form a clause. In this case all clauses have size 2 and correspond to the formula

$$(x_i \leftrightarrow x_j) \quad \text{resp.} \quad (x_i \vee \overline{x_j}) \wedge (\overline{x_i} \vee x_j)$$

A physical configuration K would, in the Boolean context, be called an assignment α. An analogue to the energy function $H(K)$ would be (up to some linear transformation) a function that counts the number of falsified clauses under the given assignment:

$$H(\alpha) = \text{number of falsified clauses under } \alpha$$

A ground state would correspond to an assignment that produces the smallest number of falsified clauses. In the case of a satisfiable formula this would be a satisfying assignment.

In principle, although the Ising model leads to a 2-*SAT* problem with very regularly distributed clauses corresponding to the underlying lattice structure, it should be possible to apply the concept to more complex clauses with arbitrary sizes and structure.

In statistical physics the occurrence of a configuration is assigned a probability that can be calculated from its energy value. This probability can depend on a further parameter t of the physical system called the temperature. That is, the probability of a configuration K with energy value $H(K)$ is proportional to $e^{-H(K)/t}$, which is called the *Boltzmann probability*. It is a difficult problem to determine the underlying proportionality factor needed such that all probabilities add up to 1. This requires to computing $S = \sum_K e^{-H(K)/t}$, which is called the *partition function*, so that the probability of K becomes $\frac{e^{-H(K)/t}}{S}$. Although the correct probability value of a configuration K is hard to compute, since it requires to computing the partition function, it is easy to compute the relative quotient when comparing two configurations (like a configuration K and its neighboring configuration K' when flipping one variable). This quotient is $\frac{e^{-H(K)/t}}{e^{-H(K')/t}} = e^{-(H(K)-H(K'))/t}$. Calculations like this can be used in the above described simulation of a physical system. We sketch a calculation based on these relative probabilities below.

The parameter t in these formulas is the *temperature*. Observe that high values of t cause all configurations to have almost the same probability. In other words, the spins behave as uniformly distributed (among "up" and "down") and independently of each other. Whereas in the case of low temperature ($t \to 0$), the only configurations which obtain a non-zero probability are those in the ground state. It is possible to simulate by computer a system of particles that starts at high temperature. The variables are selected at random and flipped (or not flipped) according to the probabilities of the underlying configurations. Very slowly the temperature is decreased. Finally, the system reaches a ground state (with high probability). In the above model this means total magnetization (either upwards or downwards). Interestingly, during this cooling process a phase transition behavior can be observed (and determined mathematically). Starting from a more or less "chaotic" system, at a certain temperature, suddenly areas ("clusters") within the material show up in which all particles have the same spin orientation. Physically motivated calculations like the ones sketched here can also be used to provide good estimations for the k-*SAT* thresholds.

Let us look more precisely into the details of a computer simulation of such an annealing process. At a given temperature t the following is repeated many times. One chooses a random particle x_i and inspects the 4 spins of its neighboring particles. These spins are added:

$$m_i = \sum_{j:\, i \sim j} x_j$$

This value m_i lies in the set $\{-4, -2, 0, 2, 4\}$. If the spin of x_i would be set to $+1$, regarding this local neighborhood, we would get the energy value $E_+ = -m_i$. If the spin of x_i would be set to -1, we would get the energy value $E_- = +m_i$. Now we decide randomly about the future spin of x_i, in a biased way (also called *Gibbs sampling* or *Glauber dynamics*), by

$$x_i := \begin{cases} +1, & \text{with probability } \dfrac{e^{-E_+/t}}{e^{-E_+/t} + e^{-E_-/t}} = \dfrac{1 + \tanh(m_i/t)}{2} \\[2mm] -1, & \text{with probability } \dfrac{e^{-E_-/t}}{e^{-E_+/t} + e^{-E_-/t}} = \dfrac{1 + \tanh(-m_i/t)}{2} \end{cases}$$

Observe that for high temperature values of t both probabilities are close to $\frac{1}{2}$, whereas for $t \to 0$ almost the whole probability mass goes to that decision which produces a lower energy.

It is just a small step from this kind of a computer *simulation* of a physical annealing process to a computer program that solves a difficult combinatorial problem when this problem can be put into the framework of energy values, probabilities of configurations, and local alterations of configurations. Algorithms and methods like this are called *simulated annealing* or a variant of the *Metropolis algorithm*, see (Kirkpatrick et al., 1983; Brémaud, 1999; Schneider, Kirkpatrick, 2006).

The idea of the method is as follows. First, a temperature parameter t is initialized with a high value. In a random fashion a starting configuration (i.e., an assignment of the underlying variables) is produced. In an outer loop which has to be cycled many times the temperature is lowered just slightly each time, like $t := (1 - \varepsilon) \cdot t$. Within the loop, each time it is tested whether the actual assignment is already a satisfying assignment. If not, some variable x_i is selected at random. The energy value of the actual assignment is compared with the one which results by flipping the assigned value of variable x_i. In other words, it is analyzed whether flipping x_i would result in more or in fewer falsified clauses. If it means fewer falsified clauses (a smaller energy value) then the flipping is done unconditionally. But still, if there are not fewer falsified clauses, a flipping is still possible. It is done with probability $e^{-(H(\alpha') - H(\alpha))/t}$. This can be implemented by using a real-valued random number $random \in [0, 1]$, uniformly distributed, and doing the flip operation, if $random \leq e^{-(H(\alpha') - H(\alpha))/t}$. Here α and α' are the assignments before and after the flip, and H calculates their respective energy values. Also, the temperature parameter t plays a role. The higher the t value is, the more likely is the flip. On the other hand, if t is close to 0, which is the case after many loops have been performed, the algorithm's behavior is more strictly greedy; only improving flips are allowed. A possible variant is to consider only those variables x_i for possible flipping which are located in falsified clauses. This particular strategy is sometimes called *focused local search*.

Another kind of physically motivated algorithms for solving *k-SAT*, especially 3-*SAT*, has been considered just a few years ago. For more details, the reader should consult the papers by the authors Braunstein, Cocco, Mézard, Monasson, Montanari, Parisi, Zecchina. These algorithms are called *belief propagation* and *survey propagation*. They seem to be quite successful below the satisfiability/unsatisfiability threshold. These algorithms are based on ideas that where used before in artificial intelligence applications (cf. Pearl, 1997) and in decoding low density parity check codes (see MacKay, 2003; Zecchina, 2005). Each variable x_i is associated with a real value $p_i \in [0, 1]$. These values are initially set to 0.5. Then some computation process is started, call it B, and iterated many times modifying the sequence $(p_1, p_2, \ldots, p_n)$ each time by a small amount until no change occurs any more. That is, the final sequence $(p_1, \ldots, p_n)$ is a fixpoint under the transformation B:

$$B(p_1, \ldots, p_n) = (p_1, \ldots, p_n)$$

The idea is here that p_i converges to a *marginal probability* – but this cannot be guaranteed each time. A marginal probability, with respect to the set of satisfying assignments, is

$$p_i \approx \frac{\text{number of sat. assignments where } x_i \text{ is assigned 1}}{\text{number of all satisfying assignments}}$$

This process can be understood as a Monte Carlo simulation of a Markov random field (see appendix).

During a calculation like this it is possible that some of the p_i receive values very close to 0 or to 1. In such a case it is almost certain that setting those variables to the respective values will be a sat-equivalent transformation (and especially a simplification). For example, if $p_i \approx 1$, even with a certain potential of error, it seems that most satisfying assignments α will have $\alpha(x_i) = 1$. Therefore, $F \mapsto F\{x_i = 1\}$ is a sat-equivalent transformation which eliminates at least one variable. This method is called *variable decimation*. Observe that such a decision of setting x_i to 1 is irreversible: there is no backtracking involved. After such variables whose assignment is clearly 0 or 1 (which we call *backbone variables* or *frozen variables*) are set, the process of calculating the p_i values of the remaining variables can start over again. More problematic are variables x_i with $p_i \approx \frac{1}{2}$. Such variables are said to be in a *joker state*. Experiments show that it is better to stop the decimation process in this case and to hand the formula containing only variables in joker states over to another traditional *SAT*-solving algorithm.

It should be clear that an algorithm which assigns all variables their correct values successively probably does not exist. If we can always find a variable x and a truth value a such that F and $F\{x = a\}$ are sat-equivalent, then this hypothetical algorithm would solve *SAT* within polynomial time, and it would follow that P = NP.

Next we present a possible update rule for the p_i values (i.e. the above mentioned computation B). We use the following notation: $\mathcal{C}_i^+$ (resp. $\mathcal{C}_i^-$) represents the set of clauses which contain x_i (resp. $\overline{x_i}$). Furthermore, $\mathcal{V}_C^+$ (resp. $\mathcal{V}_C^-$) represents the set of variables (rather, their indices) which occur in C positively (resp. negatively). Now we repeat applying the following update rule where the variable x_i is selected at random:

$$p_i := \frac{\displaystyle\sum_{C \in \mathcal{C}_i^-} \left[1 - \prod_{j \in \mathcal{V}_C^+} (1 - p_j) \prod_{j \in \mathcal{V}_C^- \setminus \{i\}} p_j \right]}{\displaystyle\sum_{C \in \mathcal{C}_i^-} \left[1 - \prod_{j \in \mathcal{V}_C^+} (1 - p_j) \prod_{j \in \mathcal{V}_C^- \setminus \{i\}} p_j \right] + \sum_{C \in \mathcal{C}_i^+} \left[1 - \prod_{j \in \mathcal{V}_C^+ \setminus \{i\}} (1 - p_j) \prod_{j \in \mathcal{V}_C^-} p_j \right]}$$

Observe that $1 - \prod_{j \in \mathcal{V}_C^+}(1 - p_j) \prod_{j \in \mathcal{V}_C^-} p_j$ is the probability that clause C becomes true when using the probabilities p_j to assign the respective variables x_j to 1. The numerator of this fraction as well as the left summand in the denominator determine the expected number of true clauses that contain $\overline{x_i}$ (hereby not taking into account occurrences of $\overline{x_i}$). Similarly, the right summand of the denominator determines the expected number of true clauses that contain x_i (hereby not taking into account occurrences of x_i). This concept of leaving out x_i in the calculation of the new value for p_i is sometimes called the *cavity method*. In this way, the resulting value p_i suggests whether it would be for the variable x_i more "urgent" to be set to 1 or to be set to 0.

Our approach in this chapter is based on the paper by (Hsu, McIlraith, 2006), see also chapter 18 in the handbook (Biere et al., 2009). Regarding the notion of random formulas and phase transitions see also chapters 6 and 8 in the handbook (Biere et al., 2009).

8 Heavy Tail Distributions and Restarts

Many of the algorithms considered in this book are probabilistic. Think especially about those algorithms based on a random walk in the search space. The running time T of such an algorithm should be considered as a random variable (see appendix). Often we observe the phenomenon that the values that T can take are distributed over a very large scale. Possibly, the expectation of T does not exist since $T = \infty$ is possible with probability greater than 0. It is possible (and likely) that the distribution of T shows a so-called *heavy tail* behavior. Formally, one can describe this by

$$\mathbb{E}(T) < \mathbb{E}(T - t \mid T > t)$$

provided that these expectations exist. This means that the expected running time increases once the algorithm runs already for more than t steps. An explanation of such behavior is that it might be the case that the algorithm has taken some bad random decisions right from the beginning that led the algorithm in an area of the search space where there is no solution or many traps in form of local optima. On the other hand, in most of the other cases, the algorithm's decisions are well and lead to a quick solution. The DPLL-like algorithm might quickly find a backdoor, then unit propagation will do the rest.

The following diagram illustrates the probability distribution of a heavy tailed random variable T.

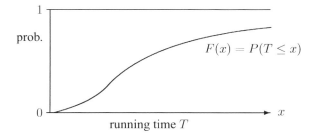

A different characterization of heavy tail behavior considers the "survival probability" $P(T > x) = 1 - F(x)$. Whereas for "normal" probability distributions this is a function approaching zero exponentially, like $1 - F(x) \sim c^{-x}$, a heavy tail distribution shows only a polynomial convergence rate, that is, $1 - F(x)$ is proportional to x^{-c}, for some constant c.

An escape from this dilemma of having extremely long running times is to select a point in time $x = \tau$, and perform a complete restart once T reaches the value τ, and possibly this has to be done many times. In particular this is advantageous if the various runs of the algorithm can be done in parallel. The probability that the algorithm finds a solution within τ time steps is $F(\tau) = P(T \leq \tau)$. The expected number of restarts until the algorithm succeeds is therefore geometrically distributed with an expected number $\frac{1}{F(\tau)}$ of restarts. This means, the expected total running time is at most $\tau \cdot \frac{1}{F(\tau)} = \frac{\tau}{F(\tau)}$.

Let $F_\tau(x)$ be the distribution function of this new algorithm with restarts after τ unsuccessful steps. For $x = n \cdot \tau$ we obtain the "survival probability" at time x: $1 - F_\tau(x) = (1 - F(\tau))^n = ((1 - F(\tau))^{1/\tau})^x$. This function (of x) converges exponentially to zero. Therefore, the running time of this new algorithm is no longer heavy tailed.

The distribution function $F_\tau(x)$ of this new algorithm with restarts can be described as follows.

$$F_\tau(x) = \begin{cases} F(x), & x \leq \tau \\ (1 - F(\tau))^n + (1 - (1 - F(\tau))^n) \cdot F(x - n\tau), & n\tau < x \leq (n+1)\tau \end{cases}$$

That is, if the original density function $f(x)$ of the running time T is as follows (which is the derivative of the distribution function $F(x)$)

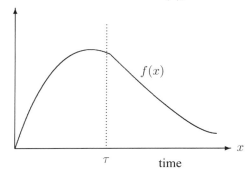

then the probability density function of the new algorithm with restarts looks like this.

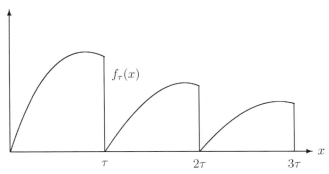

We need to determine the optimal restart point τ. The value of τ should be chosen such that $\frac{\tau}{F(\tau)}$ becomes minimal. Assuming that the functions can be differentiated, the derivative of this function can be set to zero, and one obtains the following condition

$$\frac{F(\tau) - \tau \cdot f(\tau)}{F^2(\tau)} = 0$$

From this the condition $F(\tau) = \tau \cdot f(\tau)$, $\tau > 0$, follows, where f is the probability density function of the distribution of T, hence the derivative of F.

Let us look at a simple example: assume m is the median of the distribution of T, i.e. $F(m) = \frac{1}{2}$. It is possible that the expectation of T is vastly larger than m (which is another indication of a heavy tail distribution). If we choose $\tau = m$, then the new algorithm with restarts has an expected running time of $\frac{\tau}{F(\tau)} = 2m$. Suppose further that the curve of function F below the point m is concave such that, say, $F(\frac{m}{2}) = \frac{1}{3} > \frac{1}{2} F(m)$. Now, if we choose instead $\tau = \frac{m}{2}$, then we get a new expected running time of $\frac{\tau}{F(\tau)} = \frac{3}{2}m$.

These calculations are only possible when the distribution function F or its derivative, the density function f of the running time random variable T, are known. Mostly, this is not the case. There are several possibilities to proceed without knowledge of the exact distribution. Firstly, it is possible to perform computer experiments with various benchmark formulas to figure out a good value of τ. Another approach is similar to methods in statistics. We start out with the hypothesis that the distribution of T follows a certain class of (heavy tail) distributions F_Θ (like the Pareto distribution, the Weibull distribution, the lognormal distribution, or a distribution according to Zipf's law). Such a class of distributions is determined by a (possibly multi-dimensional) parameter Θ. By performing a few tests, a good value for Θ can be determined by the maximum likelihood method. This method looks for such a Θ which minimizes the difference between the theoretical running times according to F_Θ and the observed running times during the experiment. Finally, using F_Θ as a hypothetical distribution function, the optimal choice of τ can be determined by solving the equation $F_\Theta(\tau) = \tau \cdot f_\Theta(\tau)$, as described above.

If no knowledge about the distribution of the running time T is available, then (Luby, Sinclair, Zuckerman, 1993) suggest to use various restart periods, according to the scheme $(1, 1, 2, 1, 1, 2, 4, 1, 1, 2, 1, 1, 2, 4, 8, 1, \ldots)$ (see also Knuth, 2013). It is shown that such a procedure is worse than the optimal restart by at most a logarithmic factor.

Results in (Hartmann, Rieger, 2004, page 170) suggest that a restart point τ being equal (or proportional) to the size of the input, which could mean the number of variables in the case of *SAT*, would yield good results. This is in accordance with the random walk algorithm (chapter 5.4) where a restart is performed after every n steps of a random walk (where n is the number of Boolean variables). Experiments with the ProbSAT algorithm (for 3-*SAT*) described in chapter 5.6 on random formulas near the threshold show a good algorithm behavior when a restart is done after $20n$ random walk steps. In general, it can be observed that various implementations of *SAT* solvers use astonishingly short restart periods.

The considerations of this chapter are not necessarily restricted to probabilistic algorithms. Actually, the motivation for restarts originally came from the DPLL-type algorithms which are deterministic in their basic version. This seems strange at first sight since the repetition of a deterministic algorithm on the same input will lead to exactly the same computation as before. But what makes such restarts indeed expedient is the concept of learning clauses as described with the CDCL extension of DPLL. The learned clauses are kept after a restart so that the course of computation can indeed be different when the algorithm is repeated. The same memorization can take place regarding the f values in the VSIDS heuristic (cf. page 77). Also, inserting a small amount of probabilism, for example when selecting the next branching variable, can be advantageous for the effect of restarts.

Even the algorithm by Paturi-Pudlák-Zane (see chapter 4.3) can be understood as a DPLL-like algorithm that follows just a single (randomly selected) path in the backtracking tree of DPLL, and if it does not find a solution there it does an immediate restart.

On the other hand, we remark that τ should not be chosen too small. Both DPLL-type and local search type algorithms have an initial phase during which it is virtually impossible that a solution can be found: symbolically there is a $\tau_0 > 0$ such that $F(\tau_0) \approx 0$. During this phase data structures need to be initialized, the recursive backtracking tree needs to be built, and so on. Regarding local search as applied to instances of 3-*SAT* having m clauses, after the initial guess of an assignment there will be $m/8$ falsified clauses, on average. After this initial guess usually it happens quite rapidly that there will be just a "handful" of falsified clauses left. Only starting from this moment there is a certain realistic chance that a satisfiying assignment can be found. As a rule, each variable should be "touched" at least once before a restart should be taken into account. That is, as a lower bound, $\tau \geq cn$ should be respected for some constant c.

Especially interesting are algorithms which dynamically adapt the next restart time. This can be done by monitoring some crucial parameters like the number of falsified clauses over the time scale.

For writing this chapter the following papers and book chapters were helpful: (Luby, Sinclair, Zuckerman, 1993), (Gomes, Selman, Crato, Kautz, 2000), (Williams, Gomes, Selman, 2003), (van Moorsel, Wolter, 2004, 2006), chapter 8.3 in (Hartmann, Weigt, 2005), (Wu, 2006), (Schöning, 2007), chapter 9.3 in (Battiti, Brunato, Mascia, 2008), as well as chapter 9 in the handbook (Biere et al., 2009).

9 Final Discussion

We want to give an account of the various methods, ideas and concepts which were used to design and analyze algorithms for $(k\text{-})SAT$.

Probabilism and Determinism Some of the algorithms in this book are probabilistic, i.e. they use random numbers. In some cases it is possible to derandomize such algorithms, which means to stick to the underlying concepts but transform the algorithm into a deterministic one. For example, this was the case with the algorithms that use covering codes (instead of random guessing). In principle, a deterministic algorithm is more desirable than a probabilistic one, especially if it attains the same complexity. A deterministic algorithm does not make mistakes, a probabilistic one might – with arbitrarily small probability. On the other hand, the probabilistic algorithms are very often more elegant, and the derandomized deterministic one is typically much more elaborate.

There are cases when the random approach is unavoidable since it provides much better (average) complexity as compared to deterministic algorithms, for example when comparing a greedy deterministic local search algorithm with a probabilistic one like ProbSAT. Probabilism simply helps to find one's way out of the maze.

Complete and Incomplete SAT-Solvers – under Realistic Conditions On page 87 we discussed the concepts of complete solvers in contrast to incomplete solvers. Complete solvers should always produce a correct answer ("satisfiable" or "unsatisfiable"), at least in principle, within finite time. This is what we have in theory. But in reality, a large or complex input formula might lead to no definite answer within any reasonable amount of time. Let us denote by "?" the fact that the algorithm did not obtain a result within the given time bound. Taking more realistic events into account, the difference between complete and incomplete SAT solvers diminishes. The following figure illustrates the various possibilities:

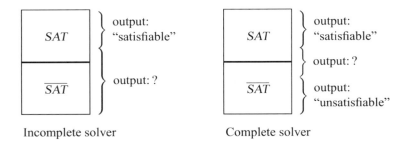

Incomplete solver   Complete solver

Computation Space vs. Time An interesting observation is that in some solver scenarios, a time space trade-off can be noticed. Using more space (i.e. storage), the necessary amount of computation time can be reduced, and vice versa. One can see this, for example, with the BDD based algorithms. Having more computation space available helps the algorithm to solve the problem. A similar effect can be observed with the CDCL type algorithms, which might use a lot of space for the learned clauses. There are also theoretical studies showing time-space trade-offs for some concrete proof systems, like resolution, cf. (Beame, Beck, Impagliazzo, 2012).

Backtracking vs. Random Walk Backtracking follows the philosophy that a decision for setting a variable to 0 or 1 should be done very carefully. If a decision later turns out to be wrong, the correction will be very expensive because variable assignments have to be set back. A lot of the computation up to this point was in vain and has to be repeated (with different assignments). In the case of random walk algorithms, the setting of variables to assignments is unproblematic. If an assignment turns out to be unfavorable, it is simply flipped back. The problem with random walks is located on a different scale: it might get stuck in local (but non-global) optima.

Calculi and Algorithms Calculi can be considered as nondeterministic algorithms and, therefore, they cannot be used immediately for a computation. What is needed is a deterministic strategy that determines the evaluation order and sorts the nondeterministic decisions in some way as efficient as possible. One such possible strategy, applied to resolution calculus, is to prefer short clauses, especially unit clauses, to be parent clauses for resolution. Another example of such a strategy is the Davis-Putnam algorithm.

For some calculi, like resolution, it is possible to prove exponential lower bounds for the proof length, using particular formula instances such as the pigeonhole formulas. Such a lower bound proof holds also for every deterministic strategy when it is based on the resolution calculus.

Meta-Heuristics and Logical Simplifications   The final goal is to find algorithms for *SAT* (and variants of *SAT*) that are more efficient than those currently available. On the one hand, this can be done by applying powerful metaheuristic methods that proved to be useful also for other problems, like local search (cf. Hoos, Stützle, 2005), simulated annealing, backtracking or branch-and-bound. On the other hand, *SAT* has the structure of a logical problem, and admits logical simplifications like unit propagation, or the application of autark assignments. The best algorithms for *SAT* arise when both approaches accompany each other.

Discrete vs. Continuous   Backtracking and random walk algorithms, at each time step in their computations, have an associated concrete assignment (possibly a partial one) which defines their actual status. Therefore, the "states" or "configurations" of such algorithms are discrete.

The "physical" algorithms and the ones with the cross entropy method use continuous values $r_i \in [0, 1]$ for each variable x_i, which express how "likely" it is that the respective variable has to be set to 0 or to 1 in order to reach a satisfying assignment. Such algorithms have the character of algorithms in numerics. Some formula or algorithmic process is iteratively applied until some fixed point is reached. At the end, by using the decimation technique, or randomized rounding, some discrete value from $\{0, 1\}$ is achieved.

Autarkies, Backbones and Backdoors   All these concepts fulfill the task of identifying certain variables which can be assigned in a certain way such that the formula can be simplified – without losing the satisfiability property.

The (partial) autark assignments α, as being used in the Monien-Speckenmeyer algorithm, have the property that applying α sets every clause to true which is "touched" by α. In this case it is a sat-equivalent transformation to move from F to $F\alpha$.

A backbone variable x, together with an appropriate assignment, say $\{x = a\}$, has the property that this partial assignment is part of all (or most) satisfying assignments of the formula F. Again, moving from F to $F\{x = a\}$ is a sat-equivalent transformation which is called variable decimation.

A set of backdoor variables, once identified, has the property that every assignment to these variables results in a simplified formula that belongs to a polynomial-time solvable class of formulas, like Horn formulas (cf. page 63).

Restarts vs. Carry-On   We have argued that restarts can drastically improve the running time behavior of an algorithm whenever a heavy tail distribution is present. Still, this stands in some contrast to the common opinion that it is better to carry on execution, not to give up, and to finish a task that has been begun. Some algorithmic methods, like simulated annealing, stick to this paradigm, and try to get around local minima which cause a computation process to get stuck, and so try to keep on going. Our experiments with concrete algorithms show that it is better to give up at some early stage and to restart the algorithm.

k-SAT vs. SAT   All algorithms in this book benefit from the fact that the input is indeed a k-*SAT* problem, and not a general *SAT* problem. The respective running times are typically shorter as compared to the general case. The theoretical analyses in this book show that there are constants $1 \leq c_3 \leq c_4 \leq c_5 \leq \cdots \leq 2$ such that the running time on k-*SAT* formulas is $O^*((c_k)^n)$. Here n is the number of variables. On the one hand, it is possible to solve the NP-complete problem 3-*SAT* in time $O^*((4/3)^n)$, say. Up to very recently (see (Seto, Tamaki, 2012)), it was not possible to find an algorithm for the general *SAT* problem that has a running time of $O^*(c^n)$, for some $c < 2$.

Random Formulas and Worst Case Formulas   The definition of random formulas was aiming for testing algorithms with respect to their average-case behavior. Accordingly, such algorithms (especially those using local search or the "physical" algorithms) are optimized to have a good running time behavior on such random formulas.

Worst-case formulas, on the other hand, are constructed in such a way that particular algorithms, or classes of algorithms, have a hard time solving them. We considered two types of such worst case formulas in this book: one was the pigeon-hole formula being designed for giving the resolution calculus, and all algorithms being based on resolution, a hard time. The other hard formulas were constructed in chapter 5.7 which make the most trouble for local search type algorithms.

It is interesting to observe that "real life" formulas that occur in practice might neither be random formulas nor worst-case formulas.

Theory and Practice   We have analyzed algorithms, like for 3-*SAT*, that achieve a worst-case running time of order $O^*((4/3)^n)$ and so belong to the best among those algorithms where a worst-case upper bound can be proven. On the other hand, such "theoretical" algorithms will not have a chance on such *SAT*-competitions where these algorithms are tested against certain formulas stemming from industrial applications, or being randomly generated. Those algorithms equipped with a lot of heuristics, like CDCL for industrial formulas, or ProbSAT for random formulas, when all critical parameters are optimally tuned, will be among the winners. These algorithms are like sophisticated racing cars. But typically we do not have theoretical analyses for such algorithms.

Both approaches and viewpoints on *SAT* algorithms have their utility, the theoretical one and the practical one. In fact, it is remarkable that, particularly in this research field, both communities profit from each other. Practitioners profit from new theoretical insights and constructions, and theoreticians can find new challenges by analyzing new heuristics invented for practice.

Appendix: Programming in Pseudo Code

Programs in this book are denoted in *pseudo code*, which allows expressing the behavior of an algorithm in a compact way, more or less independent of a particular programming language. Pseudo code has a certain resemblance with some traditional imperative languages like PASCAL or MODULA-2. In addition to the formal programming constructs (as described below) pseudo code allows commands expressed as common English phrases such as: "Choose an arbitrary clause C."

A main component of such an imperative programming language is the *assignment command*, as for example $x := e$, where the program variable x receives a (new) value e where e can be a complex arithmetic expression. It is allowed that e contains x which refers to the former value of x, as in $x := x + 1$. This particular example means that the value of x should be increased by 1.

The occurring program variables can be of different *types*. Our pseudo code programming language provides some standard types, like **bool** for the Boolean values 0 and 1, and **nat** for the natural numbers (including zero). Furthermore, we use some self-explanatory types like **formula**, **clause**, **assignment**. In this book we do not consider the implementation of complex data structures. In fact, the design of appropriate data structures will have a significant impact on the efficiency of the algorithms discussed.

A further simple command is the *test statement*

$$\textbf{if } B \textbf{ then } A \qquad \text{resp.} \qquad \textbf{if } B \textbf{ then } A \textbf{ else } A'$$

Here B is a *condition* (i.e. an expression of type **bool**) and A, A' are commands. If there should be several commands within such an **then**-case or **else**-case then one has to embrace them with **begin** and **end**:

$$\textbf{begin } A_1; A_2; \ldots; A_k \textbf{ end}$$

This principle also holds in the case of the following loop statements supplied in our pseudo code programming language. The *for-loop* has the syntax:

$$\textbf{for } i := a \textbf{ to } b \textbf{ do } A$$

This means that the variable i is initiated with the value a and then takes all values between a and b. Hereby, each time the statement A is executed.

The *while-loop* has the form

$$\textbf{while } B \textbf{ do } A$$

First the condition B is tested. If B is true, then A is executed. Afterwards B is tested again, and if true, A is executed again, and so on, until B fails to be true.

The definition of a *subroutine* (also called *procedure*) is started with the key word **proc**. Then it follows a freely selectable procedure name, followed by a parameter list, enclosed in parentheses.

We distinguish *function procedures* which compute a value (of a certain type which is listed after the parameter list) and give it back into the calling program. The key word **return** is used to jump out from the procedure and return an appropriate value. A call to a function procedure can be used in the calling program like an expression of the respective type.

Example of a function procedure (which delivers a natural number as value, and assumes there are 2 parameters which are natural numbers as well):

> **proc** max (x : **nat**, y : **nat**) : **nat**
> **if** $x > y$ **then return** x
> **return** y

Additionally, there are *command procedures*, which can be used in the calling program like a command.

Example of a command procedure:

> **proc** display (x : **nat**)
> **output** "The result is:", x

As can be seen, sometimes we use also the key words **input** and **output** to indicate a transfer of data into or out of some program.

In this book we write essentially main programs without procedures. Procedures are only used in cases when they are recursive, that is, if they call themselves, as in the following example. Recursive procedures can be much more succinct, comprehensive, and "elegant" than non-recursive ones.

> **proc** factorial (n : **nat**) : **nat**
> **if** $n = 0$ **then return** 1
> **return** ($n *$ factorial ($n - 1$))

Appendix: Graphs

A *graph* is given by a pair $G = (V, E)$, where V is a finite set, the set of *vertices*, and the set E defines the set of *edges*. An edge is represented by its two endpoints from the vertex set. It can be either *directed* or *undirected*. One speaks in the first case about a *directed graph*, and in the second case about an *undirected graph*. Formally, we write $E \subseteq V \times V$ in the case of directed graphs and $E \subseteq \binom{V}{2}$ for undirected graphs, where $\binom{V}{2}$ represents the set of all subsets of V with two elements.

Example: The picture on the left shows the directed graph ($\{a, b, c\}$, $\{(a, b), (b, a), (b, c), (c, c)\}$), while the one on the right shows the undirected graph ($\{a, b, c\}$, $\{\{a, b\}, \{b, c\}\}$).

A sequence of vertices $v_1, v_2, \ldots, v_k$ $(k > 1)$ from a graph G, with the property that for every $i < k$ there is an edge (directed or undirected) between v_i and v_{i+1}, is called a (directed or undirected) *path* in G. If v_1 is equal to v_k, then this path is called a *cycle*.

Let $G = (V, E)$ be an undirected graph. A *k-clique* in G is a subset T of V with k elements such that every two vertices in T are connected by an edge. In succinct terms: $\binom{T}{2} \subseteq E$.

A function $f : V \to \{1, 2, \ldots, k\}$ satisfying $\{x, y\} \in E \Rightarrow f(x) \neq f(y)$ is called a (proper) *k-coloring* of G.

The problem of computing the size of the largest clique in a graph, as well as the problem of finding the smallest number k such that a given graph has a proper k-coloring (the *chromatic number* of the graph), are complex algorithmic questions. The corresponding decision versions are NP-complete.

A graph that is colorable with just two colors is also called *bipartite*. This means that its vertex set can be partitioned into two disjoint sets, a "left set" and a "right set," so that every edge connects a left vertex with a right one (but never a right vertex with a right one or left vertex with a left one).

The concept of *matching* is interesting in the context of bipartite graphs. A matching M is a subset of the edges, $M \subseteq E$, so that every pair of different edges in M has disjoint endpoints. Formally:

$$\{u, v\}, \{x, y\} \in M \land u = x \quad \Rightarrow \quad v = y$$

The following picture shows a bipartite graph, with a left and a right set of vertices. The set of edges is represented by the continuous and discontinuous lines. The continuous lines alone show a matching M. In this example it can be seen that *all* vertices on the left side (with the corresponding edge) are part of the matching. Hall's *marriage theorem* states, that such a matching involving all left vertices exists if and only if for *every* subset T of the left set of vertices the inequality $|T| \leq |N(T)|$ holds. Here $N(T)$ is the set of neighbors of T on the right side.

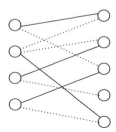

In general, only graphs are considered in which multiple edges between two vertices are not allowed. For some applications, however, it can be advantageous to allow such multiplicity. In these cases the deviation from the "standard definition" is explicitly pointed out. This is, for example, the case with the *series-parallel graphs* considered in Section 1.3. These are directed graphs that have a uniquely determined start vertex x and an end vertex y. In the simplest case the graph consists only of a directed edge from x to y: $G = (\{x, y\}, \{(x, y)\})$. One can construct from a given series-parallel graph G more complicated series-parallel graphs by choosing one of the edges in G and performing one of the following two possible actions that transform G into a new, bigger graph G' respectively G'':

G' is obtained by inserting a second copy of the chosen edge; instead of this edge from G one would have now two parallel edges. G' has the same number of vertices as G, but one more edge. For the construction of G'', the chosen edge, say (u, v), is split in two consecutive edges (connected in series) (u, w) and (w, v) with a new vertex w in between. The new graph G'' then has one more vertex and one more edge than G.

A graph is called series-parallel if it can be constructed by the application of a finite number of the mentioned rules starting from the simplest series-parallel graph (with 2 vertices and one edge).

Appendix: Asymptotic Notation and Recurrences

As it is usual in algorithmics, we express, for those algorithms for which it is possible, the running times in O-notation. Since the O-notation ignores constant factors and low order terms, this has the advantage that one can abstract from concrete implementations and machine models in this way.

One writes $f(n) = O(g(n))$, if there is a constant $c > 0$ so that, for each suitably large natural number n, $f(n) \leq c \cdot g(n)$. The functions f and g are defined on the set of natural numbers and their ranges are also positive numbers (in some cases real numbers).

Example: $5n^3 + 2n^2 + 7n \log n + 11 = O(n^3)$.

Actually, we denote by $O(g(n))$ the *set* of all functions with the properties defined above. According to this, the correct notation should be $f(n) \in O(g(n))$. "Equations" as in the example above can only be understood being read from left to right.

When dealing with *lower* bounds the Ω-notation, dual to the O-notation, is needed. One writes $f(n) = \Omega(g(n))$, if there is a constant $c > 0$ so that, for every natural number n, $f(n) \geq c \cdot g(n)$. We have, therefore, $f(n) = \Omega(g(n))$ if and only if $g(n) = O(f(n))$.

Efficient algorithms are identified as those having a polynomial running time, thus $O(n^k)$, for some constant k. Here n is the length of the input instance, or n is some other relevant parameter that should be polynomially related to the input length. This can be, for example, the number of variables in a formula or the number of vertices in a graph.

Since the satisfiability problem *SAT* is NP-complete (see the corresponding appendix), the running times for the different kinds of *SAT* algorithms are usually given as $O(a^n)$ for a constant $a > 1$. Because an exponential function of this kind grows faster than every polynomial, not only constant factors, but also polynomial factors are not really of interest, at least in this context. Because of this, sometimes we write $f(n) = O^*(a^n)$. This should denote that there is a polynomial $p(n)$ with $f(n) \leq p(n) \cdot a^n$.

Considered as sets of functions, we have, for every $\varepsilon > 0$, the following strict inclusion hierarchy:

$$O(a^n) \subsetneq O^*(a^n) \subsetneq O((a + \varepsilon)^n)$$

Many of the algorithms in this book are formulated recursively. Certain parameters (usually the number of variables) decrease at least by 1 with every recursive call. The recursion finishes on the first invocation when this value is equal to 0. We obtain in this way, for example, estimations of the kind

$$T(n) \leq T(n-2) + 2 \cdot T(n-3)$$

This expression means that a procedure call with parameter n produces (or can produce) another recursive call with parameter $n-2$, plus two further calls with parameter $n-3$. The function T gives the number of leaves in the corresponding recursion tree, and it is polynomially related to the computational cost. This means that the computation time can be estimated to be $O^*(T(n))$. The value of the function is obtained analyzing the recursion $T(n) = T(n-2) + 2 \cdot T(n-3)$ (to remain at the same example). We achieve the solution as $T(n) = a^n$ for some constant $a > 1$. To this end, the equation $a^n = a^{n-2} + 2 \cdot a^{n-3}$ is analyzed, and after dividing by a^{n-3}, the so called characteristic equation $a^3 = a + 2$ is obtained. Its solution is a constant $a \le 1.5214$. The running time of the corresponding algorithm (in this example) is $O^*(1.5214^n)$.

Appendix: Efficient Algorithms, P and NP

In the theory of the complexity classes P and NP and in the theory of NP-completeness, the concept of "efficiently computable" is usually identified with the notion of *computable within polynomial running time*. The estimation of the running time is a worst-case estimation and must consider the most difficult input of length n (respectively, the hardest formula with n variables). For this, one has to define first a computation model, like the Turing machine or the register machine (together with the corresponding "programming language"), and one should also formalize the concept of "computation step" in this model. The number of computation steps executed by such an algorithm is then the *running time*. *Polynomial running time* (or polynomial computation time) means that the number of computation steps, relative to the input length n (thus, for *every* input of length n) is a function of type $O(n^k)$ for some constant k.

In computability theory, "Church's thesis" states that all "reasonable" computation models are equivalent to each other – and therefore are equivalent to the computability concept defined by Turing machines. In this way, the intuitive concept of computability is adequately formulated in terms of (for example) Turing computability.

The "extended Church's thesis" is the corresponding statement for the concept of polynomial time (efficient) computability. All reasonable concepts of computability (meaning by this the different machine models as well as their programming languages) with their corresponding concept of running time lead to the same class of efficiently computable (namely in polynomial time) algorithmic problems. The class of problems with this robust definition is called P. In other words, an algorithmic problem belongs to the class P if there is an algorithm (formulated here generally in pseudo code) solving the problem so that, for some constant k, every input of length n can be computed within running time $O(n^k)$.

Since every exponential function of the form c^n, $c > 1$, for large enough n, is at some point bigger than every polynomial n^k, algorithms with exponential running time are (under the definition given here) not considered to be efficient, in theory. There is, of course, some criticism to this simplistic division of the algorithmic world in "good" and "bad" algorithms (more about this idea on page 15). On the one hand, the constant k can be very large, while the constant c can be very small (very close to 1), so that the input length where the exponential function starts to grow larger than the polynomial function lies out of the range of any practical relevance. In this case, the exponential algorithm is faster for all the relevant inputs.

On the other hand, one should think that everything being said about running times has to do with the worst-case. On "average," that is, considering randomly chosen inputs (average-case), even the running times of the (worst-case) exponential algorithms can, in fact, be acceptable. A further consideration is that the "practically relevant" inputs do not need to correspond either with the worse-case nor with the average-case.

We come now to the class NP. The classification of algorithmic problems in NP makes sense only for the so called *decision problems*. These are algorithmic questions admitting only a "yes" or "no" answer (respectively 1 or 0). The most important example for this book is the satisfiability problem: on input a Boolean formula F, output 1 if F is satisfiable, and 0 otherwise.

Such a decision problem can be identified with the set of inputs for which the correct output is 1. In our example, this is the set *SAT*.

Definition

A decision problem L belongs to the class NP if there is an efficient algorithm A that receives together with the normal input x a second input y, and for some polynomial p and every input string x fulfills the following property:

- If $x \notin L$, then algorithm A, on input x and *any* second input y produces always the output 0.

- If $x \in L$, then *there is* a second input y of length at most $p(n)$, where n is the length of x, so that A with this input combination outputs 1.

Implicit in the second input (more concretely, in the right selection for it in the case $x \in L$) is the concept of *nondeterminism*: naming this class NP denotes nondeterministic polynomial time. Informally, one says that on input x one "guesses" a second input y and then, with algorithm A, one tests that x and y match, or more formally, that y is a "witness" for the fact that x belongs to L. In view of this, one can also say that NP is the class of decision problems for which the (proposed) solutions can be checked in polynomial time.

SAT satisfies this definition and is located in NP, since by considering a (potentially) satisfying assignment α as the second input, together with the standard input F, the algorithm A can check in polynomial time whether it is true that $F\alpha = 1$, and output 1 if this holds. Moreover, the description of an assignment requires only n bits, where $n = |Var(F)|$. This shows that the length of the second input is linear in the size of the formula $|F|$.

It follows directly from the definitions that $P \subseteq NP$. The big open question is whether $P = NP$, or $P \neq NP$ (this is the P-NP problem).

Since no polynomial time algorithm has yet been found for many problems in NP, including *SAT*, it is commonly suspected that $P \neq NP$.

The definition of the class NP is asymmetric with respect to $x \in L$ and $x \notin L$. One does not expect that the class NP is closed under complementation. It is not clear how one should use the fact $L \in NP$ for some decision problem L in order to show $\overline{L} \in NP$. One conjectures, therefore, that NP and co-NP $:= \{L \mid \overline{L} \in NP\}$ are incomparable sets as shown in the following diagram. Observe that P is obviously closed under complementation, therefore $P \subseteq NP \cap co\text{-}NP$.

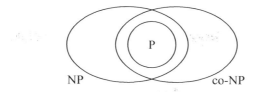

It is also open whether $P = NP \cap co\text{-}NP$ or not. One conjectures that these classes are different (from this result, $P \neq NP$ would follow). But, in principle, it could happen that $P = NP \cap co\text{-}NP$ and at the same time $P \neq NP$ and $NP \neq co\text{-}NP$. This last situation would mirror the situation in computability theory, considering the class of recursive sets instead of P, and the class of recursively enumerable sets instead of NP.

The definition of the class NP is only suitable for decision problems. From the algorithmic point of view, however, we are more interested in methods that output a satisfying assignment (provided the input formula is a satisfiable formula). This can be called the *construction problem*. The decision problem *SAT* has the *self-reducibility* property, which means that the question of whether $F \in SAT$ can be reduced to easier questions, namely whether $F\{x = 0\} \in SAT$ or $F\{x = 1\} \in SAT$, meaning "easier" in the sense that both $F\{x = 0\}$ and $F\{x = 1\}$ have fewer variables than F. An algorithm A for the decision problem *SAT* with running time $t(n)$ can be used for solving the construction problem in the following way: if the algorithm A confirms that $F \in SAT$, one can run A on the input $F\{x = 0\}$, for some variable $x \in Var(F)$; if $F\{x = 0\} \in SAT$, one assigns x value $a = 0$, and value $a = 1$ otherwise. One continues in the same way, running algorithm A on the input $F\{x = a, y = 0\}$, in order to find out the assignment of the next variable y, and so on. This means, in this way an algorithm for the construction problem can be designed with running time $O(n \cdot t(n)) = O^*(t(n))$.

The problems in the class NP are often strongly related to corresponding *optimization problems*. In the case of *SAT*, the corresponding optimization problem is called *MaxSAT*. In this case, the maximum number of clauses of an input *CNF* formula that can be simultaneously satisfied is computed. From a solution $z \in \mathbb{N}$ for the *MaxSAT* problem one can easily obtain a solution for the decision problem *SAT* since F is satisfiable if and only if $z = |F|$, that is, when z is the number of clauses in F. With some more effort one can also get a connection in the other direction. The problem

$$SAT' = \{(F, r) \mid \text{there is an assignment satisfying at least } r \text{ clauses in } F\}$$

is in the class NP, and it is therefore reducible to *SAT* (see the appendix on the NP-completeness of *SAT*). Let m be the number of clauses in F. With $O(\log m)$ many queries of the form $(F, r) \in SAT'$, $1 \leq r \leq m$, translated into the corresponding queries to *SAT* after the reduction $SAT' \preceq SAT$, one can obtain, with the help of binary search, the maximal k for which $(F, k) \in SAT'$ is true.

If $t(n)$ is the running time of a decision algorithm for *SAT*, one can then solve *MaxSAT* in time $O(\log(m) \cdot t(p(n))) = O^*(t(p(n)))$, for some polynomial $p(n)$. Here p corresponds to the running time, and lengthening, needed in the reduction from *SAT'* to *SAT*.

A difference between the decision problem *SAT* and the optimization problem *MaxSAT* is that one can try to efficiently *approximate* the second up to a certain factor, that is, one just tries to obtain a solution that is close to the optimal one, while the decision problem only admits a yes-no answer. One speaks in this case about an *exact problem*, respectively, about an *exact algorithm*. In the terminology from page 87 one could also say that an exact algorithm for *SAT* is the same as a *complete SAT* solver.

In the case of *MaxSAT* it is possible to approximate the maximum number of satisfiable clauses up to a constant factor (denoted by *MaxSAT* $\in$ APX). For example, for every assignment α we have that either α or $\overline{\alpha}$ (that is, all assignments inverted) satisfies at least half of all clauses. On the other hand, assuming $P \neq NP$, there is a constant $\varepsilon > 0$, such that no polynomial-time approximation algorithm is able to find an assignment that satisfies at least a fraction of $1 - \varepsilon$ of the maximal number of satisfiable clauses (denoted *MaxSAT* $\notin$ PTAS). This is a consequence of the celebrated PCP theorem. For an overview of this field see (Mayr, Prömel, Steger, 1998).

Appendix: Probabilistic Algorithms and the Class RP

We describe in this book probabilistic algorithms of several kinds. These are algorithms that use random numbers during their execution or, stated differently, take some of their decisions randomly. Examples for these decisions are: the random choice of an initial assignment, or the random choice of the next variable to flip within a zero clause, as it is done in some algorithms based on local search, or the choice or a random variable sequence, as it is done in the Paturi-Pudlák-Zane algorithm, and the decisions taken in the algorithmic principle of randomized rounding.

The use of randomness in a computation causes that both the computation time, even for a single concrete input, as well as the outcome of the algorithm, become random variables.

In some probabilistic algorithms it is possible to calculate the "success" probability (for example the probability of finding a satisfying assignment when the input formula is satisfiable), or at least to bound this probability from below. Let $\beta = \beta(n)$ be this probability for inputs of length n (respectively, for formulas with n variables). For example, in Sections 4.3, 5.2 and 5.4 such probabilities are estimated. The expectation for the number of times the algorithm has to be repeated in order to get a solution can be calculated as

$$\sum_{i=1}^{\infty} i \cdot (1 - \beta)^{i-1} \cdot \beta = \frac{1}{\beta}.$$

Repeating the algorithm *exactly* $\frac{1}{\beta}$ times does not provide sufficiently high confidence that a solution will be found, if one exists. For this we must spend an additional constant factor of repetitions as follows: Let t be the number of intended repetitions. The probability of not finding any solution even after t repetitions is $(1 - \beta)^t \leq e^{-t\beta}$. Let us suppose that for some constant $c > 0$, e^{-c} is an acceptable, tolerated error probability, that we would like to achieve. By setting $e^{-t\beta} = e^{-c}$, we obtain an equation on t with the solution $t = c \cdot \frac{1}{\beta}$.

This means that for a given success probability $\beta(n)$ we obtain an overall running time $O(l(n) \cdot \frac{1}{\beta(n)})$ for the algorithm to reach the error probability e^{-c}. The constant c is hidden here in the O-notation, and $l(n)$ is the running time for a single iteration of the algorithm.

The outcome of the algorithm (considered as a random variable) shows then the following behavior:

$$\boxed{\text{input formula is satisfiable}} \quad \longrightarrow \quad \boxed{\text{output: satisfying assignment found}}$$

$$\boxed{\text{input formula is unsatisfiable}} \quad \longrightarrow \quad \boxed{\text{output: no satisfying assignment found}}$$

The diagonal arrow pointing down to the right describes the possibility of making a mistake. One should notice that there is no possible transition from the lower box on the left to the upper box on the right. One speaks in this case of a randomized algorithm with *one-sided error*. This situation happens very often in probabilistic algorithms. This has to do with the fact that the claim of having found a satisfying assignment can be easily verified by applying it to the input formula. In this way, one can avoid declaring an unsatisfiable formula as "satisfiable." This one-sided verification possibility applies to every problem in NP.

The class of all problems that can be efficiently solved by probabilistic algorithms with one-sided error is denoted RP (random polynomial time).

Definition

A decision problem L lies in RP if there is a randomized algorithm producing the outputs 1 or 0, with the following behavior:

$$\boxed{\text{input } x \in L} \quad \rightarrow \quad \boxed{\text{output: } 1}$$
$$\searrow$$
$$\boxed{\text{input } x \notin L} \quad \rightarrow \quad \boxed{\text{output: } 0}$$

The probability of an erroneous output 0 on an input $x \in L$ is at most ε. The value of ε should be a constant (thus independent from x and n) with $\varepsilon \in [0, 1)$, otherwise at most a dependence of the form $1 - \varepsilon = \frac{1}{p(n)}$, for some polynomial p, is allowed. Moreover, the running time of the algorithm on any input of length n and for every choice of the random numbers in the execution of the algorithm must be bounded by a polynomial in n.

The definition of the class RP can be seen as a special case of the definition of NP where the additional second input y, with $|y| = p(n)$, is taken as a uniformly distributed random string (letting n be the length of the main input x). In the case of $x \in L$, the probability of hereby obtaining the correct output 1 should be at least $1 - \varepsilon$. Therefore, it holds that $P \subseteq RP \subseteq NP$.

In many cases, randomized algorithms are easier to design and to implement than their deterministic counterparts, and sometimes it is also possible to analyze their running times (as we just described, this boils down to an estimation of the error probability). Nevertheless, a deterministic algorithm is somehow preferable to a randomized one because it does not allow the possibility of an error. In some cases, it is possible to transform a probabilistic algorithm into a deterministic one based on the same underlying ideas. In this case, one speaks of a *derandomization* of the corresponding randomized algorithm. In this book there are several examples of this, like the use of covering codes in order to avoid the use of randomly chosen initial assignments (see sections 5.3 and 5.5).

Appendix: Boolean Circuits

Boolean circuits provide a compact way to represent Boolean functions, and have considerable practical relevance since such circuits can really be "built." First, one has to fix the building blocks (also called gates) that are allowed in such a combinatorial circuit. These are usually the elements of the "standard basis" $\{\wedge, \vee, \neg\}$, formed by the gates with two inputs and one output computing the *and* and *or* functions, together with the gate with one input and one output computing the *negation* function:

Other representations for these gates are sometimes used. One can connect gates from this set in order to construct circuits, whose inputs we represent by $x_1, x_2, \ldots$. There is also at least one output in the circuit (denoted here by y).

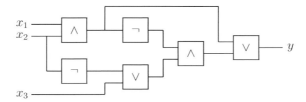

One can describe formally such a circuit using a directed graph, with some vertices labeled with the variable names x_i, representing the inputs, and in which every internal node is labeled with a Boolean function. The number of edges pointing to a vertex must coincide with the arity of the corresponding Boolean function. This graph is acyclic, which means that it does not contain any cycle. In the diagram shown above, one should understand the direction of the edges pointing from left to right.

The Boolean function corresponding to any vertex in the circuit can be inductively defined, starting from the input vertices, and applying, for each internal vertex, the function labelling it to the Boolean functions defined by its predecessor vertices.

Such a Boolean circuit is different from a Boolean formula because, in the circuit case, the out-degree of a gate can be greater than 1. This means that the function computed in a vertex can be used again in other places in the circuit. A formula, by contrast, would correspond to a circuit in which every gate has out-degree 1. In this case, the circuit has a tree structure. There are explicit families of Boolean functions for which the shortest formula representation is exponentially larger than the representation as a Boolean circuit.

Definition

A decision problem $L \subseteq \{0,1\}^*$ has *polynomial circuit complexity* if there is an infinite sequence of circuits $(S_1, S_2, S_3, \ldots)$ (one for each length) and a polynomial p so that circuit S_n has size at most $p(n)$. The circuit S_n has the inputs $x_1, \ldots, x_n$ and represents (or computes) the decision problem L, restricted to inputs of length n. This means that for all $a_1 a_2 \ldots a_n \in \{0,1\}^n$ we have:

$$S_n(a_1, a_2, \ldots, a_n) = 1 \quad \text{if and only if} \quad a_1 a_2 \ldots a_n \in L$$

The construction in the appendix on the NP-completeness of *SAT* shows as a byproduct that every problem in P has polynomial circuit complexity. This result is true in fact also for the class RP. This can be seen as follows. Given a decision problem $L \in$ RP, it is possible to reduce the error probability to strictly less than 2^{-n}, where n is the input length. Then there must exist a string y, used as random bits in the probabilistic algorithm, or as additional second input according to the comment following the definition of RP (on page 154), such that with this y, the outcome of *all* computations on inputs x of length n will be correct (since there are 2^n inputs). As in the NP-completeness proof of *SAT* (see appendix) polynomial-size circuits can be constructed for L where for each input length n the appropriate additional y-input is "hardwired" in the circuit.

On the other hand, one conjectures that not all the problems in NP have polynomial size circuits. This conjecture is based on evidence almost as strong as the P $\neq$ NP conjecture (see Karp, Lipton, 1980). The following picture shows the (conjectured) inclusion structure of these classes (where P/poly is the notion used in the literature for polynomial circuit complexity).

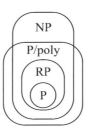

The NP-complete problems, like *SAT*, are in NP, but are (conjectured to be) out of P/poly. Even the conjecture that not all problems in NP $\cap$ co-NP have polynomial size circuits seems to be plausible.

We have mentioned the "standard basis" $\{\wedge, \vee, \neg\}$, which is sufficient for the representation of *every* Boolean function. One speaks in this case about a *complete* basis. A way to see this fact is by noticing that every Boolean function can be represented in *CNF*, and the *CNF* representation uses only operations from the set $\{\wedge, \vee, \neg\}$. One should observe that the constants 0 and 1 can be used "for free" and generally are not considered to be part of a basis. In fact, is $\{\wedge, \neg\}$ respectively $\{\vee, \neg\}$ already a complete basis since the missing operation in each case can be expressed by the other two operations using the deMorgan rules:

$$
\begin{aligned}
x \vee y &= \neg(\neg x \wedge \neg y) \\
x \wedge y &= \neg(\neg x \vee \neg y)
\end{aligned}
$$

Another complete basis is $\{\oplus, \wedge\}$. The representation of a Boolean function (as a sum of products) in this basis is also called *ring sum expansion*. A further complete basis is $\{sel\}$. The *sel* function (for selection, sometimes also called *ite* function, for if-then-else, or *mux* function for multiplex) is defined in the following way: $sel(1, y, z) = y$ and $sel(0, y, z) = z$. By using the constants 0 and 1, the basic Boolean functions can be expressed:

$$
\begin{aligned}
\neg x &= sel(x, 0, 1) \\
x \wedge y &= sel(x, y, 0) \\
x \vee y &= sel(x, 1, y)
\end{aligned}
$$

The function *sel* is used for the so called *Shannon expansion*. Every Boolean function $f : \{0, 1\}^n \to \{0, 1\}$ can be represented as:

$$
f(x_1, x_2, \ldots, x_n) = sel(x_1, f(1, x_2, \ldots, x_n), f(0, x_2, \ldots, x_n))
$$

One can compute f in this way, using $2^n - 1$ *sel* gates.

Further results on Boolean circuits can be found in the books (Clote, Kranakis, 2002), (Jukna, 2012), (Vollmer, 1999) and (Wegener, 1987).

Appendix: SAT is NP-complete

We show that *SAT* belongs to the hardest problems within the class NP. In order to compare the complexity of different problems, we use the concept of reducibility. Given two decision problems, A and B, we say that A is *reducible* to B (in symbols: $A \preceq B$) if there is a polynomial time computable function f, transforming every possible input x for A into an input $f(x)$ for B, with the property:

$$x \in A \quad \text{if and only if} \quad f(x) \in B.$$

We call function f a *transformation* or *reduction* between the given problems.

If there is an efficient algorithm for problem B, then there is also an efficient algorithm for problem A. This algorithm can be described in the following way: on input x, compute first $f(x)$ and use then the algorithm for B on $f(x)$. Based on this observation, problem A cannot be "harder" than problem B. The relation between decision problems defined by the reduction concept is transitive since the composition of two reductions is again a reduction (thus, if $A \preceq B$ and $B \preceq C$, then $A \preceq C$).

One says that a problem L is *NP-complete* if L is in NP and, moreover, every problem L' in the class NP is reducible to L in the way defined above, $L' \preceq L$. In the appendix on P and NP it is shown that *SAT* belongs to NP. We show now that every problem in the class NP is reducible to *SAT*. This proves that *SAT* belongs to the hardest problems within NP. This important result was proved independently by (Cook, 1971) and (Levin, 1973).

The status of the NP-complete problems is closely related to the P-NP question since:

Observation

For every NP-complete problem L,

$$L \in \text{P} \quad \text{if and only if} \quad \text{P} = \text{NP}.$$

Proof: If P = NP, then since $L \in$ NP, it follows that $L \in$ P.

In the other direction, if $L \in$ P, and L' is any problem in NP, then, because of the NP-completeness of L, it follows that $L' \preceq L$. We can conclude from this that $L' \in$ P, thus P = NP. $\qquad\square$

We give now a proof for the NP-completeness of *SAT* in two steps. First, we show that every problem L in NP is reducible to the decision problem *CIRCUIT-SAT*. In a second step we reduce *CIRCUIT-SAT* to *SAT*. We have in fact already shown this second reduction in Section 1.3 (Page 21). The composition of both reductions transforms L to *SAT* (actually, even to 3-*SAT*).

The problem *CIRCUIT-SAT* is defined in the following way: given a Boolean circuit over the standard basis $\{\vee, \wedge, \neg\}$ with exactly one output gate, is there a $0, 1$ assignment for the circuit inputs producing a 1 at the output gate of the circuit?

Theorem

Every problem L in the class NP is reducible to *CIRCUIT-SAT*.

Proof: In order to prove the result we must fix some concrete, formal computation model for the problems in NP. Without wanting to go too much into detail, let us consider the Turing machine model, see for example (Garey, Johnson, 1979) or (Wegener, 2005), and let us concentrate on the aspects that are important for the reduction. A Turing machine computation can be described as a sequence of configurations (instant descriptions). For a Turing machine with one work tape (with read-write head) a configuration consists of a sequence of symbols (from a finite alphabet) specifying the symbols written on the tape, the state of the machine (from a finite set of states), and the position of the head on the tape. For every polynomial time Turing machine, one can fix an alphabet Δ so that every possible configuration on an input of size n can be written as a word of $p(n)$ symbols over Δ, for some polynomial p. At any moment during the computation, the successor configuration differs from its predecessor configuration in at most 2 positions, namely in the positions of the read-write head, and in one of the positions left or right from it. The changes from one configuration to the next one are, therefore, very local. Because of this fact, one can define a function $g : \Delta^3 \to \Delta$, computing a symbol in the successor configuration from the corresponding symbol and its left and right neighbor in the preceding configuration. The inputs for the function g can be encoded as a sequence of bits so that the (binary encoding of) function g can be computed by a finite Boolean circuit.

At the beginning of a computation for an input x of a problem L (and an additional input y according to the definition of NP) there is a binary encoding of x and y written on the machine tape. The machine is at this point in its initial state and the read-write head is on the first symbol of x. These are the contents of the initial configuration. In the course of the computation the configuration changes step by step in the way described above.

We construct now, for every input x for L, a Boolean circuit S_x, built basically from g-gates, simulating the computation of the Turing machine on input x and y. One should observe that the bits from x are hardwired in the circuit while the y inputs are real circuit inputs. The output of S_x on an input y corresponds to the output of the Turing machine on inputs x and y.

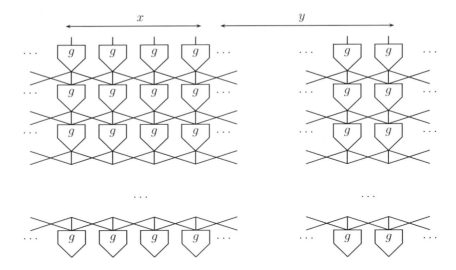

The circuit contains polynomially many levels of gates computing function g (computing in this way the transitions in the configurations). From the outputs in the last level, further connections can be constructed, producing a single output indicating whether the output of the Turing machine is 1.

The complete circuit S_x has $O(p^2(|x|))$ many gates and we have $x \in L$ if and only if there is a y with $S_x(y) = 1$. In other words, the function transforming x to S_x is a polynomial time computable reduction from L to *CIRCUIT-SAT*. $\square$

From this result, together with the results in Section 1.3 where a polynomial transformation from *CIRCUIT-SAT* to *3-SAT* was presented, it follows that *SAT* as well as also *k-SAT*, for $k \geq 3$, are NP-complete.

Appendix: Branching Programs and Binary Decision Diagrams

A *branching program* is a representation for Boolean functions, whose size is located between Boolean circuit size and Boolean formula size (over the standard basis $\{\wedge, \vee, \neg\}$). (Originally, an alternative name for branching program is *binary decision diagram*, or BDD, for short.) But nowadays the term BDD is used solely for a special case, which is discussed below, namely branching programs which are reduced and obey some variable order (see Knuth, 2011).

The above introductory sentence means that a branching program can be transformed without much effort into a circuit computing the same function while from a Boolean formula, one can construct the corresponding branching program (but this does not necessarily hold in the other direction).

A branching program is a directed, acyclic graph with exactly one input vertex and (at most) two output vertices. The output vertices are labeled with 0 and 1. We call these the 0-vertex and the 1-vertex (or 0-endnode and 1-endnode). All other vertices (the inner vertices and the input vertex) are labeled with variable names x_i and have out-degree exactly two, labeled with $x_i = 0$ and $x_i = 1$ (or shorter: with 0 and with 1). A branching program "computes" a Boolean function in the obvious way: applied to an assignment α of the variables appearing in the branching program, say $\alpha = \{x_1 = a_1, \ldots, x_n = a_n\}$, starting at the input vertex, one runs through a uniquely determined path in the graph by following the labels of the edges according to α. One arrives in this way either to the 0-vertex or to the 1-vertex in the output. This vertex determines the value of the function f represented by the branching program on α (namely $f(\alpha) \in \{0, 1\}$).

Example: The following is a branching program for the parity function on 4 inputs: $f(x_1, x_2, x_3, x_4) = 1$ if and only if an odd number of the x_i's has value 1.

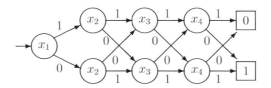

Let us suppose that a Boolean function $f : \{0, 1\}^n \to \{0, 1\}$ is given (or computed) by a branching program on the variables $x_1, \ldots, x_n$. One could wrongly assume at first sight that it is possible to decide the satisfiability of f, solving the corresponding *SAT* problem, by testing whether there is a path from the input vertex to the 1-endnode. This is wrong since it also has to be tested as to whether this path is consistent. It cannot be the case that one edge on the path is labeled with $x_i = 1$ while another edge on the path is labeled with $x_i = 0$. In fact, the satisfiability problem for branching prgrams, in general, is NP-complete as in the cases for formulas or for circuits.

This can be easily seen with a reduction from 3-*SAT* to the satisfiability problem for branching programs. First, consider a single clause $(x \vee y \vee z)$ in the given formula. This clause can be equivalently represented by the following branching program:

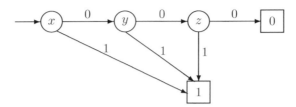

Instead of including the 1-vertex at this point, one can connect the edges pointing to it in the figure with the input vertex of other branching programs for the rest of the clauses. In this way one constructs a branching program representing the function of the formula in which, in general, several queries for the same variable can happen on a single path. This shows that 3-*SAT* $\preceq$ satisfiability for branching programs.

The situation is different when on every path from the input vertex to an endnode each variable can be queried at most once. This kind of branching program is called a 1-branching program. Indeed, in this case, one can easily test the satisfiability of the represented Boolean function by checking whether there is a path from the input vertex to the 1-endnode.

A special subclass of the 1-branching programs is formed by the so called BDD's (cf. the remark about denotation in the beginning of this appendix). In a BDD the variables are ordered according to some permutation π so that they are queried in the order given by the permutation. More formally, for a BDD it must hold that there is a permutation π defined on the set of variable indices $\{1, 2, \dots, n\}$, $\pi \in S_n$, so that, in every path starting at the input vertex, the ordering defined by the permutation, namely $x_{\pi(1)}, x_{\pi(2)}, \dots, x_{\pi(n)}$, is kept (it can happen that some variables do not appear in the path). That is, when x_i and x_j are two subsequent variable labelings in such a path, then it must hold that $\pi^{-1}(i) < \pi^{-1}(j)$. For example, the branching program given above for the parity function is a BDD. Additionally, we require that a BDD is *reduced* (see below).

BDD's strongly resemble finite automata. With every query of a variable bit (this corresponds to reading a symbol from the input word in a finite automaton) one obtains a transition between states. On the other hand, contrary to finite automata, BDD's (and branching programs, in general) do not have any loops (the corresponding graph is acyclic). Also, similar to the automata case (even easier), BDD's can be minimized (or "reduced") to a unique minimal BDD, this is what we actually call a BDD. For this, one starts from "behind", namely the output vertices, and moves to the input vertex applying the following two simplification (or reduction) rules, called *elimination rule* and *merging rule*, whenever possible:

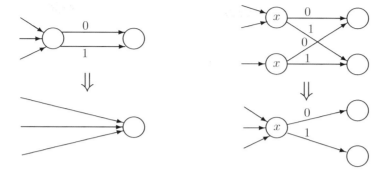

Apart from the fact, that for BDD's the satisfiability problem can be decided trivially, there are other operations that can be done efficiently in this model, like the *synthesis operation*. Given two BDD's representing the Boolean functions f and g, it is possible to construct efficiently a BDD for the function $f \circ g$. Here $\circ$ can be any Boolean function on two inputs. The size of the obtained BDD is at most the product of the sizes of the two input BDD's. The construction is similar to the product construction for finite automata, used to build (for example) an automaton for the intersection of the two accepted languages. In many cases it is even so that after applying the above given minimization rules the resulting BDD is not much larger than the initial BDD's. In Section 6.3 this construction, for the example of the AND function, is presented.

More information on branching programs, in general, and BDD's, in particular, can be found in (Wegener, 2000) and (Knuth, 2011).

Appendix: Random Variables

A *random variable* X (usually written in capital letters) is a variable whose value is determined by the outcome of a random experiment. We restrict ourselves here to random variables with a finite (or countable) range $x_1, \ldots, x_n \in \mathbb{R}$, $n \in \mathbb{N} \cup \{\infty\}$. There is a probability p_i associated with each of these values x_i, fulfilling $\sum_{i=1}^{n} p_i = 1$. We state this situation in shorthand as:

$$X \sim \begin{pmatrix} x_1 & x_2 & \ldots & x_n \\ p_1 & p_2 & \ldots & p_n \end{pmatrix}$$

The specification on the right side is called a *probability distribution*. One writes also $P(X = x_i) = p_i$ to describe the fact that X takes value x_i with probability p_i.

One can also "compute" with random variables and use them in formulas. For example, $Y = f(X)$ is a new random variable, taking values in the set $\{f(x_i) \mid i \in \{1, \ldots, n\}\}$. Then, variable Y takes value y in this set with probability

$$P(Y = y) = \sum_{i \,:\, f(x_i) = y} p_i.$$

In some applications the range of f is the two element set $\{0, 1\}$. That is, for some set M,

$$f(X) = \begin{cases} 1, & X \in M, \\ 0, & \text{otherwise.} \end{cases}$$

When the random variable X we are dealing with is clear from the context then, instead of $P(f(X) = 1)$ or $P(X \in M)$, we only write $P(M)$. When the set M is defined by some property E then we write also $P(E)$.

Some probabilistic distributions occur so often that they have their own name, for example, the *uniform distribution* on a given finite set $A = \{a_1, a_2, \ldots, a_n\}$:

$$U(A) := \begin{pmatrix} a_1 & a_2 & \ldots & a_n \\ \frac{1}{n} & \frac{1}{n} & \ldots & \frac{1}{n} \end{pmatrix}$$

A random variable X representing the result of the throw of a die can be denoted as $X \sim U(\{1, 2, 3, 4, 5, 6\})$, or $X \sim U(\{\,\boxdot, \boxdot, \boxdot, \boxdot, \boxdot, \boxdot\,\})$. When one speaks of *randomly* choosing an element from a set A, without further specification, then the uniform distribution $U(A)$ is meant.

In a *binomial distribution* with parameters n and p, the random variable can take integer values between 0 and n. The distribution is based on the following random process: a single experiment that "succeeds" with probability p and does "not succeed" with probability $1 - p$ (this is called a *Bernoulli trial*) is repeated n times. The binomial distribution assigns to the number j the probability q_j that exactly j out of the n Bernoulli trials are successful. We have:

$$Bin(n, p) := \begin{pmatrix} 0 & 1 & \ldots & n \\ q_0 & q_1 & \ldots & q_n \end{pmatrix} \quad \text{with} \quad q_j = \binom{n}{j} p^j (1 - p)^{n-j}$$

Example: Success in a Bernoulli trial could mean that, in an execution of a probabilistic algorithm, a satisfying assignment for a given formula is found. If p is the success probability in this case, and n the number of repetitions of the algorithm, then the probability that in none of the trials a satisfying assignment is found is:

$$P(X = 0) = \binom{n}{0} p^0 (1-p)^{n-0} = (1-p)^n \leq e^{-pn}$$

If one wants to keep this probability below a certain threshold e^{-c}, for some constant c, then the number of repetitions of the algorithm has to be selected as $n \geq \frac{c}{p}$ (this brings an $O(\frac{1}{p})$ factor to the running time of the algorithm).

The *expectation operator* $\mathbb{E}$, applied to a random variable, indicates its "average" value. Written in a formula:

$$X \sim \begin{pmatrix} x_1 & x_2 & \cdots & x_n \\ p_1 & p_2 & \cdots & p_n \end{pmatrix} \quad \Rightarrow \quad \mathbb{E}(X) := \sum_{i=1}^{n} p_i \cdot x_i$$

For the uniform distribution, we have

$$X \sim U(\{1, 2, \ldots, n\}) \quad \Rightarrow \quad \mathbb{E}(X) = \sum_{i=1}^{n} \frac{1}{n} \cdot i = \frac{n+1}{2}$$

and for the binomial distribution,

$$X \sim Bin(n, p) \quad \Rightarrow \quad \mathbb{E}(X) = p \cdot n$$

If f is a linear (affine) function of random variables $X_1, \ldots, X_k$, thus

$$f(X_1, \ldots, X_k) = a_1 \cdot X_1 + \cdots + a_k \cdot X_k + b$$

then, by of the *linearity of the expectation operator*, we have

$$\mathbb{E}(f(X)) = a_1 \cdot \mathbb{E}(X_1) + \cdots + a_k \cdot \mathbb{E}(X_k) + b$$

For a non-linear function f this is, in general, not true. We can estimate some concrete cases, as for example, $\mathbb{E}(2^X) \geq 2^{\mathbb{E}(X)}$, which is a special case of the *Jensen inequality*. More generally, we have $\mathbb{E}(g(X)) \geq g(\mathbb{E}(X))$ for every *convex* function g, and $\mathbb{E}(g(X)) \leq g(\mathbb{E}(X))$ for every *concave* function g. For example, $\mathbb{E}(\sqrt{X}) \leq \sqrt{\mathbb{E}(X)}$.

Let X be an arbitrarily distributed random variable, with the only constraint that $X \geq 0$. The following *Markov inequality* holds:

$$P(X \geq a) \leq \frac{\mathbb{E}(X)}{a}$$

Proof:

$$\mathbb{E}(X) = \sum_{x} x \cdot P(X = x) \geq \sum_{x \geq a} x \cdot P(X = x) \geq a \cdot \sum_{x \geq a} P(X = x) = a \cdot P(X \geq a) \quad \square$$

Markov's inequality is often used in the form $a = t \cdot \mathbb{E}(X)$. The formulation is then:

$$P(X \geq t \cdot \mathbb{E}(X)) \leq \frac{1}{t}$$

In words, the probability that a random variable X gets a value that is a factor t larger than its expected value is at most $\frac{1}{t}$.

Since Markov's inequality does not make any assumption about the distribution of X – it just uses its expected value – the estimation is, in general, not very sharp. We give a very useful and much sharper estimation that is especially suited for the case of binomially distributed random variables. This is the so called *Chernoff inequality*. Observe that in this case $\mathbb{E}(X) = pn$.

Theorem

$$X \sim Bin(n,p) \quad \Rightarrow \quad P(X \geq (1+\delta) \cdot \mathbb{E}(X)) \leq \left(\frac{e^{\delta}}{(1+\delta)^{1+\delta}} \right)^{\mathbb{E}(X)}$$

Proof: Since $X \sim Bin(n,p)$ we have $X = X_1 + \cdots + X_n$ with $X_i \sim \begin{pmatrix} 0 & 1 \\ 1-p & p \end{pmatrix}$. The 0-1-valued random variable X_i is an indicator for the i-th Bernoulli trial. Let $t > 1$ be a constant that will be specified later in order to make the inequality as sharp as possible. Observe that $\mathbb{E}(t^{X_i}) = (1-p) \cdot t^0 + p \cdot t^1 = 1 - p + pt = 1 + (t-1)p$. Using Markov's inequality, it follows:

$$
\begin{aligned}
P(X \geq (1+\delta) \cdot \mathbb{E}(X)) &= P(t^X \geq t^{(1+\delta) \cdot \mathbb{E}(X)}) \\
&\leq \frac{\mathbb{E}(t^X)}{t^{(1+\delta) \cdot \mathbb{E}(X)}} = \frac{\mathbb{E}(t^{X_1 + \cdots + X_n})}{t^{(1+\delta) \cdot \mathbb{E}(X)}} \\
&= \frac{\mathbb{E}(t^{X_1} \cdots t^{X_n})}{t^{(1+\delta) \cdot \mathbb{E}(X)}} = \frac{\mathbb{E}(t^{X_1}) \cdots \mathbb{E}(t^{X_n})}{t^{(1+\delta) \cdot \mathbb{E}(X)}}
\end{aligned}
$$

(since the X_i variables are independent)

$$
\begin{aligned}
&= \frac{(1 + (t-1)p)^n}{t^{(1+\delta) \cdot \mathbb{E}(X)}} \leq \frac{e^{(t-1)pn}}{t^{(1+\delta) \cdot \mathbb{E}(X)}} \\
&= \left(\frac{e^{t-1}}{t^{1+\delta}} \right)^{\mathbb{E}(X)}
\end{aligned}
$$

Setting $t = 1 + \delta$ we obtain the Chernoff inequality. $\qquad \square$

Example: Markov's inequality states that a positive random variable X can take a value that is twice as large as its expectation with probability at most $\frac{1}{2}$. If X follows a binomial distribution with parameters $(n, \frac{1}{3})$ its expectation is $\mathbb{E}(X) = \frac{n}{3}$. From Markov's inequality it follows that the probability of X being larger than $\frac{2n}{3}$ is at most $\frac{1}{2}$. Compared to this, Chernoff's inequality states that the probability of X being larger than $\frac{2n}{3}$ is at most $(e/4)^{n/3} \leq 0.88^n$. For $n = 100$ this is 0.000003.

Sometimes it is necessary to consider continuous random variables. Such a random variable X could take values, for example, in the range of the positive real numbers. Then, one describes the probabilistic behavior of X with a *density function* $f_X : \mathbb{R}_+ \to [0,1]$, with $\int_0^\infty f_X(t)dt = 1$. The *distribution function* of X is defined as $F_X(x) = \int_0^x f_X(t)dt$. The probability that the value of X is in the interval $I = [a,b]$ is then $F_X(b) - F_X(a) = \int_a^b f_X(t)dt$. The expectation of X is defined as $\mathbb{E}(X) = \int_0^\infty t f_X(t)dt$ in case this integral exists.

For example, we need sometimes a real random number R being uniformly distributed in the interval $[0,1]$. This means that R has the density function $f_R(x) = 1$, if $x \in [0,1]$, and $f_R(x) = 0$, otherwise.

Appendix: Markov Chains

A *stochastic process* is a family of random variables $\{X_t \mid t \in T\}$. We want to assume here that the "time" T is discrete, thus t takes the values $0, 1, 2, 3 \ldots$. We also assume that the range of the random variables X_t is discrete, and even finite. The value $X_t = x$ describes that the process is in "state" x at the point in time t. We want to associate such stochastic processes with the execution of probabilistic algorithms. The values of the random variables X_t reflect then in numbers some quantities related to the "quality of the solution" or the "position in the search space" or similar.

The distribution of the random variables X_{t+1} should depend in some way on the distributions of $X_0, \ldots, X_t$ (and sometimes also on t). The easier these dependence structures are, the easier the analysis of such a process becomes. If we suppose that the distribution of X_{t+1} depends only on X_t, and that this functional dependence is the same for every t, then we are dealing with a (finite and homogeneous) *Markov chain*. Its properties can be described by its transition matrix $P = (p_{i,j})$ (with $0 \leq p_{i,j} \leq 1$, and for all i, $\sum_j p_{i,j} = 1$): when i is the state at time t ($X_t = i$), then the subsequent state is $X_{t+1} = j$, with probability $p_{i,j}$.

One can intuitively understand a Markov chain as a *stochastic finite automaton*. For every pair of states i, j, there is an edge labeled with $p_{i,j}$ and pointing out of vertex i to vertex j (provided that $p_{i,j} > 0$).

Example: Here is a simple daily weather forecast, with $P = \begin{pmatrix} 0.8 & 0.2 \\ 0.4 & 0.6 \end{pmatrix}$:

A further example can be found on page 66.

When $(q_1, q_2, \ldots, q_n)$ is the probability distribution of X_t (written as row vector), and $P = (p_{i,j})$ is the transition matrix of the underlying Markov chain, then the distribution $(r_1, r_2, \ldots, r_n)$ of X_{t+1} can be computed as the result of a vector-matrix multiplication: $(q_1, q_2, \ldots, q_n) \cdot P = (r_1, r_2, \ldots, r_n)$.

Let $s = (s_1, s_2, \ldots, s_n)$ be the initial distribution, that is, the distribution of X_0 (in many cases one starts from a *deterministic distribution*, that is, $s_i = 1$ for some i, and $s_j = 0$ for all $j \neq i$). The distribution of X_t is then: $(s_1, s_2, \ldots, s_n) \cdot P^t$.

The Markov chain model is no longer valid from the moment in which the algorithms we are analyzing start using concepts with a "memory" component, like taboo lists, or dynamically changing "scores" for variables or clauses.

When the Markov chain satisfies certain conditions (see Behrends, 2000; Brémaud, 1999; Häggstrom, 2002; Norris, 1997) then the distribution $s \cdot P^t$ converges for $t \to \infty$ towards a steady limit distribution (independent from the initial distribution s). The limit distribution $q = (q_1, \ldots, q_n)$, if it exists, can be calculated by solving the equation system $q \cdot P = q$ with the additional condition $q_1 + \cdots + q_n = 1$. The limit distribution is a *fixed point* under the linear transformation given by the matrix P. In the example given above, the limit is $(q_1, q_2) = (\frac{2}{3}, \frac{1}{3})$, that is, considered over a long period, the probability of sun is $\frac{2}{3}$ while the rain probability is $\frac{1}{3}$.

When instead of just a random variable X_t, depending on a time parameter t, we consider a sequence of random variables $(X_1, \ldots, X_m)_{t=0,1,2,\ldots}$, one calls this a *Markov random field*. In many cases, the distribution of X_i at time $t + 1$ depends only on X_i at time t, as well as on some other "neighboring variables" $X_{i_1} \ldots, X_{i_k}$ (also at time t).

In some cases, the Markov chain or the Markov random field can be conceived in such a way that it tends to a desired limit distribution. However, since it is hard to obtain a random sample from the corresponding limit distribution, especially in the case of the Markov field, one often uses a probabilistic algorithm to simulate the process for a certain number of steps, taking the configuration obtained in this way as a random sample. This is called a Markov chain Monte Carlo simulation (in short: MCMC). For example, trying to find a satisfying assignment for an input formula on n variables, one could start with the uniform distribution on $(X_1, \ldots, X_n) \in \{0, 1\}^n$ at time 0. At this initial point the probability that the n random variables correspond to a satisfying assignment for the given formula can be exponentially small. After the simulation of the stochastic transitions in the Markov random field over a sufficiently large number of steps, it could be that the probability to obtain a satisfying assignment is much larger than initially (of course, for this to happen, there has to be some dependency between the transition probabilities and the structure of the formula). Some of the algorithms based on local search, or the physically based algorithms, can be understood from this perspective.

Appendix: Estimations with Binomial Coefficients

The following estimations are needed for the algorithms based on local search in a "Hamming ball" (let $\delta \leq \frac{1}{2}$ and let δn be a natural number):

$$
\begin{aligned}
1 = (\delta + (1 - \delta))^n &= \sum_{i=0}^{n} \binom{n}{i} \delta^i (1 - \delta)^{n-i} \\
&= (1 - \delta)^n \sum_{i=0}^{n} \binom{n}{i} \left(\frac{\delta}{1 - \delta}\right)^i \\
&\geq (1 - \delta)^n \sum_{i=0}^{\delta n} \binom{n}{i} \left(\frac{\delta}{1 - \delta}\right)^i \\
&\geq (1 - \delta)^n \sum_{i=0}^{\delta n} \binom{n}{i} \left(\frac{\delta}{1 - \delta}\right)^{\delta n} \\
&= \delta^{\delta n} (1 - \delta)^{(1-\delta)n} \sum_{i=0}^{\delta n} \binom{n}{i}
\end{aligned}
$$

From this it follows that:

$$
\sum_{i=0}^{\delta n} \binom{n}{i} \leq \left[\left(\frac{1}{\delta}\right)^\delta \cdot \left(\frac{1}{1 - \delta}\right)^{1-\delta}\right]^n = 2^{h(\delta) \cdot n}
$$

where $h(\delta) = -\delta \log_2(\delta) - (1 - \delta) \log_2(1 - \delta)$ is Shannon's *binary entropy function*, cf. (Ash, 1965). The next figure shows the graph of the entropy function.

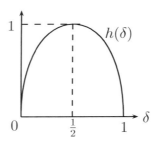

For an estimation in the opposite direction we obtain:

$$
\begin{aligned}
1 = (\delta + (1 - \delta))^n &= \sum_{i=0}^{n} \binom{n}{i} \delta^i (1 - \delta)^{n-i} \\
&\leq (n + 1) \cdot \max_i \left\{ \binom{n}{i} \delta^i (1 - \delta)^{n-i} \right\} \\
&= (n + 1) \cdot \binom{n}{\delta n} \cdot \delta^{\delta n} (1 - \delta)^{(1-\delta)n} \\
&= (n + 1) \cdot \binom{n}{\delta n} \cdot 2^{-h(\delta)n}
\end{aligned}
$$

Here it was used that the term $\binom{n}{i}\delta^i(1-\delta)^{n-i}$ takes its maximum for $i = \delta n$. This can be seen by considering the quotient

$$\frac{\binom{n}{i}\delta^i(1-\delta)^{n-i}}{\binom{n}{i-1}\delta^{i-1}(1-\delta)^{n-i+1}} = \frac{(n-i+1)\cdot\delta}{i\cdot(1-\delta)}$$

and analyze for which values of i this quotient is greater or equal to 1. This leads to the condition $(n-i+1)\cdot\delta \geq i\cdot(1-\delta)$ which is equivalent to $i \leq \delta n + \delta$. Since δn is supposed to be a natural number, and $\delta \leq 1/2$, the proof is complete.

Now the calculation above implies:

$$\sum_{i=0}^{\delta n}\binom{n}{i} \geq \binom{n}{\delta n} \geq \frac{1}{n+1}\cdot 2^{h(\delta)n}$$

A better estimation with the help of the Stirling formula (Ash, 1965) gives:

$$\sum_{i=0}^{\delta n}\binom{n}{i} \geq \frac{1}{\sqrt{8n\delta(1-\delta)}}\cdot 2^{h(\delta)n}$$

We can summarize the estimations from below and from above by writing:

$$\sum_{i=0}^{\delta n}\binom{n}{i} \overset{poly}{=} 2^{h(\delta)n}$$

The symbol $\overset{poly}{=}$ should indicate, that the exponential behavior of the two functions being compared, ignoring polynomial factors, is identical. More formally, we write $f(n) \overset{poly}{=} g(n)$, if there is a polynomial $p(n)$, so that $f(n) \leq p(n)\cdot g(n)$ and $g(n) \leq p(n)\cdot f(n)$.

One could also write instead:

$$\sum_{i=0}^{\delta n}\binom{n}{i} = O^*(2^{h(\delta)n}) \quad \text{and} \quad 2^{h(\delta)n} = O^*\left(\sum_{i=0}^{\delta n}\binom{n}{i}\right)$$

The following also holds $\binom{n}{\delta n} \overset{poly}{=} 2^{h(\delta)n}$ for all $\delta \in (0,1)$.

Bibliography

E. Aarts, J.K. Lenstra (Eds.): *Local Search in Combinatorial Optimization.* Princeton University Press, 1997.

R. Aharoni, N. Linial: Minimal unsatisfiable formulas and minimal two-colorable hypergraphs. *Journal Combinatorial Theory* 43 (1986) 196–204.

R.B. Ash: *Information Theory.* Dover, 1965.

B. Aspvall, M.F. Plass, R.E. Tarjan: A linear-time algorithm for testing the truth of certain quantified boolean formulas. *Inform. Proc. Letters* 8 (1979) 121–123.

A. Auger, B. Doerr (Eds.): *Theory of Randomized Search Heuristics – Foundations and Recent Development.* World Scientific, 2011.

A. Balint, U. Schöning: Choosing probability distributions for stochastic local search and the role of make versus break. *Proc. 15th Intern. Conference on Theory and Applications of Satisfiability Testing,* Springer 2012, pages 16–29.

R. Battiti, M. Brunato, F. Mascia: *Reactive Search and Intelligent Optimization.* Springer, 2008.

M. Bauer, D. Brand, M. Fischer, A. Meyer, M. Paterson: A note on disjunctive form tautologies. *SIGACT News* 5(2) (1973) 17–20.

S. Baumer, R. Schuler: Improving a probabilistic 3-SAT algorithm by dynamic search and independent clause pairs, *Theory and Applications of Satisfiability Testing, 6th International Conference,* SAT 2003, Lecture Notes in Comp. Sci. 2919, Springer, 2004, 150–161.

P. Beame, T. Pitassi: Simplified and improved resolution lower bound. *37th Sympos. on Foundations of Computer Science (FOCS),* IEEE, 1996, 274–282.

P. Beame, C. Beck, R. Impagliazzo: Time-space tradeoffs in resolution: superpolynomial lower bounds for superlinear space. *Proceedings of the 44th Symposium on Theory of Computing,* 2012, pages 213–232.

E. Behrends: *Introduction to Markov Chains.* Vieweg, 2000.

R. Beigel, D. Eppstein: 3-coloring in time $O(1.3289^n)$. *J. Algorithms* 54(2) (2005) 168–204.

A. Bernasconi: *Mathematical Techniques for the Analysis of Boolean Functions.* Ph.D. Thesis, Universitá di Pisa. Technical Report TD-2/98, (1998).

A. Biere, M. Heule, H.v. Maaren, T. Walsh (Eds.): *Handbook of Satisfiability.* IOS Press, 2009.

G. Biroli, S. Cocco, R. Monasson: Phase transitions and complexity in computer science: an overview of the statistical physics approach to the random satisfiability problem. *Physics* A 306 (2002) 381–394.

G. Boole: *An Investigation of the Laws of Thought on which are Founded the Mathematical Theories of Logic and Probabilities.* Dover, 1973.

A.R. Bradley, Z. Manna: *The Calculus of Computation – Decision Procedures with Applications to Verification.* Springer, 2007.

G. Brassard, P. Bratley: *Fundamentals of Algorithmics.* Prentice Hall, 1996.

A. Braunstein, M. Mézard, R. Zecchina: Survey propagation: an algorithm for satisfiability. *Random Structures and Algorithms* Vol. 27, 2 (2005) 201–226.

P. Brémaud: *Markov Chains, Gibbs Fields, Monte Carlo Simulation, and Queues* (Chapter 7: Gibbs Fields and Monte Carlo Simulation). Springer, 1999.

J. Brownlee: *Clever Algorithms – Nature-Inspired Programming Recipes.* Lulu, 2011.

T. Brüggemann, W. Kern: An improved deterministic local search algorithm for 3-SAT. *Theoret. Computer Science* 329 (2004) 303–313.

U. Bubeck, H. Kleine Büning: A new 3-*CNF* transformation by parallel-serial graphs. *Information Processing Letters* 109, 7 (2009) 376–379.

V. Chandru, J. Hooker: *Optimization Methods For Logical Inference.* Wiley, 1999.

C.L. Chang: The unit proof and the input proof in theorem proving. *J. Assoc. Comput. Mach.* 17 (1970) 698–707.

V. Chvátal, B. Reed: Mick gets some (the odds are on his side). *Proc. 33rd Foundations of Computer Science* (FOCS), IEEE, 1992, 620–627.

V. Chvátal, E. Szemerédi: Many hard examples for resolution. *Journal of the Association for Computing Machinery* 35 (1988) 759–768.

P. Clote, E. Kranakis: *Boolean Functions and Computation Models.* Springer, 2002.

G. Cohen, I. Honkala, S. Litsyn, A. Lobstein: *Covering Codes.* North-Holland, 1997.

S.A. Cook: The complexity of theorem-proving procedures. *Proc. Third Ann. ACM Sympos. Theory of Comput.* ACM 1971, 151–158.

S.A. Cook, R.A. Reckhow: The relative efficiency of propositional proof systems. *Journal of Symbolic Logic* 44 (1979) 36–50.

W. Craig: Three uses of the Herbrand-Gentzen theorem in relating model theory and proof theory. *The Journal of Symbolic Logic* 22 (1957), no. 3, 269–285.

E. Dantsin, A. Goerdt, E.A. Hirsch, U. Schöning: A deterministic algorithm for k-SAT based on covering codes and local search. *Intern. Colloq. on Automata, Languages and Computation*, ICALP 2000, Lecture Notes in Computer Science 1853. Springer 2000, 236–247

E. Dantsin, A. Goerdt, E.A. Hirsch, R. Kannan, J. Kleinberg, C. Papadimitriou, P. Raghavan, U. Schöning: A deterministic $(2 - 2/(k + 1))^n$ algorithm for k-SAT based on local search. *Theoretical Computer Science* 289/1 (2002) 69–83.

S. Dasgupta, C. Papadimitriou, U. Vazirani: *Algorithms* (Chapter 8+9). McGraw-Hill, 2008.

M. Davis, H. Putnam: A computing procedure for quantification theory. *Journal of the ACM* 7 (1960) 201–215.

M. Davis, G. Logemann, D. Loveland: A machine program for theorem proving. *Communications of the ACM* 5 (1962) 394–397.

P.T. De Boer, D.P. Kroese, S. Mannor, R.Y. Rubinstein: A Tutorial on the Cross-Entropy Method. Annals of Operations Research, 134 (1) (2005) 19–67.

D. Du, J. Gu, P.M. Pardalos (Eds).: *Satisfiability Problem: Theory and Applications.* DIMACS Series in Discrete Mathematics and Theoretical Computer Science. American Mathematical Society, 1997.

S. Edelkamp, S. Schrödl: *Heuristic Search: Theory and Applications.* Elsevier, 2012.

S. Eggersglüß, R. Drechsler: *High Quality Test Pattern Generation and Boolean Satisfiability.* Springer, 2012.

W. Feller: *Introduction to Probability – Theory and Its Applications.* Vol I & II. Wiley 1966/68.

F.V. Fomin, D. Kratsch: *Exact Exponential Algorithms.* Springer, 2010.

N.G. Fournier: Modelling the dynamics of stochastic local search. *J. Heuristics* 13 (2007) 587–639.

E. Friedgut: Sharp thresholds for graph properties, and the k-SAT problem. *J. Amer. Math. Soc.* 12 (1999) 1017–1054.

M.R. Garey, D.S. Johnson: *Computers and Intractability – A Guide to the Theory of NP-Completeness.* Freeman, 1979.

E. Giunchiglia, T. Walsh (Eds.): *SAT 2005 – Satisfiability Research in the Year 2005.* Springer, 2006.

A. Goerdt: A threshold for unsatisfiability. *J. Comp. Syst. Sci.* 53 (1996) 469–486.

A.T. Goldberg: *On the Complexity of the Satisfiability Problem.* Courant Institute, New York, 1979.

C.P. Gomes, H. Kautz, A. Sabharwal, B. Selman: Satisfiability Solvers. In: *Handbook of Knowledge Representation.* Elsevier, 2008.

C.P. Gomes, B. Selman, N. Crato, H. Kautz: Heavy-tailed phenomena in satisfiability and constraint satisfaction problems. *Journal of Automated Reasoning* 24 (2000) 67–100.

R.L. Graham, D.E. Knuth, O. Patashnik: *Concrete Mathematics – A Foundation for Computer Science.* Addison-Wesley, 1989.

J. Gu, P. Purdom, J. Franco, B. Wah: *Algorithms for the Satisfiability Problem.* Cambridge University Press, 2010.

M. Habib, C. McDiarmid, J. Ramirez-Alfonsin, B. Reed (Eds.): *Probabilistic Methods for Algorithmic Discrete Mathematics.* Springer, 1998.

O. Häggström: *Finite Markov Chains and Algorithmic Applications.* Cambridge University Press, 2002.

A. Haken: The intractability of resolution. *Theor. Comput. Sci.* 39 (1985) 297–308.

A.K. Hartmann, H. Rieger: *Optimization Algorithms in Physics.* Wiley-VCH, 2002.

A.K. Hartmann, H. Rieger (Eds.): *New Optimization Algorithms in Physics.* Wiley-VCH, 2004.

A.K. Hartmann, M. Weigt: *Phase Transitions in Combinatorial Optimization Problems – Basics, Algorithms and Statistical Mechanics.* Wiley-VCH, 2005.

L. Henschen, L. Wos: Unit refutations and Horn sets. *J. Assoc. Comput. Mach.* 21 (1974) 590–605.

T. Hertli, R.A. Moser, D. Scheder: Improving PPSZ for 3-SAT using Critical Variables. arXiv:1009.4830, 2010.

T. Hertli: 3-SAT Faster and Simpler – Unique-SAT Bounds for PPSZ Hold in General. In *Proc. 52nd IEEE Symp. on Foundations of Computer Science (FOCS)*, pages 277-284, 2011.

J. Hertz, A. Krogh, R.G. Palmer: *Introduction to the Theory of Neural Computation.* Addison-Wesley, 1991.

E.A. Hirsch: SAT local search algorithms: worst-case study. *J. Automated Reasoning* 24 (2000) 127–143.

T. Hofmeister, U. Schöning, R. Schuler, O. Watanabe: A probabilistic 3-SAT algorithm further improved, *Proc. of the 19th Sympos. on Theoretical Aspects of Computer Science* (STACS02), Lecture Notes in Comp. Sci. 2285, Springer 2002, 193–202.

T. Hofmeister, U. Schöning, R. Schuler, O. Watanabe: Randomized algorithms for 3-SAT. *Theor. Comput. Sci.* 40 (3) (2007) 249–262.

J. Hooker: *Logic-Based Methods for Optimization.* Wiley, 2000.

J. Hooker: *Integrated Methods for Optimization.* Springer, 2007.

H. Hoos, T. Stützle: *Stochastic Local Search – Foundations and Applications.* Morgan Kaufmann, 2005.

J. Hromkovič: *Algorithmics for Hard Problems.* Springer, 2001.

E. Hsu, S.A. McIlraith: Characterizing propagation methods for Boolean satisfiability. *Proceedings of The Ninth International Conference on Theory and Applications of Satisfiability Testing* (SAT'06), Springer Lecture Notes in Computer Science, Vol. 4121, 2006, 325–338.

M. Huth, M. Ryan: *Logic in Computer Science.* Cambridge University Press, 2004.

M. Iosifescu: *Finite Markov Processes and Their Applications.* Dover, 1980.

K. Iwama, S. Tamaki: Improved upper bounds for 3-SAT, *Electronic Colloquium on Computational Complexity*, Report No. 53, 2003.

K. Iwama, K. Seto, T. Takai, S. Tamaki: Improved Randomized Algorithms for 3-SAT. *ISAAC* (1) 2010: 73–84.

H. Jia, C. Moore, D. Strain: Generating hard satisfiable formulas by hiding solutions deceptively, *Journal of Artificial Intelligence Research*, Vol. 28 (2007) 107–118.

S. Jukna: *Boolean Function Complexity – Advances and Frontiers.* Springer, 2012.

M.Y. Kao: *Encyclopedia of Algorithms.* Springer, 2008.

R.M. Karp, R.J. Lipton: Some connections between non-uniform and uniform complexity classes. *Proc. 12th ACM Symposium on Theory of Computing* 1980, 302–309.

R. Kindermann, J.L. Snell: *Markov Random Fields and Their Applications.* American Mathematical Society, 1980.

S. Kirkpatrick, C. D. Gelatt, M. P. Vecchi: Optimization by Simulated Annealing. *Science* Vol. 220, No. 4598 (1983) 671–680.

H. Kleine Büning, T. Lettmann: *Propositional Logic: Deduction and Algorithms.* Cambridge University Press, 1999.

D.E. Knuth: *The Art of Computer Programming*, Vol. 4a. Addison-Wesley, 2011.

D.E. Knuth: *The Art of Computer Programming*, Vol. 4b, Section 7.2.2.2: Satisfiability, manuscript 2013.

J. Krajíček: Lower bounds to the size of constant-depth propositional proofs. *Journal of Symbolic Logic* 59,1 (1994) 73–86.

W. Krauth: *Statistical Mechanics: Algorithms and Computations.* Oxford University Press, 2006.

L. Kroc, A. Sabharwal, B. Selman: Message-passing and local heuristics as decimation strategies for satisfiability. *SAC* 2009, ACM, 1408–1414.

M.R. Krom: The Decision Problem for a Class of First-Order Formulas in Which all Disjunctions are Binary, *Zeitschrift fr Mathematische Logik und Grundlagen der Mathematik* 13 (1967) 15-20.

D. Kroening, O. Strichmann: *Decision Procedures – An Algorithmic Point of View.* Springer, 2008.

D.P. Kroese, T. Taimre, Z.I. Botev: *Handbook of Monte Carlo Methods.* Wiley, 2011.

O. Kullmann: Investigating a general hierarchy of polynomially decidable classes of CNF's based on short tree-like resolution proofs. *ECCC* 1999, TR99–041.

O. Kullmann: Upper and lower bounds on the complexity of generalised resolution and generalised constraint satisfaction problems. *Ann. of Math. and Artif. Intelligence* 40 (2004) 303–352.

O. Kullmann: Present and Future of Practical SAT Solving. *Complexity of Constraints.* Lecture Notes in Comp. Sci. 5250, Springer, 2008, 283–319.

K. Kutzkov, D. Scheder: Using CSP to improve deterministic 3-SAT. *CoRR*, abs/1007.1166, 2010.

D.A. Levin, Y. Peres, E.L. Wilmer: *Markov Chains and Mixing Times.* American Mathematical Society, 2009.

L. Levin: Universal sequential search problems. *Problems of Information Transmission* 9 (1973) 265–266.

H.R. Lewis: Renaming a set of clauses as a Horn set. *J. Assoc. Comput. Mach.* 25 (1) (1978) 134–135.

C.M. Li, W.Q. Huang: Diversification and determinism in local search for satisfiability. *Proc. SAT*, Lecture Notes in Computer Science 3569, Springer 2005, 158–172.

M. Li, P. Vitanyi: *An Introduction to Kolmogorov Complexity and Its Applications.* Springer, 2008.

J.S. Liu: *Monte Carlo Strategies in Scientific Computing.* Springer, 2008.

M. Luby, A. Sinclair, D. Zuckerman: Optimal speedup of Las Vegas algorithms. *Information Proc. Letters* 47 (1993) 173–180.

D.J.C. MacKay: *Information Theory, Inference, and Learning Algorithms.* (Ising Model, Monte Carlo, Propagation methods). Cambridge University Press, 2003.

K. Makino, S. Tamaki, M. Yamamoto: Derandomizing HSSW Algorithm for 3-SAT. arXiv:1102.3766v1, 2011.

H. Mannila, K. Mehlhorn: A fast algorithm for renaming a set of clauses as a Horn set. *Inform. Proc. Letters.* 21 (1985) 269–272.

V.W. Marek: *Introduction to the Mathematics of Satisfiability.* Chapman & Hall, 2009.

E.W. Mayr, H.J. Prömel, A. Stger: *Lecture Notes on Proof Verification and Approximation Algorithms.* Lecture Notes in Computer Science, Vol. 1367, Springer, 1998.

D. McAllester, B. Selman, H. Kautz: Evidence for invariants in local search. *Proc. of the 14th Nat. Conf. on Artificial Intelligence* MIT Press, 1997, 321–326.

M. Mézard: Optimization and physics: on the satisfiability of random Boolean formulae. *Ann. Henri Poincaré* 4, Suppl. 1 (2003) 475–488.

M. Mézard, G. Parisi, R. Zecchina: Analytical and algorithmic solution of random satisfiability problems. *Science* 297 (2002) 812.

M. Mézard, A. Montanari: *Information, Physics, and Computation.* Oxford University Press, 2009.

M. Mézard, G. Parisi, M. Virasoro: *Spin Glass Theory and Beyond.* World Scientific, 2004.

W. Michiels, E. Aarts, J. Korst: *Theoretical Aspects of Local Search.* Springer, 2007.

D.G. Mitchell: A SAT solver primer. *Bulletin of the EATCS* 85 (2005) 112–132.

M. Mitzenmacher, E. Upfal: *Probability and Computing – Randomized Algorithms and Probabilistic Analysis.* Cambridge University Press, 2005.

B. Monien, E. Speckenmeyer: Solving satisfiability in less than 2^n steps. *Discrete Applied Math.* 10 (1985) 287–295.

C. Moore, S. Mertens: *The Nature of Computation.* Oxford University Press, 2011.

A.P.A. van Moorsel, K. Wolter: Analysis and algorithms for restart. citeseer.ist.psu.edu/vanmoorsel04analysis.html, 2004.

A.P.A. van Moorsel, K. Wolter: Analysis of restart mechanisms in software systems. *IEEE Transactions on Software Engineering*, Vol. 32, No.8, 2006.

R.A. Moser: A constructive proof of Lovász local lemma. *41st Sympos. on Foundations of Computer Science*, IEEE, 2009, 343–350.

R.A. Moser: *Exact Algorithms for Constraint Satisfaction Problems.* PhD Dissertation, ETH Zürich, 2012. Published by logos Verlag, Berlin, 2013.

R.A. Moser, G. Tardos: A constructive proof of the general Lovász Local Lemma. arXiv:0903.0544v3 [cs.DS], 2009.

R.A. Moser, D. Scheder: A Full Derandomization of Schöning's k-SAT Algorithm. CoRR abs/1008.4067: (2010). *Proceedings 63rd Ann. ACM Sympos. on Theory of Computing* 2011, 245–252.

R. Motwani, P. Raghavan: *Randomized Algorithms*. Cambridge University Press, 1995.

D. Mundici: NP and Craig's interpolation theorem. In: *Proceedings Logic Colloquium '82* , Studies in Logic and the Foundations of Mathematics, North-Holland, Amsterdam, 1984, pp. 345–358.

R.M. Neal: *Probabilistic Inference Using Markov Chain Monte Carlo Methods.* Technical Report CRG-TR-93-1, Dept. of Computer Science, University of Toronto, 1993.

H. Nishimori: *Statistical Physics of Spin Glasses and Information Processing: An Introduction.* (Chapter 9: Optimization Problems), Clarendon Press, 2001.

J.R. Norris: *Markov Chains.* Cambridge University Press, 1997.

C.H. Papadimitriou: On selecting a satisfying truth assignment. *Proc. 32nd Sympos. on Foundations of Computer Science.* FOCS 1991, IEEE, 163–169.

C.H. Papadimitriou: *Computational Complexity*, Addison-Wesley, 1994.

R. Paturi, P. Pudlák, F. Zane: Satisfiability coding lemma. *Proc. 38th IEEE Sympos. on Foundations of Computer Science*, IEEE, 1997, 566–574.

R. Paturi, P Pudlák, M.E. Saks, F. Zane: An improved exponential-time algorithm for k-SAT. *Proc. of the 39th Ann. IEEE Sympos. on Foundations of Comp. Sci.*, IEEE, 1998, 628–637.

R. Paturi, P. Pudlák, M.E. Saks, F. Zane: An improved exponential-time algorithm for k-SAT, *Journal of the ACM*, Vol.52, No.3, 2005, pp. 337–364

J. Pearl: *Probabilistic Reasoning in Intelligent Systems: Networks of Plausible Inference.* Morgan Kaufmann, 1997.

A. Percus, G. Istrate, C. Moore (Eds.): *Computational Physics and Statistical Physics.* Oxford University Press, 2006.

D.A. Plaisted, Y. Zhu: *The Efficiency of Theorem Proving Strategies – A Comparative and Asymptotic Analysis.* Vieweg, 1997.

P. Pudlák: Satisfiability – algorithms and logic. *Proc. Mathematical Foundations of Computer Science* (MFCS), Lecture Notes in Computer Science 1450, Springer, 1998, 129–141.

P. Pudlák: Lower bounds for resolution and cutting plane proofs and monotone computations. *Journal of Symbolic Logic* 6 (1997) 981–998.

A.A. Razborov: Lower bounds on the monotone complexity of some boolean functions. *Soviet. Mathem. Doklady* 31 (1985) 354–357.

R. Rodošek: A new approach on solving 3-satisfiability. *Artif. Intelligence and Symbolic Mathematical Computation.* Lecture Notes in Computer Science 1138, Springer, 1996, 197–212.

R. Rubinstein: The cross-entropy method for combinatorial and continuous optimization. *Methodology and Computing in Applied Probability* 1 (1999) 127–190.

L. Saitta, A. Giordana, A. Cornuéjols: *Phase Transitions in Machine Learning.* Cambridge University Press, 2011.

T.J. Schaefer: The complexity of satisfiability problems. *Sympos. on Theory of Computing.* ACM 1978, 216–226.

D. Scheder: Guided search and faster deterministic algorithm for 3-SAT. *Proc. 8th Latin American Symposium on Theoretical Informatics* (LATIN 08), Lecture Notes in Computer Science 4957, Springer 2008, 60–71.

J.J. Schneider, S. Kirkpatrick: *Stochastic Optimization.* Springer, 2006.

U. Schöning: Resolution proofs, exponential lower bounds, and Kolmogorov complexity. *Proceedings Symposium on Mathematical Foundations of Computer Science 1997,* Lecture Notes in Computer Science 1295, Springer 1997, 110–116.

U. Schöning: *On the complexity of constraint satisfaction problems.* Tech. Report, University of Ulm, 1998.

U. Schöning: A probabilistic algorithm for k-SAT and constraint satisfaction problems. *Proc. 40th Sympos. on Foundations of Computer Science.* FOCS 1999, IEEE, 410–414.

U. Schöning: New algorithms for k-SAT based on the local search principle. *Proceedings Math. Foundat. Comput. Theory,* MFCS 2001, Lecture Notes in Computer Science 2136, Springer 2001, 87–95.

U. Schöning: *Logic for Computer Scientists.* Birkhäuser, 2008.

U. Schöning: A probabilistic algorithm for k-SAT based on limited local search and restart. *Algorithmica* 32,4 (2002) 615–623.

U. Schöning: Principles of stochastic local search. *Unconventional computation. 6th international conference,* UC 2007. Lecture Notes in Computer Science 4618, Springer 2007, 178–187.

U. Schöning, R. Schuler: *Renamable-Horn Clauses and Unit Resolution.* Techn. Report, University Koblenz, 1989.

U. Schöning, J. Torán: A note on the size of Craig interpolants. *Circuits, Logic, and Games.* Dagstuhl Seminar Proceedings 06451, 2007.

S. Seitz, M. Alava, P. Orponen: Focused local search for random 3-satisfiability. *J. Stat. Mech.* P06006, 2005.

B. Selman, H. Levesque, D. Mitchell: A new method for solving hard satisfiability problems. *Proc. of the 10th Nat. Conf. on Artificial Intelligence,* MIT Press, 1992, 440–446.

B. Selman, H. Kautz, B. Cohen: Noise strategies for improving local search. *Proc. of the 12th Nat. Conf. on Artificial Intelligence,* MIT Press, 1994, 337–343.

J.P. Sethna: *Statistical Mechanics: Entropy, Order Parameters, and Complexity* (Chapter 8: Calculation and Computation). Oxford University Press, 2006.

K. Seto, S. Tamaki: A satisfiability algorithm and average-case hardness for formulas over the full binary basis. *27th Conference on Computational Complexity 2012.* IEEE, 2012, pages 107–116.

M. Sheeran, G. Stålmarck: A Tutorial on Stalmärck's Proof Procedure for Propositional Logic. *FMCAD '98: Formal Methods for Computer-Aided Design,* Springer 1998, 82–99.

R.W. Shonkwiler, F. Medivil: *Explorations in Monte Carlo Methods.* Springer, 2009.

Y.C. Stamatiou: Threshold Phenomena: The Computer Scientist's Viewpoint, *Bulletin of the European Association of Theoretical Computer Science* 80, 199–234, June 2003.

D.L. Stein, C.M. Newman: *Spin Glasses and Complexity.* Princeton University Press, 2013.

C.A. Tovey: A simplified NP-complete satifiability problem. *Discrete and Applied Mathematics* 8 (1984) 85–89.

K. Truemper: *Design of Logic-Based Intelligent Systems.* Wiley, 2004.

K. Truemper: *Effective Logic Computation.* Leibniz, 2010.

G. Tseitin: On the complexity of derivation in the propositional calculus. *Automation of Reasoning: Classical Papers in Computational Logic 2.* Springer, 1983, 466–483.

A. Urquhart: Hard examples for resolution. *Journal of the Assoc. Comput. Mach.* 34 (1987) 209–219.

A. del Val: On 2-SAT and renamable Horn. In *AAAI: 17th National Conference on Artificial Intelligence.* MIT Press, 2000.

H. Vollmer: *Introduction to Circuit Complexity.* Springer, 1999.

I. Wegener: *The Complexity of Boolean Functions.* Wiley-Teubner, 1987.

I. Wegener: *Branching Programs and Binary Decision Diagrams.* SIAM, 2000.

I. Wegener: *Complexity Theory: Exploring the Limits of Efficient Algorithms.* Springer, 2005.

D.J.A. Welsh: *Complexity: Knots, Colourings and Counting* (Chapter 4: Statistical Physics, and Chapter 8: Approximisation and Randomisation). Cambridge University Press, 1993.

E. Welzl: *Boolean Satisfiability – Combinatorics and Algorithms.* Lecture Notes, ETH Zürich, 2005.

R. Williams, C.P. Gomes, B. Selman: On the connection between backdoors, restarts, and heavy-tailedness in combinatorial search. *Proceedings SAT 2003, 6th Intern. Conf. on Theory and Application of Satisfiability Testing,* Springer 2003, pages 222–230.

H. Wu: *Randomization and Restart Strategies.* Master Thesis, University of Waterloo, Ontario, Canada, 2006.

J. Wu, A.C.S. Chung: Markov random field energy minimization via iterated cross entropy with partition strategy. *ICASSP* 2007, IEEE, 457–460.

R. Zecchina: Statistical physics, optimization and source coding. *Pramana - Journal of Physics,* Vol. 64, 6 (2005) 1161–1173.

W. Zhang: *State Space Search: Algorithms, Complexity, Extensions, and Applications.* Springer, 1999.

A. Zhigljavsky, A. Žilinskas: *Stochastic Global Optimization.* Springer, 2008.

Index